Emphasis on Assessment

Readings from NCTM's School-Based Journals

Edited by

Diana V. Lambdin
Indiana University

Paul E. Kehle
Indiana University

Ronald V. Preston
East Carolina University

National Council of Teachers of Mathematics
Reston, Virginia

ISBN 0-87353-428-X

Printed in the United States of America

CONTENTS

PREFACE

This book is a collection of articles on assessment selected from among the January 1990–May 1995 issues of three of the journals of the National Council of Teachers of Mathematics (NCTM): the *Arithmetic Teacher* (from January 1990 to its final issue in May 1994), *Teaching Children Mathematics* (from its beginning in September 1994 as a replacement for the *Arithmetic Teacher* to May 1995), the *Mathematics Teacher* from January 1990 to May 1995, and *Mathematics Teaching in the Middle School* (from its inaugural issue in April 1994 to May 1995). During that time period, attention to assessment in the mathematics education community increased significantly. In May 1995, the NCTM published *Assessment Standards for School Mathematics*, a document written to complement its earlier *Curriculum and Evaluation Standards for School Mathematics* (1989) and *Professional Standards for Teaching Mathematics* (1991). Changes in the content and in the methods of teaching mathematics discussed in the earlier *Standards* documents brought about a need for changes in assessment strategies and practices, which are elaborated in the *Assessment Standards*.

The *Assessment Standards* provides guidelines for judging the appropriateness and the quality of assessments as well as selected examples of tasks and classroom scenarios to illustrate these points. However, the document is not intended to be used to debate issues or to offer specific suggestions for teacher practice. Providing opportunity to debate issues and share concrete examples is one role of the NCTM's school-based journals: *Teaching Children Mathematics* (formerly known as the *Arithmetic Teacher*), *Mathematics Teaching in the Middle School*, and the *Mathematics Teacher*. In fact, even before the publication of the *Assessment Standards*, these journals had already published numerous articles on assessment.

Ninety-six articles on assessment were published in the school-based NCTM journals from January 1990 to May 1995 as well as eleven papers dealing with assessment in the *Journal for Research in Mathematics Education* (*JRME*). At the end of this book, each of these 107 articles is briefly described in an annotated bibliography as well as cross-listed in an article-by-topic matrix. (Boldfaced titles in a bibliography indicate that the articles are reproduced in this book.) If you are looking for an article that deals with a particular assessment topic, the three matrices in the back of this book provide a place to start. (In compiling the annotated bibliographies, we used the *Current Index to Journals in Education* [produced by the ERIC Clearinghouse for Science, Mathematics, and Environmental Education—ERIC/CSMEE] to search for appropriate articles. With permission from the clearinghouse, we have adapted ERIC's article abstracts for use in our bibliographies. Many thanks to ERIC for permitting this use of their abstracts.)

This book is composed of a subset of the entire collection of articles on assessment from the NCTM school-based journals, January 1990–May 1995. This subset was selected to provide classroom teachers with help in understanding the vision of assessment articulated in the *Assessment Standards for School Mathematics*. These articles include resources that teachers might like to have at their fingertips for ready reference or that organizers of teacher in-service workshops on assessment might find particularly useful. They also include papers that present new ideas, issues, or topics on assessment to the NCTM membership.

However, the collection in this book is neither definitive nor exhaustive and represents only a part of the articles available in the NCTM journals. Furthermore, an examination of the entire 107 articles reveals significant gaps. For example, although authentic assessment and performance assessment are being experimented with in many states, there were no NCTM articles dealing broadly with these topics. Perhaps this volume can serve as a catalyst to NCTM members to share ideas in these and other missing areas through future articles in NCTM journals.

The book is divided into four sections. Section I (Rationale for Changes in Assessment) contains articles that provide background, rationale, or a point of view about the many changes in assessment that teachers face today. Section II (Looking at Testing and Grading) presents a diverse collection of ideas concerning these very common assessment concerns. Some of the articles in Section III (Looking at Alternative Assessment) raise issues about the use of alternative forms of assessment, whereas others offer practical tips for getting started. Finally, Section IV (Looking Within—Evaluating Our Own Effectiveness) focuses on how teachers can reflect on the current status of the assessment movement and judge their own progress in responding to the call for change.

SECTION I

Rationale for Changes
in Assessment Practices

Teachers, students, parents, and many others with an interest in high-quality mathematics education frequently ask why new and different methods of assessment are seen as so important. The articles in this section were chosen because they may help in furnishing rationales for recent calls for, and efforts to make, changes in assessment.

In "Evaluation: A New Vision," Frank Lester and Diana Lambdin Kroll point out that (in the vision of the *Curriculum and Evaluation Standards*) classroom assessment must be concerned with much more than its traditional focus on testing and grading. Their article identifies four very different reasons for collecting assessment information, then proceeds to provide an overview of alternative methods for accomplishing these goals. It is interesting to note that this paper, published in 1991, actually never uses the term *assessment* at all. Instead, it refers throughout to *evaluation*, which was customary at that time. In subsequent years, some mathematics educators have begun to use these terms in slightly different ways. *Assessment*, as defined in the *Assessment Standards* (NCTM 1995), is "the process of gathering evidence about a student's knowledge of, ability to use, and disposition toward mathematics and of making inferences from that evidence for a variety of purposes," whereas *evaluation* is "the process of determining the worth of, or assigning a value to, something on the basis of careful examination and judgment… Evaluation is one use of assessment information" (pp. 87–88).

David Clarke's forward-looking 1992 article, "Activating Assessment Alternatives in Mathematics," identifies a set of eight principles for restructuring school mathematics, several of which seem to foreshadow NCTM's 1995 *Assessment Standards*. Building on the foundation that these principles provide, Clarke clarifies the new, but increasingly important, distinction between formal and informal classroom assessment. Formal assessment, he says, "involves cessation of instruction, typically for the whole class while an 'assessment event' is held, [whereas] informal assessment … involves the collection of information about students' learning coincident with instruction and without disrupting the learning process." The assessment movement has increasingly come to value informal assessment, embracing the notion that, as Clarke points out, "good assessment equals good instruction."

Mark Driscoll similarly emphasizes the importance of systematically integrating assessment into instruction in "The Farther Out You Go," an article that takes its title from a student who once told Driscoll that "the farther out you go in a decimal, the smaller the number." Driscoll aptly uses this incident to illustrate how his own views about what he wants students to know and be able to do have changed over the years. He argues that these changes are reflections of much broader transformations in the mathematics education community at large and that they have significant implications for how teachers plan classroom activities, gather and interpret evidence about students' understanding, and use their findings to cycle back to planning for subsequent lessons.

Jay Greenwood's article, "On the Nature of Teaching and Assessing 'Mathematical Power' and 'Mathematical Thinking,'" discusses these often abstract and elusive concepts and proposes a set of seven criteria that teachers and students may use for assessing their growth in these areas. He illustrates his discussion of the seven criteria with specific examples of assessment techniques.

Finally, Constance Kamii and Barbara Ann Lewis use several examples to support their contention that new methods of assessment are essential when new types of learning are valued, since traditional achievement tests place too much emphasis on the mastery of symbolic, rule-based knowledge. In an article entitled "Achievement Tests in Primary Mathematics: Perpetuating Lower-Order Thinking," Kamii and Lewis compared second graders taught mathematics in a constructivist environment with those taught in a traditional environment. Although the traditionally taught students scored slightly better on achievement test items, they performed significantly worse when asked in an interview setting to show what place value and double-column addition meant and to work nonroutine word problems.

EVALUATION: A NEW VISION

FRANK K. LESTER, JR., and DIANA LAMBDIN KROLL

Teaching according to the vision of the NCTM's *Curriculum and Evaluation Standards* will involve numerous changes in the content and instruction of the school mathematics program. Moreover, this vision will also require a change in testing procedures and methods for evaluating the effectiveness of instructional practices (Clarke, Clarke, and Lovitt 1990; EQUALS and California Mathematics Council 1989; NAEP 1987; NCTM 1989). As is pointed out in NCTM's curriculum standards, an evaluation program that is properly aligned with the proposed curriculum standards can no longer use only written tests. Calculators, computers, and manipulatives must be included in the evaluation process.

We can no longer use only written tests.

A good evaluation program should not focus on specific, isolated skills. Evaluation is more than marking answers right and wrong. Instead, increased attention should be given to observing and questioning students, both to assess their understanding and to gain insight into their feelings and their beliefs about

Frank Lester teaches at Indiana University, Bloomington, IN 47405, where he is involved primarily in preservice teacher education. His special interests include problem solving in the elementary and middle grades and assessment of higher-order thinking in mathematics.

Diana Kroll, a former middle school and high school mathematics teacher, is administrative coordinator for the Indiana University Mathematics Education Development Center. She is particularly interested in problem solving, alternative assessment techniques, and writing to learn mathematics.

mathematics. Holistic scoring techniques are needed for better evaluation of students' written problem-solving efforts. Information should be collected through students' responses to short-answer questionnaires or through such written assignments as journal entries or brief essays. Before describing these and other techniques, we shall reflect on the goals of evaluation.

WHY DO WE EVALUATE?

Although in the past evaluation was often thought of as synonymous with testing and results of evaluation were frequently used primarily for grading, the evaluation standards recommend a broader conception. At least four reasons can be cited for collecting evaluation information:

- To make decisions about the content and methods of mathematics instruction
- To make decisions about classroom climate
- To help communicate what is important
- To assign grades

Making decisions about mathematics instruction

One of the most important reasons for gathering evaluation data is to make instructional decisions about the content of the mathematics program and the teaching methods to be used. Data from classroom observations, from analyses of students' written mathematics work, and from their writing about mathematics can be used to diagnose students' strengths and weaknesses. Clearly, the precision with which one can diagnose strengths

and weaknesses is highly influenced by the goal of the evaluation and the type of evaluation technique used. For example, if a teacher is interested in knowing more about the thought processes that students use when solving problems, interviewing them individually or in small groups will probably lend more insight than examining their written work. The more types of evaluation data teachers can collect from students, the better they can modify instruction to meet their students' needs.

Making decisions about classroom climate

To meet the goals outlined in the evaluation standards it is essential to create a classroom climate in which students are actively involved in the learning process. Classroom climate is influenced by a number of factors. Does the teacher convey to students that he or she enjoys mathematics and teaching mathematics? Are problem solving and active exploration integral parts of the class? Are students given opportunities to explore and experiment without being graded? Are more than the answers evaluated?

Perhaps the most important indicators of an appropriate classroom climate are students' attitudes and beliefs. Such assessment techniques as students' self-inventories, their self-reports, and interviews or observations of students can generate the data needed to make judgments concerning students' attitudes and beliefs about mathematics.

Communicating what is important

Students are experts at detecting what teachers consider important and unimportant. Teachers should show students that they value assigned homework by discussing it, referring to it, collecting it, reacting to it, grading it, and holding students responsible for learning from it. If students are expected to show all their work, teachers should be sure to look at more than just final answers. In general, students consider important those aspects of instruction that their teacher emphasizes and assesses regularly. The curriculum standards emphasize problem solving, reasoning, communication, and making mathematical connections as important goals for any mathematics class. Students will value progress in these areas only if teachers use evaluation techniques that indicate their importance.

Assigning grades

Finally, teachers collect evaluation data so that grades can be assigned. It is important that teachers understand that evaluation is not synonymous with grading. However, the following guidelines may be useful when grades are to be assigned:

- Advise students in advance when their mathematics work will be graded.
- Use a grading system that considers the thinking process used, not just the answers.
- Be aware that pupils may not perform as well when they are to be graded.
- Use as much evaluation data and as many different techniques as possible to help in the assignment of grades.
- Consider using a testing format that matches the instructional format used in class. For example, if students usually work in cooperative groups, consider testing their performance in cooperative groups.

For many students, grades motivate their performance. Such students will gain considerably when the system used to assign grades reflects the many facets of their mathematical performance.

OVERVIEW OF ALTERNATIVE METHODS OF EVALUATION

A variety of evaluation techniques is useful in accomplishing the goals just discussed. Four such techniques are among the most important and most useful for classroom situations: (1) observing and questioning students, (2) assessing students' mathematics work, (3) using students' writing for assessment, and (4) assessing students' work through individual portfolios. For a chart that summarizes some of the strengths and weak-

Students value what is assessed.

nesses of classroom use of a variety of evaluation methods, see Lester and Kroll (1990). Other evaluation techniques worthy of consideration and discussion include performance assessment, which many educators consider promising and which is still in the development stage (cf. Wiggins [1989]). Concept maps are another innovative technique, useful for seeing how students relate various mathematical ideas. Novak and Gowin (1984) discuss both the practical considerations of assigning concept maps and the rationale behind their use.

Observing and questioning students

Observing and questioning students while they are engaged in mathematics activities can yield invaluable information not only about their skills but also about their thinking processes, their attitudes, and their beliefs. Such observation can be done informally, as the teacher circulates around the room, or by means of a more structured, formal interview.

Teachers can learn a great deal about students by circulating unobtrusively as students work in small groups and by interjecting questions to clarify their observations. This is just one example of how evaluation data can be collected as teachers perform their normal classroom activities. No extra time is required, and evaluation becomes part of the learning process. An important consideration, however, is that teachers have a clear picture of what they want to evaluate. Gathering evaluation data through classroom observation can be difficult because so much is going on when students are working on problems. Teachers need to think ahead about what is to be evaluated so that they can focus attention

on the relevant aspects of students' work. One must decide whether to determine, for example, which problem-solving strategies students understand and use, whether they check their work regularly and efficiently, or how they feel about specific topics in mathematics or about doing various kinds of activities.

Similarly, teachers should think carefully about the types of questions they ask during observations. In everyday classroom situations, teachers ask students questions for a variety of reasons: to stimulate thinking, to offer hints, to test, or to demonstrate to other students what their peers know. When teachers are evaluating, they may need to suspend temporarily their natural tendency to teach. As evaluators, teachers should phrase questions so that students' answers yield information about whatever aspects of their mathematics understanding or behavior are being evaluated. Table 1 lists some of the kinds of questions that can be used to evaluate students' thinking as they are working on a mathematics problem. The questions are organized around key phases and aspects of problem solving, although question asking should be a part of other kinds of mathematical activity as well. It is impossible to include a comprehensive list of questions. Rather, the intent is to give readers a feel for the kinds of questions they might ask (cf. EQUALS and California Mathematics Council [1989, 24–25]).

Teachers should record their observation findings briefly, objectively, and in as timely a fashion as possible. A comment card, a checklist, a rating scale, or a journal can be used for recording observations. Observation is probably the best way to get a firsthand look at how students think about and do mathematics.

Assessing students' mathematics work

When teachers grade students' mathematics work, they usually look first at answers and then probe deeper for sources of errors if the answers are incorrect. Evaluating mathematics work according to the spirit of the evaluation standards is similar, although more emphasis is generally given to process—how the student approaches the problem—and less to product—what answer is obtained (Charles, Lester, and O'Daffer

TABLE 1
Sample Questions for Assessing Students' Thinking

Phase or Aspect of Problem Solving	Questions
Understanding	Can you tell me what this problem is about in your own words? Is there something that is missing (or that can be ignored)? What assumptions are you making about the problem?
Planning	Can you explain your plan to me? What have you tried so far? How did you organize the information? Is there a simpler problem related to this one that you could solve first? Why do you think your plan will work? Are you sure your plan fits the information given in the problem?
Carrying out plans	Can you show me how you have checked your work? Why did you put these headings in your table? Why did you draw this picture? How do you know that what you have been doing is appropriate? Correct?
Looking back	Are you sure your answer is correct? Why? Could you have solved this problem another way? What made you decide to use the plan (strategy) you used to solve this problem? If I changed the original problem to read "_____," would you solve it in the same way? Can you state another problem that could be solved in the same way that you solved this one? What did you learn by solving this problem?
Communicating mathematically	Can you reword the problem using simpler terms? Can you explain what you are doing? How would you explain what you are doing (or have done) to someone who will be in this class next year? Can you write another problem that could be solved using the same approach you used to solve this problem?
Seeing relationships	Is this problem like any others you have solved? In what ways is it the same? Different? (Show student a related but different problem.) What, if anything, is the same about the mathematics in this problem and the one you have just solved?
Assessing one's own capabilities	Is this kind of problem easy or hard for you? What makes problems like this easy? Hard? In general, what kinds of problems are especially hard for you? Easy? Why?

1987; EQUALS and California Mathematics Council 1989). Clearly, the most difficult part of evaluating students' work is deciding how to assess work that shows various types of thinking processes and various types of errors. Consider two methods for evaluating students' written work in mathematics: analytic scoring and holistic scoring

Analytic scoring. Analytic scoring is particularly useful in assessing students' problem-solving efforts. Analytic scoring involves the use of a scale to assign points to certain phases of the mathematical problem-solving process. The teacher first identifies the problem-solving phases that are to be evaluated then specifies a range of scores to be awarded for various levels of performance in each phase. For example, in evaluating students' written work on word problems, an analytic-scoring scale might assign four points to understanding the problem, four points to planning a solution, and two points to getting a correct answer. An analytic-scoring scheme usually includes specific criteria for awarding partial credit for each phase.

Analytic-scoring methods are most useful when it is appropriate to give students feedback about their performance in key categories associated with mathematical problem solving, when it is desirable to have diagnostic information about students' strengths and weaknesses, or when it is important to identify specific aspects of mathematics that may require additional instructional time. Analytic-scoring methods require considerable time to analyze each student's written work carefully. (Charles, Lester, and O'Daffer [1987] discuss an analytic-scoring scheme in detail.)

> ## Analytic scoring offers insights into students' thinking.

Holistic scoring. Unlike analytic scoring, which produces several numerical scores for each problem—each associated with a different aspect of problem-solving work—holistic scoring produces one single number assigned according to specific criteria related to the thinking processes involved in solving a particular problem. Holistic scoring is *holistic* because it focuses on the total solution as a whole, neither on the answer alone nor separately on various aspects of the solu-

tion. Table 2 gives an example of a problem and a holistic-scoring scale suitable for use in scoring students' written work on that problem. Holistic scoring is most appropriate when a relatively quick, yet consistent, evaluation technique is needed. For example, a teacher might use holistic scoring for end-of-semester examinations. However, in general, holistic scoring should be used in combination with other, more informative evaluation techniques.

Using students' writing for assessment

In recent years, as students' writing has come to be more and more an integral part of many mathematics classrooms, teachers have begun to see the value in using students' writing for purposes of assessment (Connolly and Vilardi 1989; Keith 1988; Nahrgang and Petersen 1986). From the wide variety of work that can be used for assessment, three categories of writing seem to stand out: self-reports and self-inventories, in-class and homework writing assignments, and paragraphs or essays written on quizzes and tests.

Students' self-reports. Self-reports are especially appropriate for assessing students' feelings and beliefs about mathematics and for obtaining information about how students organize and monitor their work. In a self-report, students are often asked to write a retrospective account of a mathematics activity that has just been completed. They reflect on their experience, describe their actions and their results, and make their own assessment of what they have learned. The teacher can lend some structure to the report by asking students to respond to questions that focus on selected aspects of the activity. Such questions might include these:

- Describe the tasks you did for your group.
- How did you keep track of your findings?
- How confident do you feel about what you did?
- What mathematics did you learn?
- How does this knowledge relate to what you have learned before?
- What new questions did this activity raise?

Students' self-reports are used to assess attitudes or beliefs more frequently than performance. They are not appropriate for grading purposes, since such use might affect the candidness of the reports. Clearly, the usefulness of self-report data is dependent on how accurately, completely, and candidly students report their intentions, actions, feelings, and beliefs. Because the information gathered through self-reports is subjective and can be incomplete, they should be used only in combination with other evaluation techniques, such as teacher observations or teacher-evaluated problems or test items.

In-class and homework writing assignments. Writing assigned for classwork, for homework, or for a regularly kept journal often affords students an opportunity to assess their own understanding of newly encountered concepts and gives the teacher a better sense of how to plan future lessons. Azzolino (1990) presents an extensive list of ways that writing assignments might be used in mathematics classes.

Some of the most effective writing assignments involve open-ended questions (CAP 1989; EQUALS and California Mathematics Council 1989). In open-ended questions, students might be asked to formulate hypotheses, to explain mathematical situations, to write directions, to create new related problems, or to make generalizations. Open-ended

> ## Students can explain when and why a procedure is used.

questions can assess whether students are able to do such things as organize and interpret information; report results in words, diagrams, charts, or graphs; understand fundamental concepts; use appropriate mathematical language; and draw generalizations.

Many teachers have found that when students write regularly about mathematics in a journal, the students often come to value the opportunity to reflect on what they have been learning and to attempt to relate their new learning to old. Moreover, teachers can gain valuable

insight into the understandings and beliefs of their students by reading students' journal entries (Clarke, Clarke, and Lovitt 1990; EQUALS and California Mathematics Council 1989).

Assigned topics might be quite specific or more general. The choice depends in large part on the purpose of the assessment. A specific question might be "Make up in the form $ax^2 + bx + c = 0$ a quadratic equation that has two different real roots. Explain how you constructed it and how you know what its roots are." A more general assignment might be one in which the students are asked to complete such sentences as "Today in math I learned _____ " or "What I still don't understand about logarithms is _____."

Writing done on quizzes and tests. Time is often the biggest obstacle to having students write on mathematics quizzes and tests. However, students who are accustomed to writing for in-class and homework assignments are generally much more capable of producing thoughtful written answers under test conditions. As in-class and homework

---

TABLE 2
A Sample Holistic-Scoring Scale*

James knows that half the students from his school are accepted at the public university nearby. Also half are accepted at the local private college. James thinks that these figures add to 100 percent, so he will surely be accepted at one or the other institution. Explain why James may be wrong. If possible use a diagram in your explanation.

4 points: Exemplary response
    All the following characteristics must be present:
- The answer is correct.
- The explanation is clear and complete.
- The explanation includes a mathematically correct reason for the faulty reasoning involving the assumption of disjoint sets in the problem.
- Some sort of diagram is provided that relates directly and correctly to the information in the problem.

3 points: Good response
    Exactly one of the following characteristics is present:
- The answer is incorrect.
- The explanation lacks clarity.
- The explanation is incomplete.
- No diagram is provided that relates directly and correctly to the information in the problem.

2 points: Inadequate response
    All the following characteristics must be present:
- The answer is incorrect
- The explanation lacks clarity or is incomplete but does indicate some correct and relevant reasoning.
- No diagram is provided that relates directly and correctly to the information in the problem.

1 point: Poor response
    All the following characteristics must be present:
- The answer is incorrect.
- The explanation, if any, uses irrelevant arguments (e.g., whether a student is qualified for college, whether a student has applied for college).
- No solution is attempted beyond just copying data given in the problem statement.
- No diagram is provided that relates directly and correctly to the information in the problem.

0 points: No response
- The student's paper is blank or it contains only work that appears to have no relevance to the problem.

*The problem is taken from the twelfth-grade test of the 1987–88 California Assessment Program (CAP).
This holistic-scoring scale is an adaptation of the six-point model used by CAP to score the item (CAP 1989).

---

assignments, open-ended questions usually yield more valuable information than more closed, restricted ones. For example, Azzolino (1990) suggests that asking students to write definitions on tests is not a good idea; students are likely to parrot statements memorized from the text. It is better to ask students to explain when and how to apply a definition or why a particular example does *not* fit the criteria of the definition. Asking students to explain a procedure is an excellent test question. But the question should specify that the explanation must include an explanation of *when* and *why* one would want to perform the procedure, as well as *how* to do it, for example, "State a problem for which the Pythagorean theorem would be needed for solution, then explain how you would use the theorem to solve the problem."

Assessing students' work via individual portfolios

A classroom assessment plan will be well rounded and valid if the teacher collects from each student a few samples of each o. the various types of data described in the foregoing—observations, written mathematics work, and writing. In fact, it may be possible to get the best overall picture of students' progress by having each student organize and submit an individual mathematics portfolio (CAP 1990; Clarke, Clarke, and Lovitt 1990; EQUALS and California Mathematics Council 1989). Like a professional artist's portfolio, an individual mathematics portfolio should be more than just a folder of work. It should be a collection of documents carefully selected by the student—or by the teacher and the student working together—to present a broad view of the student's range of interests and abilities in mathematics. Usually a student's portfolio includes many items that have been evaluated at an earlier date. Items in a portfolio might range from test papers to written self-reflections, from samples of homework to original problems written by the student. The teacher may choose to include samples of notes that have been made during observations of the student. However, it is important to limit the number of items that may be included in a portfolio. Students should be forced to think about which samples of their work to include so

that the teacher can survey a range of samples. The evaluation of an individual mathematics portfolio should be based on the variety and quality of the portfolio entries, not on the number of items included.

TIPS FOR GETTING STARTED

Start small

So many interesting and innovative ways to evaluate are available that it is possible to be overwhelmed. Begin by trying out just a few new ideas in your classroom. Avoid being too ambitious or setting goals too high. Teachers who have little experience in using alternative evaluation techniques and who try to do too much all at once may merely frustrate themselves and confuse their students.

Incorporate evaluation into the class routine

Try not to be paralyzed by thinking that no time is available to implement the ideas in this article. Time is definitely a consideration in the hectic schedule of a classroom teacher, but combining evaluation with other teaching activities is quite possible. For example, although individual student interviews are recommended as one of the most valid techniques for assessing students' mathematical thinking, most teachers have no time to conduct interviews on a regular basis. However, short, impromptu chats with small groups or individual students—often possible while student helpers pass out papers or materials, while the rest of the class works in small groups, or while individuals work at their seats—can furnish a wealth of information about students' mathematical development. This information, which many teachers are already gathering as they talk with students each day, is useful data for an alternative evaluation plan.

Set up an easy and efficient record-keeping system

As teachers begin to use alternative forms of evaluation, their record keeping needs to change. More than a gradebook is needed. Establish a card file, a checklist, or a folder in which to record information. If a record-keeping system facilitates teachers' making notations on the spot rather than forces them to wait until

after class or after school, they will be much more likely to use it regularly.

Establish an evaluation plan

An essential ingredient in an effective instructional program is a well-conceived evaluation plan that is developed concurrently with a teacher's instructional goals and activities. Try to establish an assessment routine in the classroom as soon as possible and attempt to make evaluation a natural, positive activity. Be sure to share the evaluation plan with students. An open, honest discussion with students about what is expected of them is essential to a successful program.

Personalize the evaluation plan

Clearly, the choice of evaluation techniques needs to be based on a multitude of factors, such as the type of mathematical skills to be assessed, the number of students to be evaluated, the amount of time available, the teacher's experience in teaching and evaluating higher-order thinking, the reason for the evaluation, and the availability of evaluation materials. The use of a variety of techniques permits a much more comprehensive evaluation of students. The choice of evaluation techniques will be quite personal, but in the end teachers need to choose techniques that are feasible for use in their particular classroom and that generate information appropriate for the goals of their own personal evaluation plan.

REFERENCES

Azzolino, Aggie. "Writing as a Tool for Teaching Mathematics: The Silent Revolution." In *Teaching and Learning Mathematics in the 1990s,* 1990 Yearbook of the National Council of Teachers of Mathematics, edited by Thomas J. Cooney and Christian R. Hirsch. Reston, Va.: The Council, 1990.

California Assessment Program (CAP). *A Question of Thinking: A First Look at Students' Performance on Open-ended Questions in Mathematics.* Sacramento: California State Department of Education, 1989.

———. *Guidelines for the Mathematics Portfolio.* Sacramento: California State Department of Education, 1990.

Charles, Randall, Frank Lester, and Phares O'Daffer. *How to Evaluate Progress in*

Problem Solving. Reston, Va.: National Council of Teachers of Mathematics, 1987.

Clarke, David J., Doug M. Clarke, and Charles J. Lovitt. "Changes in Mathematics Teaching Call for Assessment Alternatives." In *Teaching and Learning Mathematics in the 1990s*, 1990 Yearbook of the National Council of Teachers of Mathematics, edited by Thomas J. Cooney and Christian R. Hirsch. Reston, Va.: The Council, 1990.

Connolly, Paul, and Teresa Vilardi, eds. *Writing to Learn Mathematics and Science.* New York: Teachers College Press, 1989.

EQUALS and California Mathematics Council. *Assessment Alternatives in Mathematics: An Overview of Assessment Techniques That Promote Learning.* Berkeley, Calif.: Lawrence Hall of Science, 1989.

Keith, Sandra Z. "Explorative Writing and Learning Mathematics." *Mathematics Teacher* 81 (December 1988):714–19.

Lester, Frank K., and Diana Lambdin Kroll. "Assessing Student Growth in Mathematical Problem Solving." In *Assessing Higher Order Thinking in Mathematics*, edited by Gerald Kulm, 53–70. Washington, D.C.: American Association for the Advancement of Science, 1990.

NAEP (National Assessment of Educational Progress). *Learning by Doing: A Manual for Teaching and Assessing Higher-Order Thinking in Science and Mathematics.* Princeton, N.J.: Educational Testing Service, 1987.

Nahrgang, Cynthia L., and Bruce T. Petersen. "Using Writing to Learn Mathematics." *Mathematics Teacher* 79 (September 1986):461–65.

National Council of Teachers of Mathematics, Commission on Standards for School Mathematics. *Curriculum and Evaluation Standards for School Mathematics.* Reston, Va.: The Council, 1989.

Novak, Joseph D., and D. Bob Gowin. *Learning How to Learn.* New York: Cambridge University Press, 1984.

Wiggins, Grant. "A True Test: Toward More Authentic and Equitable Assessment." *Phi Delta Kappan* 70 (May 1989):703–13.

ACTIVATING ASSESSMENT ALTERNATIVES IN MATHEMATICS

David J. Clarke

The *Curriculum and Evaluation Standards for School Mathematics* (NCTM 1989, 1–2) emphasizes the role of evaluation "in gathering information on which teachers can base [their] subsequent instruction." This strong sense of assessment's informing instructional practice is also evident in the materials arising from the Australian Mathematics Curriculum and Teaching Program (Clarke 1989; Lovitt and Clarke 1988, 1989). Both projects offer their respective mathematics-education communities a set of goals much broader than those traditionally conceived for mathematics instruction. The adoption of these goals by mathematics teachers and school systems demands the use of new assessment strategies if the restructuring of the mathematics curriculum and mathematics-teaching practice is to be effected. Mathematics education must not restrict itself to those goals that can be assessed only through conventional pencil-and-paper methods.

Certain statements have emerged as guiding principles in the restructuring of assessment in Australian mathematics education. Assessment in school mathematics at all stages, whether through informal classroom assessment or external examination, should—

- relate to, and be consistent with, the full range of educational objectives,

David Clarke teaches mathematics education at the Australian Catholic University, Victoria, Australia 3116. His research activities include the interactive monitoring of students' learning, assessment alternatives, multiage instruction and communication, problem solving, and questioning techniques.

- recognize a range of learning styles,
- be fair to all groups of students and free from bias,
- enhance students' motivation and commitment to learning,
- establish starting points for further learning,
- ensure that the various learning objectives in mathematics are equally esteemed,
- be reported in a clear and meaningful way, and
- define and communicate standards to students and parents.

This article addresses these principles

The aim is better assessment, not more.

in practical terms. A central priority of the discussion is that the recommended practices involve minimal disruption of the instructional process and not impose an additional workload on the teacher. Rather, teachers are encouraged to be more discerning and selective in the assessment strategies they employ. The aim is for better, more appropriate assessment, not simply more assessment.

ASSESSMENT IS CONCERNED WITH THE EXCHANGE OF INFORMATION

Through our assessment we communicate most clearly to students which activities and learning outcomes we value (Clarke, Clarke, and Lovitt 1990).

Students have the right to explicit information about their progress that includes indications of both strengths and weaknesses; reporting to students should have this prime objective. Of immediate concern are the techniques by which assessment information is collected, interpreted, and communicated. Central to this discussion is the distinction between formal and informal assessment.

INFORMAL ASSESSMENT

Teachers formulate definite and quite accurate opinions concerning the competence of their pupils (Coladarci 1986), and formal assessment using tests commonly does little more than legitimize and quantify the assessment made through extended classroom contact.

The distinction being made here is between formal assessment, which involves the cessation of instruction, typically for the whole class while an "assessment event" is held, and informal assessment, which involves the collection of information about students' learning coincident with instruction and without disrupting the learning process. However, informal assessment generally lacks structure, and the information it produces, although it may influence the teacher's decision making (Shavelson and Stern 1981), is not systematically recorded and lacks the status accorded to a test score. A teacher constructs a picture of the pupil's competence through unplanned observations that are seldom documented. By introducing some structure into their observations, teachers can maximize the information they collect and minimize the time squandered on redundant, uninformative, and counterproductive assessment.

Two strategies have been critical in assisting Australian teachers to document systematically their students' learning in an ongoing fashion: annotated class lists and students' work folios.

Annotated class lists

It is clearly impractical for a teacher to record comments on every student every day. Hence this strategy focuses on recording only significant events.

Notes on observations by a teacher in the classroom are best restricted to significant events. Teachers can draw up a checklist of the behaviors, skills, or attitudes they would like to foster in their students. Such a list of practical learning and teaching goals should form the basis of the mathematics program at any grade level. Teachers annotate a class list as in figure 1, by recording those significant events that either challenge or extend their image of a student. The original checklist tells the teacher what to look for and also serves to summarize the significant moments in a systematic record for each student. In identifying significant moments, ask, "Will knowing this information change my subsequent teaching of that student or that lesson?"

Teachers reported success in using annotated class lists to document those fleeting insights. Experience has shown that a "breathing space" during which the students work independently gives the teacher time to jot down any insights and to carry out further observations. A related benefit arising from the use of such a procedure is that by the end of any given week, students can be identified against whose names nothing has been written. In this way, the use of annotated class lists may alert teachers to those "invisible" students present in every classroom.

Students' work folios

One of the most effective ways to document students' progress is to collect representative or significant samples of students' work, suitably dated.

How best can a teacher record the insights offered by each of the pieces of work illustrated in figure 2? To restrict our documentation to a single mark is to sacrifice precisely that detail that could most usefully inform our actions. A folio of students' work samples powerfully illustrates a student's development, which is particularly relevant for report writing or parent-teacher interviews. Experience in using student portfolios

FIGURE 1

Annotated Class List

Week beginning August 3	COMMENTS (Aberrations and Insights)	ACTION	
		REQUIRED	TAKEN
Bastow, Barry	No concept of odd and even	✳	
Carlton, Donna	Showed leadership in the group		
Carss, Marjorie			
Clements, Ken			
Caughey, Wendy			
Del Campo, Gina	Thought 63 and 36 the same	✳	✓
Ganderton, Paul	Really tired		
Grace, Neville	Sequencing problems	✳	
Howe, Peter			
Lee, Beth	Spatial thinker		
McDonough, Andrea	Recognised significance of a counter example		
McIntosh, Alistair			
Moule, Jim			
Mulligan, Joanne			
...ner, Kevin			
...er, Fay	M. A. B. ...needed... ...letters		

FIGURE 2
Students' Work Samples

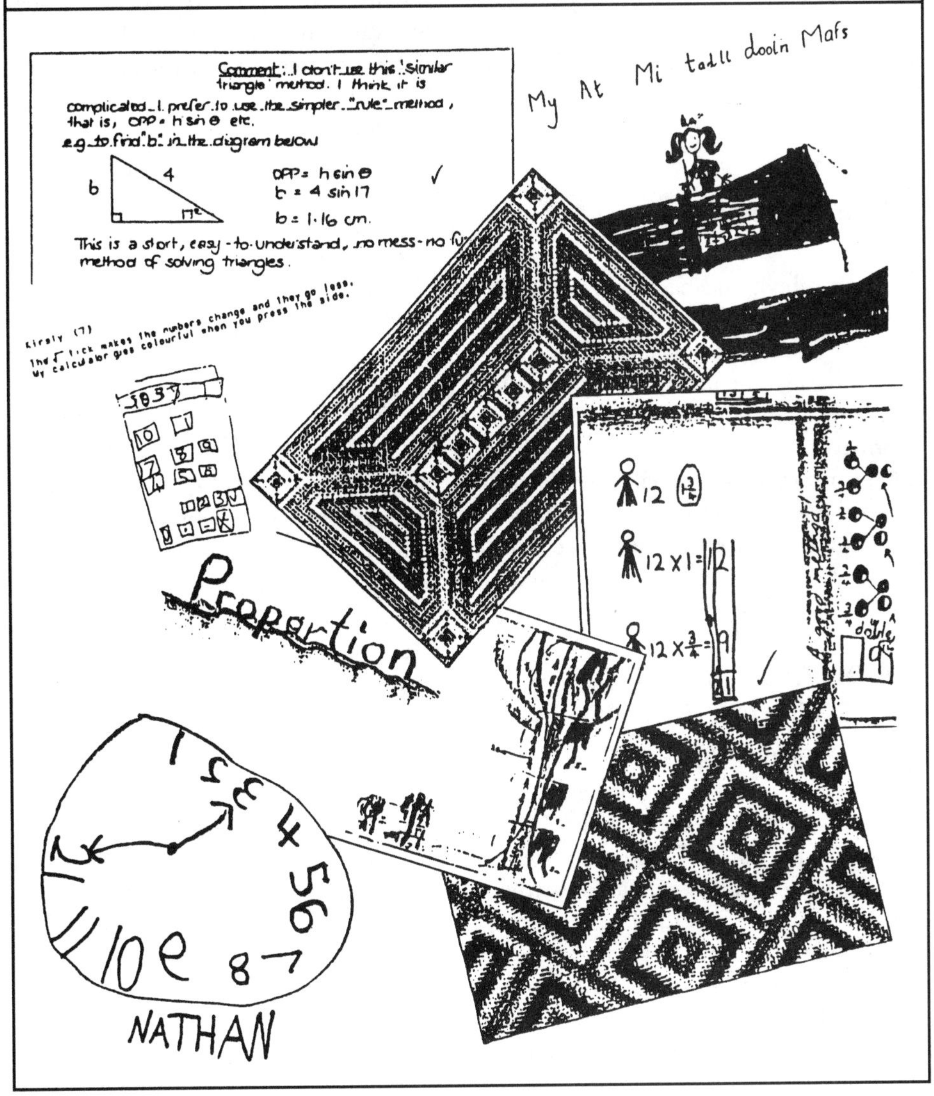

in California schools has produced some useful guidelines on the implementation of this assessment strategy (Stenmark 1989).

FORMAL ASSESSMENT

Although our use of formal assessment has been limited to the conventional pencil-and-paper test, recent field-testing of other formal assessment techniques has proved most productive. In particular, three formal assessment techniques received strong endorsement by teachers: practical tests, student-constructed tests, and students' self-assessment.

Practical tests

Practical tests offer the advantages of the provision of short-term learning goals, enhanced motivation, immediate and unambiguous feedback, and a high degree of assessment validity, since the skills are assessed in practice in the manner in which they were learned and as they will be applied.

Many topics lend themselves to a practical test, for example, topics in measurement, pattern and order, geometry, and probability and statistics. Practical test items can be included among more conventional items on a test, for example, "To complete this question, use the equipment furnished to find the volume of (1) the cube, (2) the cylinder, and (3) the stone." The equipment might include a ruler, string, grid paper, calipers, a measuring cylinder, a beaker of water, and plastic centimeter cubes.

Computing skills are best tested in a practical situation. An approach used successfully by one teacher involves distributing weekly a list of computing skills to be acquired. During a particular week, each student is asked to demonstrate one of the skills listed for the previous week; the skill is chosen by the teacher without prior notice to the student, for instance, "Write and run a simple Logo procedure to draw a regular polygon using the REPEAT command."

Student-constructed tests

Student-constructed tests offer both an effective assessment tool and a powerful review strategy to assist students in organizing their knowledge of a topic.

Administer a test made entirely, or partly, of student-constructed test items. Not only do students have a new sense of participation in the assessment process, but they have a far greater interest in discussing the solutions to their test, and the preparation of test items is a most effective review strategy.

One successful method of using student-constructed tests involves the following:

- The teacher divides the class into groups of two or three students and asks each group to make up five problems that they feel would fairly test the topic to be assessed.

- The teacher reserves the right to select from the pool of problems, but a guarantee to include at least one item from each group gives legitimacy to the exercise in the minds of the students.

- The teacher's editorial rights include the right to rephrase an ambiguous or poorly worded question while remaining true to the essential form of the students' question.

- The teacher may choose to require each group to furnish a sample solution to each of their proposed questions.

- In reviewing the class's performance on the test, it is useful to ask the group that wrote a particular question to outline the sort of solution they would consider acceptable.

Students' self-assessment

One of the most constructive and empowering educational goals we might frame would be to equip students to monitor their own progress.

Effective assessment is a continuous process predicated on the teacher's and the student's mutual recognition of the goals of the learning experience and the criteria for success. The process of reflecting on one's learning is valuable in itself. One strategy suitable for upper elementary-level and junior-secondary-level students involves the regular completion of the response sheet shown in figure 3. Teachers employing this strategy have typically administered the response sheet every three or four weeks.

This procedure (Clarke 1987) gives students the opportunity to share regularly their successes and concerns with their teacher. Certain actions by the teacher maximize the value of the procedure:

- The response sheet should be a confidential, but not anonymous, communication from the student to the teacher.
- Administration of the response sheets must be regular and reasonably frequent, at least once a month.
- The teacher must treat the procedure as an important part of the class's mathematics program and act on the students' responses when possible.
- The various response sheets from the same student should be filed together, furnishing a picture of the changing or persistent concerns of the student.

With very junior grades, a written response may be inappropriate. In such situations it is possible to combine the methods of self-assessment, practical test, students' work folio, and annotated class list in a single strategy by regularly asking each individual student, "Show me something that you have learned how to do this week in mathematics." Students' responses to this request have proved to be very revealing and can systematically be documented either by retaining and filing any written or pictorial response or by suitably annotating the teacher's ongoing observation record.

With more senior students, the regular completion of a mathematics journal has been shown to be both a powerful learning tool and a source of significant insight into students' learning (Clarke, Stephens, and Waywood, 1992).

Students reflect on their learning.

Each school and each teacher must consider the relative merits of formal and informal assessment. Attempts must be made to document the best possible assessment information, particularly if informal assessment is to acquire status similar to that of formal assessment. Given the newfound diversity of assessment strategies at our disposal, we must be selective in our use of the new techniques.

GOOD ASSESSMENT EQUALS GOOD INSTRUCTION

We are witnessing the reconciliation of assessment and instruction. Students' self-assessment strategies (Clarke 1987; Clarke, Stephens, and Waywood 1990) promise to develop metacognition while informing teachers' instruction. Students' involvement in the design of tests appears to offer dramatic educational benefits. Problem-solving activities offer both productive educational experiences and major insights into students' mathe-

matical behavior (Clarke and McDonough 1989). In particular, strategies like the "good questions" model (Sullivan and Clarke 1988) offer the possibility of effective instruction and windows into students' understanding of mathematics.

Contrast the likely student response to the questions

"Find the average of the numbers: 13.4, 18.5, 15.7, 16.3, and 19.6"
and
"Which five numbers would have an average of 17.2?"

Students' responses to the second question have included these:

- "15.2, 16.2, 17.2, 18.2, 19.2" from students for whom "average" clearly has medianlike associations, and
- "Any five numbers that add up to 86" from students confident in the use of the algorithm for the arithmetic mean.

Interestingly, the students employing either method are often astonished by the approach taken by their classmates using the other method. The use of such questions leads to a much richer learning experience than that offered by the first question while also offering assessment information not accessible through conventional questioning.

Sullivan and Clarke (1988, 1991) have suggested that such questions have three essential characteristics: they require more

---

FIGURE 3
A Sample Response Sheet

Name: _____

Class: _____

Teacher: _____

Date: _____

- Write down the two most important things you have learned in mathematics class during the past month.
- Write down at least one sort of problem that you have continued to find difficult.
- What would you most like more help with?
- How do you feel in mathematics classes at the moment? (Circle the words that apply to you.)

  a) Interested   *b)* Relaxed   *c)* Worried
  d) Successful   *e)* Confused   *f)* Clever
  g) Happy   *h)* Bored   *i)* Rushed
  j) Write down one word of your own _____

- What is the biggest worry affecting your work in mathematics at the moment?
- How could we improve mathematics class?

than recall of a fact or replication of a procedure; they are educative for the student, as well as informative for the teacher; and they are to some extent open-ended.

Other "good" questions include these:

1. Find the area of a rectangle with a perimeter of 20 centimeters.
2. Which numbers might be rounded off to 5.8?
3. Draw a triangle with an area of 12 square centimeters.
4. Draw a clock showing three o'clock.

The use of problem-solving activities reveals the mathematics the students choose to use rather than the mathematics they can demonstrate on request. This distinction is crucial and represents a new recognition of the extent to which our past assessment strategies have misled us by focusing on explicitly cued facts and procedures. In problem-solving activities, the mathematics classroom most closely approximates the real world and we are most likely to see the effective outcomes of our instruction. For some teachers and students, however, problem-solving activities can appear unfamiliar and threatening. "Good" questions can offer, among other things, a useful initiation into problem solving (Clarke and Sullivan 1990). Characteristic of this approach, and of the increased documentation of informal assessment advocated earlier, is a belief that assessment needs to be seen and practiced as an integral part of the instructional process.

ASSESSMENT SHOULD ANTICIPATE ACTION

Assessment should anticipate action. The most useful criterion when deciding whether to engage in a particular assessment activity is "What action will result from this assessment?" If the answer is "None," do not carry out the assessment.

Possible actions drawing on assessment information will include teacher decisions regarding instructional practice, program design and review, individual pupil tutoring or counseling, modified student-learning behaviors, and enhanced parental-support practices.

It is also becoming accepted that the effective monitoring of a student's learning requires the use of several different modes of assessment. To this end, some schools have adopted the policy "No student will receive a written report that does not make explicit reference to at least three different forms of assess-

Several different forms of assessment are used.

ment." It is possible to design a school program to incorporate the new initiatives in a realistic, practical manner and in a form that specifies the action to follow from each assessment strategy employed.

A simple procedure that a teacher might employ in planning a year's integrated instructional and assessment program would be one of the following, depending on the grade level:

1. Identify the three or four assessment strategies that you think are most likely to yield useful assessment information.
2. Design a year's time line on which you specify—
   - how and when each strategy will be put into practice;
   - what action will follow as a consequence of each assessment strategy and when this action will be taken.

Schools are finding local answers to the question "What is a complete, coherent, achievable, and defensible assessment-and-reporting package?" The resultant school mathematics programs increasingly employ the strategies outlined in this article and take as guiding principles the integration of assessment with instruction and the requirement that assessment should anticipate action.

REFERENCES

Clarke, David J. *Assessment Alternatives in Mathematics.* Canberra: Curriculum Development Centre, 1989.
———. "The Interactive Monitoring of Children's Learning of Mathematics." *For the Learning of Mathematics* 7 (February 1987):2–6.
Clarke, David J., and Andrea McDonough. "Assessing Problem Solving: A Challenging Problem." In *Every One Counts*, edited by Brian Doig. Parkville, Australia: Mathematical Association of Victoria, 1989.
Clarke, David J., Doug M. Clarke, and Charles J. Lovitt. "Changes in Mathematics Teaching Call for Assessment Alternatives." In *Teaching and Learning Mathematics in the 1990s*, 1990 Yearbook of the National Council of Teachers of Mathematics, edited by Thomas J. Cooney and Christian R. Hirsch, 118–29. Reston, Va.: The Council, 1990.
Clarke, David J., W. Max Stephens, and Andrew Waywood. "Communication and the Learning of Mathematics." In *Mathematics Assessment and Evaluation: Imperatives for Mathematics Educators*, edited by Thomas A. Romberg. Albany: State University of New York Press, 1992.
Clarke, David J., and Peter A. Sullivan. "Initiating Students into Problem Solving and Assessing Mathematics Learning Using Everyday Content through the Use of Effective Questions." In *Mathematical Turning Points—Strategies for the 1990s*, edited by Ken Milton and Hugo McCann, 164–72. Conference book of the thirteenth biennial conference of the Australian Association of Mathematics Teachers. Hobart, Australia: Mathematical Association of Tasmania, 1990.
Coladarci, T. "Accuracy of Teacher Judgements of Student Responses to Standardized Test Items." *Journal of Educational Psychology* 78 (April 1986):141–46.
Lovitt, Charles J., and Doug M. Clarke. *MCTP Professional Development Package: Activity Bank.* Vol. 1. Canberra: Curriculum Development Corporation, 1988.
———. *MCTP Professional Development Package: Activity Bank.* Vol. 2. Canberra: Curriculum Development Corporation, 1989.
National Council of Teachers of Mathematics, Commission on Standards for School Mathematics. *Curriculum and Evaluation Standards for School Mathematics.* Reston, Va.: The Council, 1989.
Shavelson, Richard J., and Paula Stern. "Research on Teachers' Pedagogical Thoughts, Judgements, Decisions and Behaviours." *Review of Educational Research* 51 (Winter 1981):455–98.
Stenmark, Jean. *Assessment Alternatives in Mathematics.* Berkeley, Calif.: EQUALS Project, Lawrence Hall of Science, 1989.
Sullivan, Peter A., and David J. Clarke. "Asking Better Questions." *Journal of Science and Mathematics Education in South East Asia* (June 1988):14–19.
———. "Catering to All Abilities through 'Good' Questions." *Arithmetic Teacher* 39 (October 1991):14–18.

"THE FARTHER OUT YOU GO. . .": ASSESSMENT IN THE CLASSROOM

Mark Driscoll

I can thank a student named Billy for teaching me about the importance of integrating assessment with instruction. It was the early 1970s, and I was teaching in an alternative high school that I had helped found the year before, in a converted warehouse in central St. Louis. Our students were drawn from the city's school-dropout population, and many had not been in a mathematics classroom for years. Luckily, our classes were relatively small, which permitted me on this day to reflect on what Billy had done on a task. I had put five decimals, all between 0 and 1, on the chalkboard and asked the class to rank them in order of number size—a list something like .06, .607, .6, .6707, .067. Billy arrayed them in descending order of length, longest to shortest. I asked, Which is the number with the smallest value, Billy?" He pointed without hesitation to .6707. "How come?" I asked. This time, Billy thought a bit and seemed to be looking at what he had done through the mists of school memory. "I don't know. I sort of remember one of my teachers saying, 'The farther out you go in a decimal, the smaller the number.'"

The remark stuck with me for days. Somehow, I could not dismiss it as a mere memory aberration. Evidently, Billy had been listening several years before

Mark Driscoll is Senior Project Director at Education Development Center, 55 Chapel Street, Newton, MA 02158-1060. He is a member of NCTM's Assessment Standards Writing Group and is working with two National Science Foundation–funded projects, Leadership for Urban Mathematics Reform Project and Assessment Committees of Teachers Project.

when his teacher had given what was intended to be a helpful guide to the symbol system of decimals, but the meaning he had attached—or, at least, was attaching during this activity—was distorted from what was intended. I then realized, in a way that was permanently imprinted on my teaching values, that the mathematical meaning I intended and the mathematical meaning derived by students were not necessarily the same. The realization made me a bit uneasy, but mostly I found it exciting. Years later, when I heard Dutch educator Pierre van Hiele say that a long-standing goal in his teaching has been to be surprised each day, I nodded in appreciation.

> *The intended meaning and the students' constructed meaning are not necessarily aligned*

But, of course, surprise without action is practically worthless in teaching. If my intended meaning and the students' constructed meaning are not aligned, then my instruction needs somehow to work to bring them together. This challenge is not easy. In Billy's case, I was in a fog about what to do next. I was not worried about responding immediately to Billy, because other students in the group set him straight about the ordering of decimals. However, I was concerned about being alert for other misunderstandings and about shaping my instruction systematically from then on; I did not want to depend on serendipity to get

an accurate reading of my students' understanding. With Billy, I had been lucky: he was willing to share his thinking and memories with me. I knew I could not always count on such cooperation.

THE WISDOM OF HINDSIGHT

Much has changed since that day. The field of mathematics education has been transformed by years of penetrating research and by the guiding visions set by the NCTM in the *Curriculum and Evaluation Standards* and the *Professional Teaching Standards* (1989, 1991). In the intervening years, I have had reason to think of Billy many times as I read one research account or another about students' construction of learning and the alternative conceptions they develop. One early and memorable account was Erlwanger's (1975) case study of a student named Benny, which revealed how it is possible for students to develop two different, and conflicting, systems for using mathematics—one for getting by in school mathematics and one for handling real, out-of-school mathematics challenges.

How can we account for the Bennys and Billys in making the vision in those NCTM *Standards* documents a reality? I am convinced that we cannot unless we learn to be persistent and systematic about integrating assessment into instruction. Such an approach is proposed by the most recent NCTM standards document, *Assessment Standards for School Mathematics* (1993), which addresses four purposes of assessment. In this article, "integrating assessment into instruction" is identified with two of these purposes:

making instructional decisions and monitoring students' progress.

My reminiscences about Billy will serve as a framework for one model of systematic effort. This model involves a process of inquiry that extends through several stages of questioning to form an assessment feedback loop that can help align mathematical goals with teaching practices. Adapted from the efforts of NCTM's Assessment Standards Working Group, its four steps are (1) planning the activity, (2) gathering evidence, (3) interpreting evidence, and (4) using evidence. Ideally, this process is undertaken collegially, in ongoing staff development groups of teachers looking at the products of students' work with an eye toward improving instruction. Experiences with several projects at Education Development Center—the Classroom Assessment in Mathematics project and the Regional Alliance for Mathematics and Science Education Reform, both National Eisenhower Projects, for example—have proved this approach to be a productive form of professional development.

To write this article, I imagined that I was back with Billy's class, and I used hindsight to evaluate the context from my perspective then and my perspective now. While I worked through the steps of the model, I was able to reflect on how much my thinking about mathematics education has changed since the 1970s.

STEP 1: PLANNING THE ACTIVITY

The first step, planning, begins with eliciting and articulating priorities. Any mathematics teacher's priorities are derived in good part from the personal stamp he or she brings to the classroom: knowledge and beliefs about mathematics; assumptions about the students and their capacities; beliefs about instruction; and a host of values about, and goals for, what should be learned in the mathematics classroom. By itself, this personal stamp is neither bad nor good; it is part of the human condition to let values and beliefs guide behavior. However, since value and assessment are tightly linked—for the most part, what gets assessed is

what is valued—the essential point for teachers is to learn how to manage what we bring to the classroom.

Sometimes, teachers are conscious of the personal stamps they bring and are able to manage them to their benefit and the benefit of their students. More often than not, however, these assumptions, beliefs, and values are hidden from consciousness and limit the capacity to be systematic. A key to being systematic about integrating assessment into instruction is knowing how to manage one's personal stamp, starting with a planned process of selecting assessment activities, a process that also tests one's assumptions and reflects one's values and beliefs.

> Be persistent and systematic about integrating assessment into instruction.

The following questions should be asked when planning an activity. As I recall, I intended to guide Billy and the rest of the group toward algebra but needed to see how much groundwork had to be covered. As the students progressed, I was alert for pieces of prerequisite knowledge that were missing. When gaps appeared, we spent instructional time to fill them. On reflection, I find that in a similar situation today, I

What do I want the students to know and be able to do?

Then	Now
Students should understand the correspondence between decimal notation and number value.	Students should have the same understanding, but that understanding should be set in a broader context of number notation and number value that can connect decimals with fractions.
Given a set of decimals, students should be able to compare number sizes correctly.	Students should be able to make the same comparisons, but, more important, they should be able to interpret the meaning of decimals in a variety of contexts, know when to use decimal notation, and apply a knowledge of decimals to solve a variety of problems.
Students should be able to explain their thinking out loud.	Students should be able to communicate an understanding of decimals in a variety of ways, that is, with words, pictures, symbols, and manipulatives.

would answer the questions quite differently than I would have answered them twenty years ago.

What are valuable ways to ascertain whether they understand and can perform these activities?

Then	Now
A few short, closed-ended exercises are done individually by students.	Students are given a balanced combination of closed-ended exercises, short open-ended problems, longer investigations, and written explanations.
Students explain to the teacher and to each other their decisions in doing the exercises.	Students have a variety of opportunities to reveal what thinking is involved in using decimals—orally and in writing, individually and in groups.

STEP 2: GATHERING EVIDENCE

The second step involves gathering evidence about students' understanding. This step should directly link with the decisions made in the first step. In particular, evidence should be drawn using activities that fit with how the teacher answers several key questions. As I reflect on these questions in the context of Billy's class, I recognize a real misalignment between my values and my evidence gathering: I placed a high value on discovery learning and on students' taking ownership of their own learning, which were guiding principles for the whole school, but my selection of tasks was narrow and tied to old beliefs about mathematics and learning. Reflection about key questions probably would not have led to the same answers that I give today, but they might have served to prod me into recognizing the inconsistencies and engaging in appropriate inquiry with my colleagues about alternative ways of thinking. Some key questions to ask about tasks follow.

What kinds of tasks can guide instruction and help monitor students' progress?

Then	Now
In form, they look like the decimal tasks I did when I was a student.	They invite students to enter them in a variety of ways and at different levels of experience with decimals.[1]
Their content is narrowly defined to give clear indicators for any needed instruction.	Complexity and challenge are valued, so students can learn while doing the tasks but so important dimensions of each task, such as the accessibility of the language, can be identified.
	They have the potential to show what the students can do as well as what they cannot do.
	To give a complete picture of decimal understanding, single-answer tasks are balanced with tasks for which multiple solutions exist.
	At least some tasks offer opportunities for the students to attach meaning to the use of decimals in the social, political, and economic contexts in which they live.

[1]An example that can make students' thinking explicit is the assessment task called "Decimal Dilemma" used a few years ago in the intermediate grades by Pittsburgh Public Schools: "Kiara and Jason walked home after school. They had just completed a mathematics test. It was a difficult one. Both were talking about the answers they wrote on the test. They disagreed on some of their answers. For one of the questions, they had to choose the larger decimal: .3 or .26. Jason answered .26, but Kiara though .3 was larger. Help Kiara and Jason settle their disagreement. Explain who is correct and why."

What are some important dimensions to consider in choosing tasks?[2]

Then	Now
Timeliness in the sequence of the curriculum: Does the appropriate content occur at the appropriate point in the sequence?	Mathematical context: How well do students make connections with the mathematics they have learned previously?
	Mathematical potential: How well do the tasks foreshadow future learning? In particular, how well do they foreshadow formal algebra by involving algebraic thinking with patterns, relations, and functions?
	Complexity in the task's information: How much information must the student organize and manage?
	Degree of openness: How many approaches are possible; how many solutions are possible?
	Accessibility: To what extent are the language, contextual information, and other aspects of the task accessible to the students?

[2]I am grateful to colleagues at the New Standards Project and the Vermont Institute for Science, Mathematics, and Technology for stimulating my thinking about task dimensions.

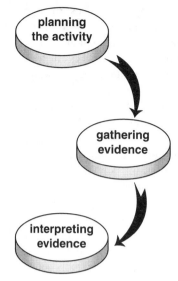

STEP 3: INTERPRETING EVIDENCE

The third step, interpreting the evidence obtained from students, is complex and is the step in which the value of collegial discussion among teachers is greatest. A student's task response can mask a wide range of intentions, understandings, and misunderstandings. Teachers acquire data about students through observations, students' answers to questions, and students' products. Viewing those data as grist for inquiry is important.

Other professions, such as business and law, have made good use of case discussions to sharpen inquiry skills related to interpreting data. This technique is useful in mathematics professional development, thanks to resources like the collection of mathematics discussion cases compiled by Barnett, Goldstein, and Jackson (1994) from their work at Far West Laboratory.

Before interpreting the evidence from students' responses, teachers should reflect on their assumptions and on the possible influence of extraneous, as well as relevant, factors.

What assumptions do I bring to my interpretation of the evidence?

Had I asked this question of myself when faced with Billy's answer about decimals, I might have noted my hidden assumption that he had not been learning anything relevant or helpful about decimals in the several years he had been out of school. I might have noted, too, my assumption that this single, decontextualized task furnished a sufficient picture of his knowledge and understanding. This reflection suggests a second ques-

tion that is important to ask because in assessment, as in any human enterprise, it is easy to blur the lines between solid evidence on the one hand and personal experience and opinion on the other.

What do I know for sure? Do I have enough information?

In the instance of Billy, I now recognize the possible usefulness of finding out, perhaps through a writing task, if and how he had been using decimals in his time away from school. The teachers in our St. Louis school regularly observed and even videotaped each other in class. The subsequent discussions allowed for more accurate interpretations of classroom evidence, but we relied on instinct and used no clear guidelines. What teachers need are instructional analogs of scoring rubrics. When the purpose of assessment is evaluating achievement, scorers of students' work are guided by scoring rubrics. Teachers can find examples of such scoring rubrics in various places, such as the California State Department of Education's *A Sampler of Mathematics Assessment* (1994). Unfortunately, when the purpose is to give students feedback and inform instruction, rubriclike guidelines are not so prevalent. Occasionally, however, scoring rubrics can be used or adapted as pointers back to instruction.

What guidelines can I use to test my interpretation of the evidence?

Then	Now
No guidelines or rubrics are used, but the other mathematics teachers in the school are a resource.	Although the other teachers are a resource, I prefer having consensus on the various indicators that constitute sufficient knowledge and know-how concerning decimals. Such an indicator might be "can write correctly about, draw an accurate explanation of, or speak accurately about the correspondence between number size and decimal notation."

In the past few years, a side benefit of various conversations sparked by the move to alternative assessment and the use of scoring rubrics has been the distinction made between the need for revision by the student and the need for further instruction. Again, although this distinction has been applied to scoring rubrics, it is beneficial to apply it to assessment that informs instruction: When does instruction need to "fix" something versus when can students fix things themselves?

In considering students' responses to the tasks, where are the needs for revision through direct feedback? Where, in contrast, are the needs for further instructional activities?

Then	Now
The need for instruction on decimals—decimal place value in particular—seems evident.	Instruction on the nature of decimals may be needed, but it is worthwhile first to treat Billy's answer on this particular task as a faulty rule that needs revision and not try to "fix" it through instruction. His reliance on distant memory probably means that he could benefit from some explorations with other students that involve making judgments about decimals and communicating about the judgments.

rately you are recalling this particular rule by trying it out over the next class or two on some activities involving decimals. If it doesn't hold up, you can revise it."

Direct instruction would consider the following:

- The need for more problems in which decimals are used in contexts that have real-world meaning for Billy and the other students
- The need to experiment with decimals in the context of problems that are open-ended enough to require judgments about the appropriate size of decimals to offer as solutions
- The parallel need to practice expressing rules in spoken and written words or in diagrams

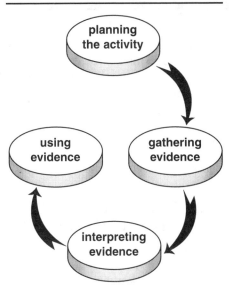

STEP 4: USING EVIDENCE

Sometimes in the assessment process, evidence based on students' work leads to actions that are evaluative: giving grades, scores, report cards, and so on. Another set of actions follows the use of assessment integrated with instruction. These actions are aimed at improving classroom interactions. If, in step 2, careful consideration has been given to the dimensions of the task, a closer look at those dimensions can point to appropriate feedback and instruction for the teacher.

What are the pointers for feedback and instruction given in the various dimensions of the task?

Then	Now
Some pointed work on the meaning of place value in decimals is assigned.	Billy would be given feedback such as this: "You're right, Billy, there are rules governing decimals. You can check on how accu-

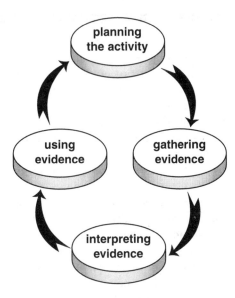

STEP 5: COMPLETING THE LOOP

Even as instruction is responding to the interpretation of evidence, planning can be renewed and priorities reviewed. As the feedback loop cycles back, it gives an opportunity to revisit this question: What *is* important for my students to learn in mathematics?

- On the basis of what I have seen in completing the cycle, what step should be next in the planning?
- What do I want to change in my goals for mathematics instruction? What do I see as important for the students to know and know how to do?

CONCLUSION

Because our St. Louis school served students like Billy who had been out of school for a while, we did not know what to

assume about their mathematics backgrounds. We needed to maintain a diagnostic posture a good part of the time. Hence, we were primed for integrating assessment with instruction. However, the efforts were far from systematic and were even rather scattershot. In addition, we were hampered by mind-sets about assessment that dictated gathering a narrow range of data, and we were locked into a linear model of teaching and learning mathematics. Ironically, we met together several times a week as a staff; we regularly observed each other's classes. We did not, however, have a framework that encouraged the systematic integration of assessment with instruction, nor did we have tools for inquiry that would let us unpack the evidence that students were presenting and incorporate it into our teaching.

Today, the prospects for teachers and for students are different. The NCTM's *Standards* documents (1989, 1991, 1995) have furnished the framework that was missing twenty years ago. They have spurred the development of tools for professional inquiry, such as the model described in this article, for use in integrating assessment with instruction. In doing so, they have benefited all students but especially those who, like Billy, walk a narrow path between learning mathematics and giving up.

REFERENCES

Barnett, Carne, Donna Goldstein, and Babette Jackson, eds. *Fractions, Decimals, Ratios, and Percents: Hard to Teach and Hard to Learn?* Portsmouth, N.H.: Heinemann Educational Books, 1994.

California State Department of Education. *A Sampler of Mathematics Assessment.* Sacramento: California State Department of Education, 1994.

Erlwanger, Stanley H. "Case Studies of Children's Conceptions of Mathematics—Part I." *Journal of Children's Mathematical Behavior* 1 (Summer 1975):157–283.

National Council of Teachers of Mathematics. *Curriculum and Evaluation Standards for School Mathematics.* Reston, Va.: The Council, 1989.

———. *Professional Standards for Teaching Mathematics.* Reston, Va.: The Council, 1991.

———. *Assessment Standards for School Mathematics.* Reston, Va.: The Council, 1995.

Pittsburgh Public Schools. *Pittsburgh Performance Assessment Program.* Pittsburgh: Author, 1992.

ON THE NATURE OF TEACHING AND ASSESSING "MATHEMATICAL POWER" AND "MATHEMATICAL THINKING"

Jonathan Jay Greenwood

Two of the first three Standards for Teaching Mathematics begin with the following statements:

The goal of teaching mathematics is to help all students develop *mathematical power* (emphasis added) and all students can learn to *think mathematically* (emphasis added). (NCTM 1991)

What exactly is "mathematical power" to someone who has always identified mathematics as being the mastery of facts, such as the multiplication tables, and procedures, such as the long division

> **Mathematical thinking can be the focus of learning rather than a by-product.**

algorithm? What does it mean to "think mathematically" to a teacher who always struggled with story problems as a student? To those teachers who fit these descriptions, and a sizable number do, assessing students' mathematical power and mathematical thinking is even more bewildering.

Piaget refers to *mathematical power* as having to do with acquiring personal "autonomy" (Kamii 1984). In this context, mathematical power is the student's ability to think and function independently from the teacher. Mathematical

Jay Greenwood teaches at Georgia Southwestern College, Americus, GA 31709, and also works with students at Sumter County Middle School.

power is attained by helping students develop thought processes that can be used to solve problems and to determine whether solutions are appropriate. Mathematical power is gained by minimizing the student's dependence on the teacher or answer key.

Mathematical thinking involves, among other things, the abilities to (*a*) recognize patterns, (*b*) generalize common problem situations, (*c*) identify errors, and (*d*) generate alternative strategies. Mathematical thinking implies a systematic approach to quantitative problems. It is a by-product of learning and doing mathematics. At the same time, it can be the *focus* of learning rather than just a by-product. This focus suggests that all mathematics lessons could benefit by monitoring not only the content being studied but the actual growth in the student's ability to think and reason.

Until recently, the means by which teachers have assessed academic progress has been through the use of paper-and-pencil tests. The assumption has been that correct answers mean mastery; wrong answers mean learning deficiencies. Offered here are some ideas and alternatives to the more traditional methods of academic assessment. The suggested procedures, however, require a rethinking of the criteria for teaching and learning so that they are better aligned with the development of mathematical thinking and power. The article begins by offering seven such learning criteria. Included in the listing are suggestions for

teaching and assessing students' progress that are compatible with each learning criterion. This discussion is followed with suggestions for assessing students' growth and grading it. Pedagogical foundations that support this approach and several content-specific applications of the methods outlined in this article can be found in Greenwood (1991, 1992).

LEARNING CRITERIA FOR MATHEMATICAL THINKING

The criteria found in table 1 are designed to be introduced to the students during the first class period to familiarize them with the notions of "mathematical thinking" and "mathematical power." They can be written on large posterboard and hung on the wall for the duration of the class. The idea is to refer to them often, daily if possible. Introducing the criteria during the first week of school helps students anticipate probing questions throughout the year because they begin to see from the start that more will be expected of them than just correct answers.

In the discussion that follows, the learning criteria themselves are enumerated. The statement that follows each criterion is the rationale that is offered to the students during the first meeting. The accompanying lesson example is given to help convey ideas pertaining to teaching and monitoring each criterion. Before turning to the task of illustrating the criteria, a word is in order about the nature of the examples used. Care has been taken to depict scenarios that cover

TABLE 1
Criteria for Mathematical Thinking

1. Everything you do in mathematics should make sense to you.
2. Whenever you get stuck, you should be able to use what you know to get yourself unstuck.
3. You should be able to identify errors in answers, in the use of materials, and in thinking.
4. Whenever you do a computation, you should use a minimum of counting.
5. You should be able to perform calculations with a minimum of rote pencil-paper computations.
6. When the strategy you are using isn't working, you should be willing to try another strategy instead of giving up.
7. You should be able to extend, or change, a problem situation by posing additional conditions or questions.

a wide range of instructional situations from basic computational exercises to more general problem solving. The intent of these examples is to show the applicability of the criteria across this range and to assist the audience most in need of these ideas.

1. Everything you do in mathematics should make sense to you.

You should be able to explain your strategies and thoughts so they are clearly understood by others, not just repeat the steps of what to do to get an answer. The only way I can determine whether something makes sense to you is by listening to you explain it to me or to others. My assumption is that you can't explain something unless you understand it yourself. Sometimes you will be asked to explain how you worked a problem by using manipulatives, diagrams, patterns, or other materials we will be using. Eventually you will be asked to describe your thoughts and the pictures you have in your mind. So you see, you will have many opportunities to show whether something makes sense to you.

Discussion and example. Imagine walking around the room as students are working on mathematics problems where they are asked to draw a rectangle with a perimeter of 18 and a length of 4. You stop to observe Doris, who seems to be progressing well. You interrupt her work quietly and ask her to explain how she arrived at the drawing of a 4 × 5 rectangle. Her first response is to erase the answer and proceed to work the problem over. Does this scenario sound familiar? In many classrooms, students have acquired the notion that the teacher asks for explanations only for incorrect

answers (Kamii 1984). To develop thinking skills, we must begin to value students' explanations for *all* work, *all* thinking—correct and incorrect alike. When students begin to see that such questions as "Are you willing to show me how you got that answer?" "How do you know?" and "Why is that so?" apply to all the mathematics they do, they will develop more confidence in their original solutions and not feel compelled to erase them so quickly. Students who react to such questions with confidence illustrate growth in this criterion.

2. Whenever you get stuck, you should be able to use what you know to get yourself unstuck.

For you to learn to think for yourself, it is important that you learn how to answer your own questions. I'm asking you to learn how to build on what you know without asking the teacher or checking the answer key. To do so, it is important that you learn how to use what you know to straighten yourself out when you run into trouble. In the beginning, I will help you out by asking you some questions that will lead you to get unstuck. Later on, you will be able to ask the questions of yourself. When you start doing that, we will both know you are learning how to get unstuck.

Discussion and example. Rafael comes to you and asks, "What is '8 × 7'? I forgot." To supply the answer (56) is to get the student "unstuck." Often it is seen as the thing to do. Because of short-term gains, supplying the answer saves time, it keeps the student on task, it minimizes errors, and the student is more apt to seek you out for help when it is needed. However, the long-term effects of consis-

tently giving answers can hinder students' ability to learn what is needed to get themselves unstuck (Bruner 1968). Therefore, this criterion suggests that students' questions be answered with *questions* that will lead to getting unstuck. In this example, an appropriate response might be, "Do you know what 8 × 8 is?" If the student answers "64," the teacher then asks, "Can you use that information to figure out what '8 × 7' is?" If the student doesn't know what 8 × 8 is or can't use the answer to figure out 8 × 7, try a follow-up question, such as "Do you know what '7 × 7' is, and if so can you use that information to figure out what '8 × 7' is?" As students anticipate your questions to their questions, they begin to ask the same kinds of questions of themselves. By the teacher's example they learn some strategies for getting unstuck. Students too can serve as "strategy teachers." They can share with the

Respond to questions with questions.

class difficulties they've encountered and tactics they've used to get unstuck. Sharing this information offers students alternatives and fosters independence in thinking.

3. You should be able to identify errors in answers, in the use of materials, and in thinking.

You can learn a great deal from your errors if you are willing to think about them once they've been spotted. At times I will ask whether you disagree with something and whether you can spot some mistake. If something is wrong and you can spot it, that will tell us both that you know how it is supposed to be. If nothing is wrong and you think there is, that will tell us something too. It will be important to listen to other students because I'm interested in how well you can help each other. We learn best when we take advantage of our mistakes because mistakes tell us a lot about what we need to work on. In a lot of ways, "mistakes" are stepping stones to learning.

Discussion and example. The class is using the fact that the sum of the measures of the three angles of any triangle is 180 degrees to find the sum of the measures of the four angles of any quadrilateral. Miguel has volunteered to come to the front of the class to demonstrate his answer of 720 degrees. He uses figure 1 to illustrate his thinking. He explains, "The quadrilateral *ABCD* is broken into four triangles, and each triangle has a total of 180 degrees. Therefore, the figure *ABCD* has 4 × 180° = 720° altogether."

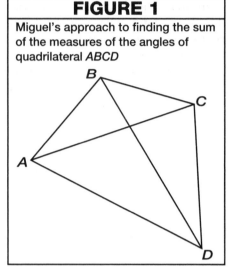

FIGURE 1

Miguel's approach to finding the sum of the measures of the angles of quadrilateral *ABCD*

Several students nod approvingly, and several others look confused. The teacher asks if any students disagree, and although none signal the recognition of an error, Maria asks to share her result, which seems to suggest a different answer. She illustrates her answer with figure 2. She explains, "I broke *ABCD* into two triangles, and therefore the figure *ABCD* has 2 × 180° = 360° altogether."

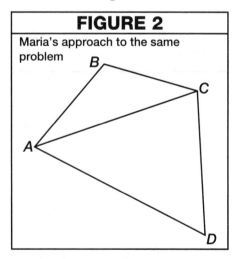

FIGURE 2

Maria's approach to the same problem

The discussion that ensues can go several ways. The teacher can, of course, point out that none of the angle measures *a, b, c, d* in figure 3 contribute to the sum of the measures of the angles of *ABCD*.

This observation suggests that Miguel's answer needs to be decreased by 360 degrees, and the adjusted answer of 720° − 360° = 360° agrees with Maria's. However, long-term advantages are gained by asking the students to discover the nature of the error in the first solution themselves (Bruner 1968; Wirtz 1976; Greenwood 1981). This criterion focuses on the importance of helping students develop the means and the confidence to question answers. Eventually, as students become more familiar with identifying errors, they also become more comfortable and articulate in demonstrating their thinking strategies.

FIGURE 3

The discrepancy between the work of Miguel and of Maria lies in the four interior angles: *a, b, c, d.* The teaching question to consider is, How should the students be led to

4. *Whenever you do a computation, you should use a minimum of counting.*

I will be interested in how well you can learn to think about numbers and how you can picture them being added, subtracted, multiplied, and divided. To help you concentrate on *thinking*, I'm going to be asking you to try not to count. What I would like you to do, as much as possible, is think your way through a computation. By doing so, you'll actually find more and more patterns that will shorten your computations and make them easier for you to do. Every time you do a lot of counting, you actually stop thinking and begin to rely on the counting process itself. If you do this enough, you stop improving, you stop growing; you just fall back to counting. The more you count, the less you think. The more you think, the less you have to count. As we move along in our work together, I'm

going to ask you to explain your work and your thinking in ways that minimize counting.

Discussion and example. This criterion is specifically meant to address the practice of counting on one's fingers to arrive at some addition or subtraction fact. Imagine the following situation occurring in a classroom. The teacher asks Marty, "What's eight plus five?" Marty is observed to use his fingers to count on from eight, moving a finger with each word, saying, "Nine, ten, eleven, twelve, thirteen. The answer is thirteen." Next imagine that twenty minutes have passed, and the teacher again asks Marty to find the answer to "eight plus five." It is not unusual to observe Marty repeat the earlier process in coming up with the answer of thirteen. In fact, when Marty is faced again with the same question, a day, week, or year later, it is not surprising that he employs the same process. The

Could you find the answer without counting?

fact that counting always leads to the correct answer can actually hinder the student's learning anything permanent about the way numbers are combined and partitioned. This idea led Wirtz to conclude that "counting confounds thinking" and that "thinking is maximized when counting is minimized" (Wirtz 1976). It has also been shown that when students have already become dependent on counting as a means for producing addition and subtraction answers, it is counterproductive to demand that they discontinue the practice without helping them develop an alternative strategy with which to replace it (Newton 1985; Greenwood 1981). Therefore, whenever counting is observed, the teacher can wait until the student is finished before asking, "I noticed how you got your answer, Marty. Could you have found it without having to count?" Additional questions posed to the class to offer alternatives could also be framed in this way: "Can someone think of another way you could figure out the answer without having to count?" As these questions are asked over time and as alternative strategies are generated by their peers, students begin to value non-counting strategies and thus begin to generate and employ thinking processes to replace counting practices.

5. *You should be able to perform calculations with a minimum of rote pencil-paper computations.*

This criterion is very similar to item 4, but it is included to give extra emphasis to mental-computational strategies and the use of calculators and computers. It is important that we explore a lot of different ways of solving arithmetic computations and become comfortable with several that go beyond paper and pencil. Exploring alternatives will also help us learn to think mathematically because we'll be concentrating on how things fit together.

Discussion and example. Consider the following set of number sentences:

$$1 + 2 = 3$$
$$4 + 5 + 6 = 7 + 8$$
$$9 + 10 + 11 + 12 = 13 + 14 + 15$$

When each number sentence is presented one at a time, the teacher pauses and asks the class if each one is true. The first two sentences are easily judged by most classes as being true. The next sentence, however, oftentimes has students reaching for their pencils and calculators. In such situations, when students are asked to perform a computation in the context of solving a larger problem or investigating a pattern, it is important to take the opportunity to focus on mental-computational techniques. Thus, this criterion provides a forum around which the teacher can ask, "Can you determine whether the sentence is true by just using your mind?" Students will propose such strategies as "On the left side, '9 + 11 = 20,' and the other two numbers add up to '22,' and '20 + 22 = 42.' On the right side, add the three '10s' together and get '30,' and '3 + 4 + 5= 12' and '30 + 12 = 42.' So the sentence is true." As other student-devised strategies are given, the point is made that many computations can be performed mentally and that a certain amount of "power" is gained by those who can learn to do so. The teacher can then ask if anyone can use the pattern of the first three sentences to describe the next sentence in this sequence. The class discussion, where students share their thinking, leads to the following:

$$1 + 2 = 3$$
$$4 + 5 + 6 = 7 + 8$$
$$9 + 10 + 11 + 12 = 13 + 14 + 15$$
$$16 + 17 + 18 + 19 + 20 = 21 + 22 + 23 + 24$$

The natural question at this point is whether this fourth sentence is true, and here again the students can be asked to try to determine the answer without using paper and pencil or calculator. The author has witnessed several very clever techniques suggested by students. One favorite was given by a fifth-grade student

If one strategy does not work, are you willing to try another?

who claimed that all such sentences formed in this way would be true. His reasoning went like this:

The first sentence is easy, so I'll start with the next one. The second sentence starts off with 4, which is 2 twos. Give one of the 2s to the 5 and one of the 2s to the 6, and you get the right side (7 + 8).

$$4 + 5 + 6 = 7 + 8$$
$$7 + 8 = 7 + 8$$

The third sentence starts off with 9, which is 3 threes. Give a 3 to the 10, a 3 to the 11, and a 3 to the 12, and you get the right side.

$$9 + 10 + 11 + 12 = 13 + 14 + 15$$
$$13 + 14 + 15 = 13 + 14 + 15$$

He continued in this way until he had shown that his method worked for the four sentences given. The class, and the author, were quite impressed. What would the next sentence in this sequence look like? Would it be a true sentence? Will this strategy be successful there too? This criterion is an attempt to help give value to these questions and these types of discussions.

6. *When the strategy you are using isn't working out, you should be willing to try another strategy instead of giving up.*

This criterion is probably the most important of all because it focuses on your learning how to think for yourself. It is also one of the hardest because it challenges you to work your way out of tight spots without the help of the teacher or the answer key. Learning how to think means you are learning how to take care of yourself. It means you don't always need someone else to solve your problems for you. Solving your own problems is the most important thing that school can teach you. It offers you a chance to develop a sort of independence and a sort of "power" that will help you learn on your own after school has taught you all it can. I want you to try to think about this criterion every time you get bogged down trying to solve a problem. Try to monitor your growth in this area and see whether you can minimize the number of times you "give up" on a problem. We will have a number of opportunities to talk about your progress throughout our work together.

Discussion and example. This criterion is similar to criterion 2, "getting unstuck," but like the earlier example of the relationship between criterion 4 and criterion 5, it too is more general than its earlier version because it refers to overall strategies rather than isolated facts or procedures. The intent of the criterion is to help students begin to think in terms of overall problem-solving strategies rather than just isolated answers to episodic problems. This example comes from an experience with a seventh-grade class that was working on geometric constructions. The class had been given a homework problem that asked them to construct a 75-degree angle. The next day, a class discussion showed that several students had solved the problem by constructing two perpendicular lines and bisecting the right angle, forming a 45-degree angle. Then by constructing an equilateral triangle, they produced three 60-degree angles. Bisecting one of the angles of the triangle formed a 30-degree angle. Copying adjacent 45-degree and 30-degree angles formed the desired 75-degree angle. See figure 4.

One of the students, who had been unable to solve the problem the night it was assigned, came to class the day following the class discussion and shared the following solution (see fig. 5). He said that after he saw what other students had done, he had begun to think about the problem after class. When he figured out his solution, he was excited and

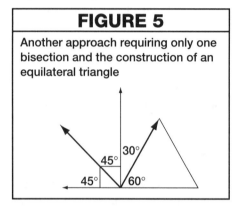

FIGURE 4

Constructing a 75-degree angle by bisecting a right angle, bisecting a 60-degree angle, and copying the two angles as adjacent angles.

wanted to share it with the class. This criterion creates a forum whereby secondary solutions and afterthoughts are an important component of mathematics.

FIGURE 5

Another approach requiring only one bisection and the construction of an equilateral triangle

7. *You should be able to extend a problem situation by posing additional conditions or questions.*

Every problem is determined by the specific conditions that it describes. By changing any of the conditions, you end up with a new and different problem. We will be trying to go beyond solving problems and coming up with answers. Part of our work will be about making up our own questions and problems. After we work a problem, we might ask, "What would happen if...?" This question usually leads to a different problem, and I want you to pay attention to how often we explore it in class and how often you ask it yourself. Albert Einstein once said, "Imagination is more important than knowledge." This criterion is about imagination.

Discussion and example. Problem posing is the ultimate expression of mathematical growth (Bruner 1968; Wirtz 1976). Consider the following problem that was given to a fourth-grade class.

$$
\begin{array}{r}
A \\
B \\
+C \\
\hline
AB
\end{array}
$$

Each letter represents a digit (0,1,2, ...,9) and the students were to find the value of C. By trial and error, most students found that $C = 9$ and $A = 1$ and that B could be any other digit. The class discussion intrigued one student, Sophia. She continued to play around with the problem after class to the extent that she removed the restriction that C be a one-digit number. The next day, she shared her findings with the class. It seems that if $A = 7$, and $B = 4$, then

$$
\begin{array}{r}
7 \\
4 \\
+C \\
\hline
74
\end{array}
$$

means that $C = 63$. Continuing in this vein, Sophia found that in each case, C would necessarily be a multiple of 9, and in fact would be $9 \times A$. By extending the problem she found another interesting property of numbers, and she was motivated to share her discovery with the class. More important in the long term, the class discussion that she prompted set a memorable example to the other students about the potential for posing one's own questions and problems.

These seven criteria, then, form the basis for establishing a classroom environment that advances the notion that "mathematics is a way of thinking." They lay a foundation whereby students can actually practice mathematical thinking while learning it themselves. The criteria go a long way in giving importance to the order and logic on which the field of mathematics is built. They depend on and support students' understandings and the ability to talk about their work in ways that will make sense to others. According to these criteria, mathematics is not seen as being just a chain of rules, each of which produces an answer. In fact, under these conditions, the student is meant to see that one's responsibility for doing a mathematics problem does not end when an answer is obtained. The process of explaining and defending one's strategy is of equal importance. Besides offering many valuable opportunities for students to learn from their own work, whether correct or incorrect, this process

is also a critical diagnostic tool the teacher can use to see "inside the student's head" to determine the extent of understanding. The seven criteria support the notion that the strength of knowledge is in the ability not only to answer questions but also to have the sense and confidence to question answers.

Establishing these seven learning criteria alone will not automatically generate instant successful learning in all students. The teacher needs to see that establishing and referring to the learning criteria is an important first step. Given time and attention, the criteria can help students bring more thought and personal responsibility to their learning.

ASSESSING STUDENTS' PROGRESS

We now shift our focus to assessing and grading students. In this area, the role of the teacher is to gather information that describes how students respond to each of these criteria; organize what is observed; and turn it into usable, accurate assessment data. The following discussion contains some ideas that have been found useful in this effort.

Whenever working or explaining finished work, the student supplies the teacher with information that can be used to gauge growth along at least one of the criteria. In the beginning, these observations can be recorded on the record sheet shown in table 2. After a while, as the assessment process is internalized by the teacher, most assessment data are more easily remembered and organized without having to record them. At any rate, in the beginning the recording sheet can be used as follows:

a. To keep an unmarked original record form, make a photocopy of it and refile the original for future use.

b. Write each student's name on the copy.

c. Make one copy of this record for each month assessment data are collected.

d. Equate each number at the top of the form with one of the criteria. For example:

1 = *Everything you do in mathematics should make sense to you.* (Understands)

2 = *Whenever you get stuck, you should be able to use what you know to get yourself unstuck.* (Gets unstuck)

3 = *You should be able to identify errors in answers in the use of materials and in thinking.* (Spots errors)

4 = *Whenever you do a computation, you should use a minimum of counting.* (Minimum of counting)

5 = *You should be able to perform calculations with a minimum of rote pencil-paper computations.* (Minimum paper-pencil use)

6 = *When the strategy you are using isn't working out, you should be willing to try another strategy instead of giving up.* (Perseverance)

7 = *You should be able to extend a problem situation by posing additional conditions or questions.* (Problem posing)

e. Select a grading and recording system to use on the student data that will be collected.

Letter grades, such as the traditional A–F, or others, such as the one offered here, can be used. If you prefer, the numbers 1–5 could be used in place of the letters and might be considered when a numerical average is desired. Several suggestions are given in table 3. Whichever code is selected, the teacher records the grade or score under the appropriate criterion when a student provides information to the teacher. For example, Su-Lin is observed working with another student, Hans. The teacher overhears the following conversation:

Su-Lin: "Wait a minute, that's not right. Six times eight isn't fifty-six."

Hans: "Yes it is."

Su-Lin: "No it's not. I'll bet you it's not."

Hans: "Okay, let's get the grid and masks" (the materials being used at the time).

They get the grid and masks, and Hans discovers that he's made a mistake. The teacher has gained valuable assess-

TABLE 2
Student Record Form

Student	Understands 1	Get Unstuck 2	Spots Errors 3	Minimum of Counting 4	Minimum Pencil-Paper Usage 5	Perseverance 6	Problem Posing 7	Tests 8

TABLE 3

Grading Codes That Might Be Used for Each Criterion

Grade	Grade	Score	Interpretation
A	E	5	*Excellent.* A superior example of a clear explanation (use of materials, gets unstuck, spots errors, etc.)
B	V	4	*Very good.* Better-than-average explanation (use of materials, gets unstuck, spots errors, etc.)
C	G	3	*Good.* Satisfactory explanation but lacking in detail (use of materials, gets unstuck, spots errors, etc.)
D	B	2	*Below Average.* Lacks detail and raises questions as to complete understanding (use of materials, gets unstuck, spots errors, etc.)
F	N	1	*Not satisfactory.* Not able to meet this criterion at this time

ment information on both students. Su-Lin spotted an error and called it to Hans's attention, so the teacher can record an "E" or "V" under the number "3" next to her name (using the middle coding system). Hans was able to focus on the question raised by Su-Lin and had some sense of how to find the correct answer. In doing so, he found his error and corrected it. The teacher needs to decide whether this occurrence was an example of getting unstuck or finding an error, or both, but it is useful information no matter where it is recorded. It should also be noted that had Hans not suggested the grid and masks as a way of finding the correct answer, or if neither of them spotted the error, this information would also have been useful and could have been translated into a "B" or "N" for both. The situation given in the foregoing dialogue would be worthy of a class discussion to help students better understand how such interactions can be used to assess learning. It might be introduced to the class like this:

"While I was walking around during your work time, I saw Su-Lin and Hans discussing a difference of opinion about one of the problems. Su-Lin and Hans, are you willing to tell the class what happened?" After the situation is described, ask the class whether they can tell which of the learning criteria was demonstrated in that example, and then go on to tell Su-Lin and Hans that they need to think about taking credit for the way in which they handled it. (See Greenwood [1991, 1992] for more examples.)

The teacher should make an effort to collect information for each criterion on every student at least once a month. Therefore, copies of the record sheet are needed for each month of use. Often, if enough information hasn't been gathered for, say, Josef and the class is approaching the end of the month, the teacher may tell him that he will be asked to share some of his work at the front of the class the next day (or soon). It is important to give students advance notice when they will be asked to do something that involves personal risk (Newton 1985). It helps them prepare their focus and they are not jolted with surprise when called on. In such situations, the teacher can also make a note to observe these students more closely. As time goes on, the teacher gets a lot better at pacing observations and spreading them around more evenly throughout the month.

At the end of each month the students can be asked to evaluate themselves according to the same seven criteria. By doing so, the students take an active part in monitoring their own growth and have a chance to compare their evaluative statements with the teacher's. Table 4 is a copy of the general form used with students.

On Monday or Tuesday of the last week of each month, the form is distributed to each student. The students are asked to consider each criterion carefully and to grade themselves, marking in the left column, according to how they think they've done over the course of the month. They are asked to use the same grading code that will be used by the teacher. The students can use the suggested code given previously in their self-evaluations. The code that follows has also been used with students because many find it easier to interpret:

A = Always
M = Most of the time
O = Occasionally
S = Seldom
N = Not at all

After sufficient time, students' self-evaluations are collected. The teacher then goes over each student's form carefully and evaluates it using the same grade codes, marking in the rightmost column. In the beginning, it is not unusual for students to be more critical of themselves and more negative with their own self-given scores than the assessments given by the teacher. Whenever these discrepancies occur, the student can be asked to try to describe how the teacher's grade was determined. That is, what information did the teacher use to assess the student's growth as being greater than that given by the student? The question is more than rhetorical, since it asks the student to reflect on how she or he is perceived by others; and since the teacher's grade is generally higher, it offers the student a chance to think about how she or he has grown. As

> *Progress against these criteria can be assessed by both teacher and student.*

time goes on, students develop a better sense for assessing themselves and seem to keep the criteria more in mind when they are working. Again over time, students lose the biting edge of self-criticism and become more kind to themselves. When the teacher finishes writing responses on the forms, they are returned to the students with the request that they be taken home and shown to their parents. They are to be returned the next day with the parent's signature and are kept until the end of the grading period. These informal assessments are intended to supplement the formal grades that are sent home at the end of each grading period. This type of monthly communication is vitally important in monitoring and reporting students' growth. It has been found that this total assessment program is effective for several reasons:

- It gives the students a chance to grade themselves, which is critical to developing a sense of personal involvement and personal responsibility in one's learning.

- It gives students an opportunity to compare their evaluative judgment

Emphasis on Assessment

TABLE 4

Student-Teacher Mathematics Evaluation Sheet

Student _____

What I'd give myself		What the teacher would give me
☐	1. I give clear and understandable explanations and can use the materials to show that the mathematics I do makes sense to me.	☐
☐	2. Whenever I get stuck, I can use what I know to get unstuck.	☐
☐	3. I am able to identify errors in answers, in the use of the mathematics materials, and in thinking.	☐
☐	4. When I do a computation, I do a minimum of counting.	☐
☐	5. When I do a computation, I don't always need paper and pencil.	☐
☐	6. When a strategy doesn't work, I try another one instead of giving up.	☐
☐	7. I can extend, or change, a problem by asking extra questions or posing different conditions.	☐
☐	8. I study and practice before tests and quizzes.	☐
☐	9. I am a helpful partner.	☐
☐	10. I take care of myself when learning mathematics.	☐

Use the following code to mark yourself in each criterion.

A = Always
M = Most of the time
O = Occasionally
S = Seldom
N = Not at all

with someone else's. This type of "reality check" helps solidify the student's "outside-in" view of self.

- The learning criteria become more familiar, more important, and more useful to the students as they learn how to apply the criteria both to learning and to the assessment of learning.

- Students are not surprised when grades come out. They are much more a part of the grading process, and they begin to see it as a "consequence" of their efforts during the previous days and weeks.

SUGGESTIONS FOR GRADING

The following discussion is difficult to broach because of the personally sensitive nature of grading students. It is also difficult because of the laudable work done recently to move assessment toward holistic parameters rather than reduce them to simplistic letter grades

of the past (Stenmark 1989). The suggestions offered here are not intended in any way as a criticism of that work, nor as implied support for letter grades and grade-point averages. The intent rather is to offer helpful suggestions to teachers who find themselves struggling with the problems of transition that will help broaden the concept of grades so that they better reflect students' growth in mathematical power and mathematical thinking and place less emphasis on procedural knowledge that is the domain of tests and quizzes.

With this intent in mind, the process of translating the foregoing discussion into recorded grades is the next step in expanding student assessment to reflect these new dimensions. It is important that students' grades reflect all the areas that have been the focus of the seven learning criteria given previously. Grades that are solely dependent on test scores and on the completion of homework assignments simply do not

capture the quality of learning that is proposed and intended by the NCTM's *Curriculum and Evaluation Standards* (1989). The teacher can quantify each of the seven learning criteria by using numbers instead of letter grades, find their sum, and add the test scores to this total. Dividing this accumulated total by 8 (the seven criteria plus the average test score—see table 2) provides the teacher a meaningful, more complete measure of the student. When weighing each area somewhat equally, a composite grade might then be determined by averaging the eight criteria. Several alternatives in weighing are given in table 5.

Responses from parents, students, and administrators have shown that such a grade reflects a more total picture of the student's progress during the grading period. It also supplies valuable information for parents in their attempts to help students at home.

TABLE 5
Suggestions for Weighting the Different Criteria

Ex. 1 weight	Ex. 2 weight	Ex. 3 weight	Criterion
13%	15%	10%	Understanding
13%	10%	15%	Getting unstuck
12%	10%	10%	Spotting errors
12%	10%	15%	Using minimum of counting
13%	20%	15%	Using minimum of paper-pencil
12%	10%	15%	Perseverance
12%	10%	10%	Problem posing
13%	15%	10%	Tests and quizzes
100%	100%	100%	Total grade

SUMMARY

Implementing the NCTM's curriculum standards and professional teaching standards (1989, 1991) requires operational definitions for such terms as *mathematical power* and *mathematical thinking*. Without a workable process for defining our work in teaching and assessing these noble goals, we stand exposed to the close scrutiny of those more interested in test scores as a means of measuring students' growth. The ideas and experiences presented in this article are shared as an attempt to contribute to this effort. They are based on the use of seven learning criteria that help put into operation the concepts of mathematical power and mathematical thinking. The criteria can be used across grade levels and for all mathematical topics as a basis for planning, teaching, and assessing students' growth.

BIBLIOGRAPHY

Bruner, Jerome S. *Toward a Theory of Instruction*. New York: W. W. Norton & Co., 1968.

Greenwood, Jonathan Jay. "The Effects of Student-conducted Error Analysis on Teacher Practices and Student Performance." Unpublished Ph.D. diss., University of Oregon, June 1981.

———. *Developing Mathematical Thinking: A Complete Unit on the Addition and Subtraction Basic Facts*. Portland, Oreg.: Multnomah Education Service District, 1991.

———. *Developing Mathematical Thinking: A Complete Unit on the Multiplication and Division Basic Facts*. Portland, Oreg.: Multnomah Education Service District, 1992.

Kamii, Constance. "Autonomy: The Aim of Education Envisioned by Piaget." *Phi Delta Kappan* 65 (February 1984):410–15.

National Council of Teachers of Mathematics. *Curriculum and Evaluation Standards for School Mathematics*. Reston, Va.: The Council, 1989.

———. *Professional Standards for Teaching Mathematics: Executive Summary*. Reston, Va.: The Council, 1991.

Newton, Fred E. *Alternatives to Failure: Resources for Improving Teaching: A Report of Two Alternative Classrooms*. Portland, Oreg.: Multnomah Education Service District, 1985.

Stenmark, Jean. *Assessment Alternatives in Mathematics*. Berkeley, Calif.: EQUALS Project, Lawrence Hall of Science, 1989.

Wirtz, Robert. *Banking on Problem Solving*. Monterey, Calif.: Curriculum Development Associates, 1976.

ACHIEVEMENT TESTS IN PRIMARY MATHEMATICS: PERPETUATING LOWER-ORDER THINKING

Constance Kamii and Barbara Ann Lewis

The *Curriculum and Evaluation Standards* (NCTM 1989) states that if we want to improve the nation's mathematics education, it is necessary to change the current method of evaluation that depends on standardized achievement tests. The National Research Council (1989) is even more explicit about the harmful effects of achievement testing. Among its criticisms are the following (p. 68):

- Tests become ends in themselves, not means to assess educational objectives. Knowing this, teachers often teach to the tests, not to the curriculum or to the children.
- Tests stress lower- rather than higher-order thinking.

In spite of the consensus among mathematics educators that standardized achievement testing encourages lower-order thinking, these tests continue to be used throughout the country as if they revealed The Truth about students' knowledge of mathematics. The purpose of this article is to present data demonstrating that achievement tests in prima-

Constance Kamii and Barbara Lewis teach at the University of Alabama at Birmingham, Birmingham, AL 35294. Kamii is working with teachers at the Hall-Kent Elementary School in Homewood, Alabama, to develop a primary-level mathematics program based on constructivism, the theory of Jean Piaget. In the summer of 1991, Lewis will direct a six-week, NSF-funded institute in mathematics education for elementary school teachers.

ry mathematics give misleading information. By comparing second graders' scores on an achievement test with their answers to questions requiring higher-order thinking, we intend to show that standardized achievement tests emphasize pupils' lower-order thinking.

The data were collected on 87 pupils in four second-grade classes in late spring. Two of the classes came from schools in which mathematics instruction was traditional, with reliance on a textbook, its accompanying workbook, and manipulatives. The other two classes' school offered the constructivist primary mathematics program described in Kamii

> ## Achievement tests give misleading information.

(1985, 1989a, 1989b). The characteristic of the constructivist program was that the teacher did not teach pupils how to do anything and, instead, asked them to invent their own procedures for solving computational and story problems. The pupils in the constructivist program also played many mathematical games requiring numerical thinking and strategies. By contrast, those in the traditional program were taught rules, or algorithms, specifying how to add and subtract two-digit numbers, and so forth. The traditional program also gave many exercises and story problems involving the application of algorithms.

All the pupils in the study attended suburban schools in lower- to upper-middle-class communities near Birmingham, Alabama. In the constructivist school the second graders were at the 79th percentile on the mathematics portion of the nationally normed achievement test mandated in the state of Alabama. The corresponding percentiles at the other schools were 85 or above. We cannot give exact percentiles, since we promised to protect the anonymity of the schools that served as comparison groups. If we compare the mathematics scores on the achievement test, traditional instruction appears to be more effective than constructivist teaching. However, the following data related to place value, double-column addition, story problems, mental arithmetic, and estimation lead to the opposite conclusion.

Place value

The achievement test has a cluster of items identified as Place Value. The mean raw score out of a possible 15 on this cluster was 12.60 for the constructivist group and 14.64 for the traditionally instructed group.

To find out how the pupils' scores on the achievement test corresponded to their understanding, we individually interviewed all the pupils in the four classes. In the interview, each pupil was first shown a card with the numeral 16 written on it and asked to count out sixteen chips. The interviewer then drew an imaginary circle around the 6 in the 16 with the blunt end of a pen and asked, "What does *this part* [the 6] mean? Could you show me with the chips what *this part* [the 6] means?" The second graders did not have any difficulty with this question.

The interviewer then circled the 1 in the 16 and asked, "What about *this part* [the 1]? Could you show me with the chips what *this part* [the 1] means?" (Note the use of the term *this part* to avoid the use of any other word.)

> ## Individual interviews reflected dramatic differences.

If the pupil showed only one chip, the interviewer continued to probe: "You showed me all these chips [pointing out the 16 chips] for this number [circling the 16 on the card] and these [pointing to 6 chips] for this part [circling the 6 on the card] and this chip [pointing] for this part [pointing to the 1 on the card]. What about the rest of the chips [pointing to the 9 or 10 chips that were not used to show the two parts on the card]? Is this how it's supposed to be, or is there something strange here?" A few pupils replied that something was strange, but most of them said that that was how things were supposed to be.

The proportions of pupils in the four classes who showed ten chips for the 1 in 16 were 67 percent of the constructivist group and only 15 percent of the traditionally instructed group (see table 1).

The reason for the contradictory finding is that achievement tests tap mainly knowledge of symbols. For example, in one test item of the Place Value cluster, pupils are shown 50019, 5019, 519, and 590 and asked to mark the one that says "five hundred nineteen." (We made up all the test items, but our examples are similar to the items on the test.) In another item, pupils are shown an expanded form of a number, such as 500 + 20 + 0, and the possible answers of 700, 520, 50020, and 5200. Second graders can manipulate written symbols to answer these kinds of questions without understanding the numerical value of each digit. The results from the interviews concerning pupils' understanding of regrouping, which are discussed next, lend further support to this statement.

Double-column addition

The cluster on the achievement test that includes double-column-addition problems is Addition of Whole Numbers. This cluster consists of 16 computational problems, some of which involve regrouping. The mean raw score on this cluster was 14.76 for the constructivist group and 15.12 for the traditionally instructed group. These data give the impression that no difference existed between the two groups, but individual interviews revealed dramatic differences (see table 2).

After asking the question about the 1 of 16 in the place-value interview, we left the card and the 16 chips on the table and presented the pupil with a card on which the following problem was written:

$$\begin{array}{r} 16 \\ +17 \\ \hline \end{array}$$

The interviewer asked the pupil to "add these numbers in your head" and to explain how he or she got the answer. Almost all the pupils in both groups gave the answer of 33. All the traditionally instructed pupils explained that they added the 6 and the 7 first, got 13, "put the '3' down here and carried the '1' there," and so on. By contrast, almost all the pupils in the constructivist group added the tens first and then the ones as follows:

$$10 + 10 = 20$$
$$7 + 6 = 13$$
$$20 + 10 = 30$$
$$30 + 3 = 33$$

The interviewer then asked the pupil to count out 17 chips. When the pupil finished, the interviewer pointed out the correspondence between the numeral 16 on the card and the 16 chips and between the numeral 17 on the card and the 17 chips. The next request was that the pupil explain, using the chips, the procedure he or she had just described.

As can be seen in table 2, 83 percent of the constructivist group correctly explained regrouping with chips, but only 23 percent of the traditionally instructed group did so. The pupils in the latter group revealed their confusion in a surprisingly wide variety of ways. Following is an example: "I take '6' from '16' and '7' from '17,' and that makes '13.' I then take '1' from '13' (see fig. 1a) and '1' and '1' [taken from one of the piles of 10], and that's how I got my answer." The interviewer protested, "I don't see '33' anywhere, and I don't understand how you got '33' with what you have here." Some pupils then arranged two sets of 3 chips, as shown in figure 1b, in an attempt to produce the written convention with chips. Almost all the traditionally instructed

TABLE 1			
Data on Place Value			
	Constructivist *n* = 46	Traditional *n* = 39*	Significance of difference
Achievement test (raw score on Place Value)	12.60	14.64	n.s.
Interview (percent showing ten chips for the 1 in 16)	67%	15%	0.001
*Two pupils were absent on the day of testing.			

TABLE 2			
Data on Double-Column Addition			
	Constructivist *n* = 46	Traditional *n* = 39*	Significance of difference
Achievement test (raw score on Addition with Whole Numbers)	14.76	15.12	n.s.
Explanation of $\begin{array}{r}16\\+17\\\hline\end{array}$ (percent explaining)	83%	23%	0.001
Misaligned digits (percent writing 99 as the answer)	11%	79%	0.001
*Two pupils were absent on the day of testing.			

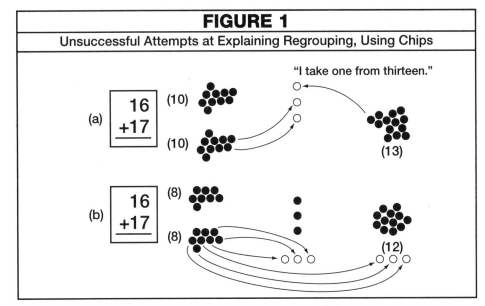

FIGURE 1
Unsuccessful Attempts at Explaining Regrouping, Using Chips

pupils thus got the correct answer, but only 23 percent could explain with chips why the answer was 33.

In the final part of the interview, we handed a sheet of paper to the pupil on which the following misaligned columns (adapted from Labinowicz 1985) appeared:

$$\begin{array}{r} 4 \\ 35 \\ +24 \\ \hline \end{array}$$

The interviewer asked the pupil to "read these numbers" and then to write the answer. When the pupil finished, the interviewer asked him or her to read the answer aloud and then inquired, "Does that sound right?"

As can be seen in table 2, the proportions who wrote 99 by mechanically following the rule of adding each column were 11 percent of the constructivist group and 79 percent of the traditionally instructed group. The percent of 79 is not surprising, since the traditionally instructed second graders generally did not understand place value, as was demonstrated in their answers about the 1 in the 16.

The reason for the large discrepancy between the findings of the achievement test and those of the interviewers is that the achievement test evaluates only if pupils can solve problems presented in the conventional forms that have been taught. Achievement tests do not ask if pupils understand why their answers are correct, nor do they ask what pupils do when a problem is presented in an incorrect form.

Story problems

On the achievement-test cluster called Problem Solving, the constructivist and traditionally instructed groups got similar raw scores of 12.62 and 12.76 out of a possible 15. The story problems on the achievement test are all easy, routine problems with small numbers, for example, Mary had 15 pieces of gum and gave 6 pieces to Peter. How many pieces does she have left?

> *Achievement tests don't ask why an answer is correct.*

The goal of the constructivist program was not for pupils to solve routine problems that had been practiced but to become able to deal with novel problems never before encountered. We made a booklet of nonroutine problems for group administration and called it the *Math Sampler*. Three of the questions in the *Math Sampler* were the following:

1. There are 26 sheep and 10 goats on a ship. How old is the captain?

2. There are 49 children who want to go to the zoo. Some of their parents are willing to drive their cars and can take 5 children in each car. How many cars will be needed to take all 49 children to the zoo?

3. There are 21 children in the class. If they each bring 14 soup labels, how many labels will there be altogether?

As can be seen in table 3, 27 percent of the constructivist group wrote that the question about the captain's age did not make sense, but none of the traditionally instructed group objected to this question. The great majority of the latter group (88%) wrote 36 as the answer because 26 + 10 = 36.

The question about the number of cars needed to take 49 children to the zoo is the kind presented in third grade as a division problem in traditional programs. As can be seen in table 3, 61 percent of the constructivist group and 29 percent of the traditionally instructed group gave the answer of 10 cars by using repeated addition.

The question about soup labels is typical of story problems involving the multiplication of a two-digit number by a two-digit number that is traditionally introduced in fourth grade. Twenty percent of the second graders in the constructivist program wrote 14 vertically 21 times and used addition to get the answer of 294. Only 2 percent of the traditionally instructed group wrote this answer.

The percents in table 3 demonstrate that pupils who have been encouraged to invent their own procedures do better on nonroutine story problems than those who have been taught how to get answers. Readers interested in further details about other story problems can find them in Kamii (1989b).

TABLE 3
Data on Story Problems

	Constructivist $n = 41$*	Traditional $n = 41$	Significance of difference
Achievement test (raw score on Problem Solving)	12.62	12.76	n.s.
Math Sampler			
1. It does not make sense	27%	0%	0.001
2. 10 cars	61%	29%	0.002
3. 294 labels	20%	2%	0.004

*Five pupils were absent on the day of testing.

Mental arithmetic

Mental arithmetic is not tested on the achievement test, but we gave the following three problems by using an overhead projector so that the pupils could see each problem for only 9 seconds: 98 + 43, 3 × 31, and 4 × 27. As can be seen in table 4, very few traditionally taught pupils could give correct answers, but 48 percent, 60 percent, and 29 percent, respectively, of the constructivist group did. By changing 98 + 43 to 100 + 41, for example, half the pupils in the latter group got the answer.

Estimation

The ability to make estimates is important not only in mathematics, in determining the reasonableness of an answer, but also in daily living. However, the achievement test does not have a single question requiring estimation. We used an overhead projector to allow pupils to see the problem for only 4.5 seconds. As table 4 shows, 64 percent of the constructivist group and 39 percent of the traditionally instructed group wrote answers for 347 + 282 in the 500–700 range.

DISCUSSION OF THE DATA

We have presented many examples showing that according to an achievement test, traditional instruction produces results that are just as good as, or better than, a constructivist program. However, other data consistently demonstrate with statistical significance the superiority of a constructivist program if higher-order thinking is evaluated.

The reason for the discrepancy lies in the fact that achievement tests are created within the framework of an obsolete conception of school mathematics. According to the old conception, mathematics is a set of symbols and rules, or algorithms, to internalize. Because traditional mathematics educators and makers of achievement tests either do not know or do not accept the difference between social, or conventional, knowledge and logicomathematical knowledge, they reduce mathematics to conventional symbols and rules. The distinction Jean Piaget (1971) made among the following three kinds of knowledge according to their ultimate sources clarifies this statement.

> *Achievement tests omit mental arithmetic and estimation.*

Physical knowledge, logicomathematical knowledge, and social knowledge

Physical knowledge is knowledge of objects in external reality. The color and weight of a bead are examples of physical properties that are in objects in external reality that can be known empirically by observation.

Logicomathematical knowledge, in contrast, consists of relationships created by each individual. For instance, when we are presented with a red bead and a blue one and think that they are *different*, this difference is a relationship created by each individual. The beads are observable, but the difference between them is not. The difference exists neither *in* the red bead nor *in* the blue one, and if a person did not put the objects into this relationship, the difference would not exist for him or her. Other examples of relationships the individual can create between the same beads are *similar* and *two*. Numerical concepts are thus relationships created mentally by each indi-vidual. In other words, physical knowledge is empirical knowledge that has its source partly in objects. Logicomathematical knowledge, however, is not empirical knowledge, since its source is in each individual's head. The individual goes on to construct relationships based on the relationships he or she previously made. Adding *three* to *four* is an example of constructing a relationship with previously constructed relationships.

The ultimate sources of social knowledge are conventions worked out by people. Examples of social knowledge are the fact that Christmas comes on 25 December and that a tree is called *tree*. The spoken words *one, two, three,* as well as such written numerals as 1, 2, 3, belong to social knowledge, but the numerical concepts underlying these conventions belong to logicomathematical knowledge. The reader interested in further details about the three kinds of knowledge is referred to Kamii (1985, 1989b).

Testing for social knowledge or for logicomathematical knowledge?

Two foregoing examples were given from the Place Value cluster of the achievement test to show that the test taps knowledge of symbols. We can now point out that symbols belong to social knowledge. For example, writing the numeral 10 requires only social knowledge, without tapping the underlying logicomathematical knowledge of being able to think *simultaneously* about 1 ten and 10 ones. This logicomathematical knowledge is difficult for second graders, and our place-value interview targeted precisely this thinking. A more detailed discussion of place value can be found in Kamii (1989b).

The other data presented show that the achievement test and the test we made produced contradictory findings because the former focused on social knowledge, whereas the latter examined pupils' logicomathematical knowledge, that is, their reasoning.

Double-column addition is now taught as a set of conventional rules for pupils to learn. Working within the framework of this old conception, achievement-test makers ask only if pupils can follow the rules to get correct

TABLE 4
Data on Mental Arithmetic and Estimation

	Constructivist $n = 42$*	Traditional $n = 41$	Significance of difference
Mental arithmetic (9 s)			
98 + 43	48%	17%	0.002
3 × 31	60%	17%	0.001
4 × 27	29%	5%	0.002
Estimation (4.5 s)			
347 + 282 = answer in 500–700 range	64%	39%	0.01

*Four pupils were absent on the day of testing.

answers. For constructivists, however, the important consideration is pupils' thinking, or their logicomathematical knowledge. Our interviews relating to double-column addition thus focused on logicomathematical knowledge, whereas the achievement test examined only pupils' knowledge of a social rule.

According to the old conception of school mathematics, story problems involve the application of rules that have been taught. The story problems in achievement tests are, therefore, easy, routine problems, as we stated earlier. Some questions in achievement tests even ask for only the conventional, written form for the question rather than ask for a numerical answer. Consider an example of this emphasis on social knowledge: Mary has 7 marbles and her brother gives her 5. Which number sentence can you use to find out how many marbles Mary now has?

$$7 + 5 = \_\_\_$$
$$7 - 5 = \_\_\_$$
$$\_\_\_ 5 + = 7$$
$$7 - \_\_\_ = 5$$

We were also interested in pupils' thinking in mental arithmetic, or their logicomathematical knowledge. For this reason we wanted to see, for example, if pupils mentally changed 98 + 43 to 100 + 41, or 3 × 31 to 90 + 3. Those who knew only to use algorithms did not think about restructuring the problem to make it easier.

In the estimation task, all the pupils were told that they would not have enough time to get the exact answer. If they were in the habit of inventing solutions, they thought of 347 + 282 as "500 and something" or "600 and something" instead of using the algorithm.

We stated at the beginning of this article that according to the National Research Council, "tests stress lower- rather than high-order thinking" (1989, p. 68). Achievement tests include an inordinate number of computational problems requiring lower-order thinking. Other examples of test items that tap lower-order thinking and social knowledge are the following:

What fraction of this shape (see fig. 2a) is shaded?

$$\frac{1}{2} \quad \frac{1}{1} \quad \frac{2}{1} \quad \frac{2}{2}$$

What time is it according to the clock (see fig. 2b)?

2:30   6:15   1:60   1:30

Which metric unit should you use to measure the length of a crayon?

kilometer liter gram centimeter

Which pair is correct?

five   nine   two   seven
( )   ( )   ( )   ( )
 4   8   3   7

The last item is from the category Concepts of Number. In reality, this item has nothing to do with the logicomathematical concept of number, since it taps only pupils' ability to read symbols.

Money is better spent on alternative assessment.

IMPLICATIONS FOR TEACHERS AND PRINCIPALS

The sale of achievement tests is completely unregulated, and test makers are not accountable to anyone to keep abreast of recent research and theory, the NCTM's *Curriculum and Evaluation Standards*, or the recommendations of the National Research Council. Yet test makers have enormous influence on classroom practices because teachers teach to the tests and textbooks are now aligned with achievement tests.

As explained in Kamii (1990), the evaluation of any instructional program takes place with reference to the goals and objectives defined for the program. The NCTM's *Curriculum and Evaluation Standards* calls for the development of logical reasoning as a major goal of mathematics programs. Achievement tests, however, measure mostly the extent to which pupils have learned symbols and rules to produce correct answers.

Achievement tests would instantly become powerless and harmless if the purchase of these tests stopped. Even though teachers and principals are held accountable to produce higher test scores, policy makers and those who purchase these tests are not held accountable to prove that the tests, in fact, improve instruction. Teachers and principals can organize themselves through the local affiliates of such professional organizations as the National Council of Teachers of Mathematics, the National Association for the Education of Young Children, and the National Association of Elementary School Principals and demand that policy makers in their states and school systems justify the purchase of achievement tests. As long as the goals and objectives defined by achievement tests remain outdated, these tests will continue to promote rote memorization and lower-order thinking.

REFERENCES

Kamii, Constance. *Double-Column Addition: A Teacher Uses Piaget's Theory*. New York: Teachers College Press, 1989a. Videotape.

———. *Young Children Continue to Reinvent Arithmetic, 2nd Grade*. New York: Teachers College Press, 1989b.

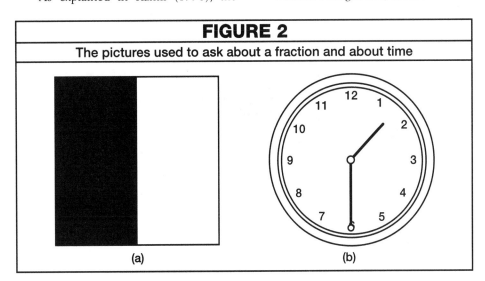

FIGURE 2

The pictures used to ask about a fraction and about time

(a)   (b)

———. *Young Children Reinvent Arithmetic.* New York: Teachers College Press, 1985.

Kamii, Constance, ed. *Achievement Testing in the Early Grades: The Games Grown-ups Play.* Washington, D.C.: National Association for the Education of Young Children, 1990.

Labinowicz, Ed. *Learning from Children: New Beginnings for Teaching Numerical Thinking.* Menlo Park, Calif.: Addison-Wesley Publishing Co., 1985.

National Council of Teachers of Mathematics, Commission on Standards for School Mathematics. *Curriculum and Evaluation Standards for School Mathematics.* Reston, Va.: The Council, 1989.

National Research Council, Mathematical Sciences Education Board. *Everybody Counts: A Report to the Nation on the Future of Mathematics Education.* Washington, D.C.: National Academy Press, 1989.

Piaget, Jean. *Biology and Knowledge: An Essay on the Relations between Organic Regulations and Cognitive Processes.* Chicago: University of Chicago Press, 1971.

SECTION II:

Looking at Testing
and Grading

Colleagues, administrators, students, parents, college admission directors, politicians, and the local community all take an interest in what occurs within the classroom. Test data have been the traditional means of communicating information both about students' progress and about school programs. A major stance taken in the NCTM *Assessment Standards* is that multiple sources of information, rather than traditional tests and grades alone, should be used to make such judgments. The articles in this section take a new look at testing and grading—examining their pros and cons and suggesting modifications that may make them more useful.

Cynthia Garnett identifies a disturbing consequence of testing. She describes how the experience of testing in the classroom can influence children's perceptions of school and learning. In particular, her children have come to believe that "schooling is testing" and "playing is not learning." Her observations in "Testing—Do Not Disturb? A Concerned Parent's View of Testing" provide strong motivation for taking a closer look at how we test and how we can supplement testing so that children gain a clearer understanding of what is really meant by learning.

Arguing that teachers have traditionally relied too heavily on timed teacher-designed tests for evaluating students' progress, Jon Manon writes about "The Mathematics Test: A New Role for an Old Friend." He suggests that tests are highly efficient for certifying procedural skills and for providing summative feedback at the end of units but recommends using a wider variety of assessment measures when formative feedback about instruction is desired. Furthermore, Manon points out that tests need not occur only at the end of instruction. Carefully crafted test questions can draw students' attention to ideas we think worthy of further discussion; they can serve as a place to "begin important mathematical conversations" rather than to end them.

In an article entitled "More than Testing," Elizabeth Badger offers a specific task that can supplement traditional tests of students' understanding of measurement. By comparing and contrasting a new process for assessing students' learning with tra-

ditional testing, she helps us understand better the strengths and weaknesses of each. Her ideas represent one step toward broader and more useful forms of assessment.

Warren Esty and Anne Teppo share their experience with an approach to grading that is based on progressive improvement, arguing that traditional test-score averaging does not take into account the cumulative nature of mathematical knowledge. In their approach, tests and quizzes are used merely for diagnostic purposes during most of the semester. Only at the end of the course do they use test scores to assign grades. In "Grade Assignment Based on Progressive Improvement," they also share feedback from students that provides further encouragement for experimenting with this approach.

Cathy Schloemer presents a grading scheme for motivating students to do more than just "get through" their homework. In "An Assessment Example," she describes a rubric for assessing verbal presentations of homework problems presented by students at the chalkboard. Knowing that they may have to present a problem formally motivates Schloemer's students to work toward a deeper understanding of the relevant concepts. Assessing homework presentations can be used to complement more traditional homework grades.

Aligning assessment with instruction is often problematic when new forms of instruction are used. For example, teachers often wonder how to assign grades when students have worked cooperatively on assignments. In "Cooperative Learning in the Mathematics Class," Diana Lambdin Kroll, Joanna Masingila, and Sue Mau suggest the use of an analytic scoring rubric for grading cooperative work. Their article includes examples of scoring sheets complete with annotations as well as practical tips for grading cooperative problem solving.

In the final article in this section, "Mirror, Mirror on the Wall … Teaching Self-Assessment to Students," Julianna Csongor discusses self-assessment as a skill that students must acquire if they are to become self-sufficient learners. She describes how she builds incentives for self-assessment into her testing and grading procedures.

TESTING—DO NOT DISTURB?
A CONCERNED PARENT'S VIEW
OF TESTING

Cynthia M. Garnett

Our children, Alexandra and Veronica, are aged seven and five, respectively, and like most of their peers, they spend much of their time playing. Their play is resourceful, inventive, and, for them, thoroughly engaging. They play, among other games, "war," a card game at which they are both expert. They play "house," during which they set the table, serve meals, sort laundry by color, and take hammer and screwdriver to fix things. They play hopscotch and jump rope and "Captain, may I?" They play Pokeno and the African stone game "mankala" with their friend from Guinea-Bissau. They sing and dance to "Miss Lucy" and "There's a Brown Girl in the Ring" and have added rhythmical hand movements to "Miss Mary Mack." Alexandra plays piano by matching numbered fingers to notes and keys. Our five-year-old self-taught swimmer, Veronica, imitates perfectly the movements of M. C. Hammer and is frustrated by her attempts to teach them to her "thirty something" parents, who are stuck somewhere between the boogaloo and the twist. The children's play reveals much

about their mathematical thinking and their problem-solving strategies. Their play reveals that mathematical ideas are being constructed in the culture-rich context of their work—"child's play."

Recently their play revealed something of their perceptions of school and school learning. Before starting, the kindergartner and first grader created the sign in figure 1 to hang on the doorway of their make-believe classroom. During play their voices and demeanor changed as they became "teacher" and "student." The one who is "teacher" is definite and authoritative, and the one who is "student" is obliging and accommodating. These children had been in school less than two years, and their behavior and their sign suggest that they are well on their way to being "schooled up." They had constructed two metaphors related to school and learning—that "schooling is testing" and that "playing is not learning."

Alexandra illustrates her perceptions about school and school learning in her essay titled "Spring" (fig. 2). Katz (1990)

reminds us that all young children know what is important to the adults around them.

Would-be-constructivist teachers, like the ones who populate our children's school, as well as many preservice and inservice educators nationwide, seem to have learned all too well that culture-rich, project-based learning; cooperative-group explorations; and individual-discovery learning are too risky to insure the required performance on the timed tests that come like taxes every spring. They seem also to have learned that allowing students to construct meaning through their own metaphoric play is not a good idea when "efficient" algorithms must be taught and rote memorization of facts must be accomplished before April arrives. The process of schooling, for teachers, becomes getting students ready for the test and the next grade level. Creative teaching gives way to telling; after all, it's April and testing time.

The natural worries that attend the occupation of parenting are not quieted

FIGURE 1

TestING
Do not DISTURb

Cynthia Garnett is an assistant professor in the Department of Early Childhood and Family Studies at Kean College of New Jersey, Union, NJ 07083. In addition to focusing on emergent literacy, she is involved in developing an African American social studies curriculum guide for the state of New Jersey. Alexandra and Veronica Garnett are in the second and first grades, respectively, at the Margaret Douglas School, P.S. 36, New York, New York.

FIGURE 2

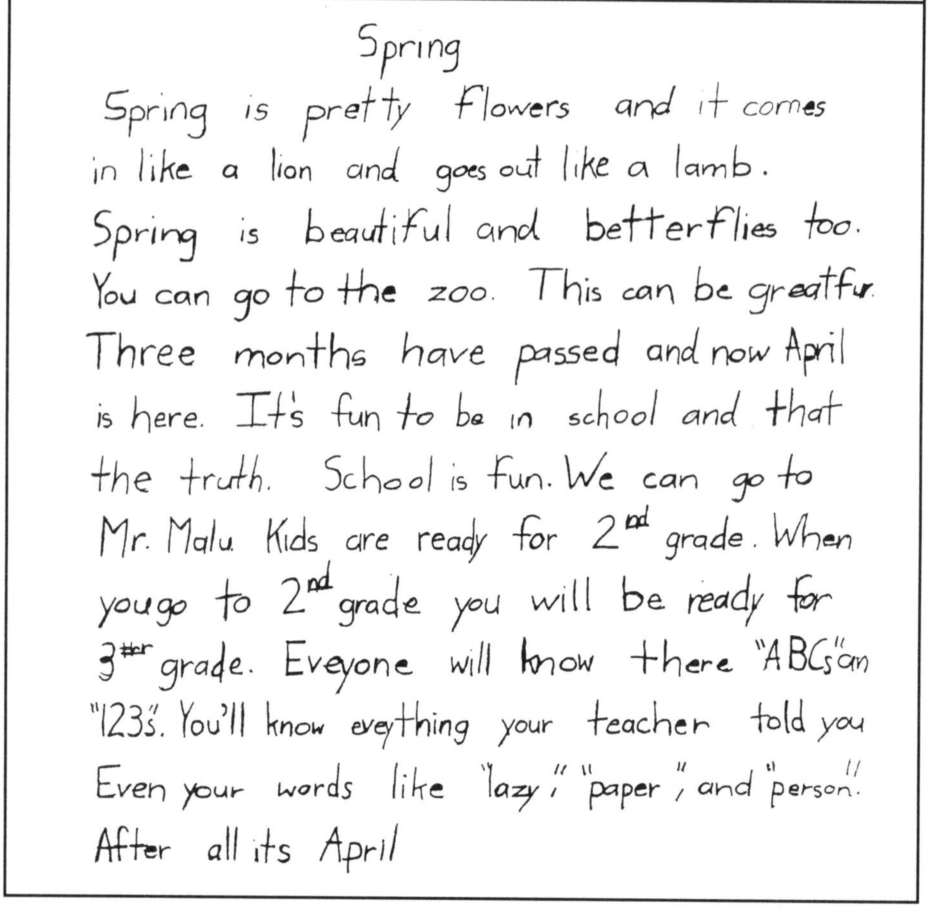

Spring

Spring is pretty flowers and it comes in like a lion and goes out like a lamb. Spring is beautiful and betterflies too. You can go to the zoo. This can be greatfu. Three months have passed and now April is here. It's fun to be in school and that the truth. School is fun. We can go to Mr. Malu. Kids are ready for 2nd grade. When you go to 2nd grade you will be ready for 3#r grade. Eveyone will know there "ABCs" an "123's." You'll know eveything your teacher told you Even your words like "lazy," "paper," and "person." After all its April

by research reported in *Childhood Education* by Thomas (1989). She reports that children who enter school eager and confident in their abilities soon begin to experience a decline in both self-concept and academic satisfaction. Standardized testing, which tends toward the devaluation of both diversity and metaphoric ways of knowing while promoting skills-based instructional objectives and competitive models of learning and teaching, seems to play a role in this decline.

Schools seem to want to change to improve their effectiveness in meeting the needs of all children. One hears and reads of educational reform, of global perspectives and multiculturalism, of constructivism and creative problem solving, of cooperative and inquiry learning. Then the "Testing, Do Not Disturb" sign is hung out, and reform is halted or, at the very least, placed on hold for the spring. Each spring reflective, creative teaching is arrested. Discovery and project-based learning are shoved aside. Educators shrug and lament that testing, like taxes, will be with us always. But shrugging and lamenting seem to abdi-

cate the responsibility that parents, teachers, and administrators share in providing for our daughters' (and our sons') futures. What exactly are we being asked not to disturb?

From the vantage point of a parent, standardized testing seems to have a stranglehold on the school, the teachers, the curriculum, and my children. The educational system seems to be asking us not to disturb this stranglehold, but *disturb we must* because our children are at risk of losing confidence in their abilities to construct meaning and solve problems.

Do not disturb means…

a diminished appreciation of diversity, a devaluing of diverse ways of knowing. It is to ignore the mathematical traditions of most cultures (Gerdes 1988). It is to deny that "doing mathematics is a universal human activity" (Zaslavsky 1991). It is to value only the "correct" application of someone else's algorithms.

Do not disturb means…

a diminished respect for autonomy and the encouragement of hegemony in the

learning environment. It is to arrest the reform movements in education that have so inspired teachers who want to teach children and not teach to a test. It is to discourage those who want to arrange environments, guide interactions, select tasks, and analyze these actions so that the elements of learning can be better aligned.

Do not disturb means…

a diminished sense of the importance of play and its natural forms of problem solving and activity-based, discovery learning in children who yet believe in the tooth fairy and the magic of Tinkerbell.

Do not disturb means…

a diminished sense of self; a diminished sense of who is meant by *everybody*, in the notion that "everybody counts" (National Research Council 1989). It is to perpetuate the myth that a single right answer from a single source for the singular purpose of pitting people against each other is needed for accountability.

As a parent I want specific things from any assessment in which my child is engaged:

- First, that my child be valued as she is being evaluated
- Second, that the "Do Not Disturb" sign be torn down and all parties to the child's education, including the child, be invited to participate
- Third, that assessment help children know what they know and value their ways of knowing; help teachers and parents know what children know, value their ways of knowing, and get direction in arranging the learning environments better to support their development; and help administrators gain insights to offer instructional leadership and derive improved strategies that foster healthy child development

NCTM's *Curriculum and Evaluation Standards* (1989) offers direction for this task. The document indicates that appropriate assessment—

- employs "complex, multifaceted tasks . . . structured to allow students to answer at different levels of sophistication" (p. 202), which best appreciates the diverse ways of knowing that children exhibit in a multiexperiential learning environment;

- measures the "generation of ideas, the formulation of problems, and the flexibility to deal with mathematical problems" (pp. 201–2), which best appreciates the creative problem-solving strategies our children develop;

- involves the "process of trying to understand what meanings students assign" (p. 203), which best appreciates that each child constructs her or his own knowledge; and

- produces "judgments that are evolutionary in nature" (p. 203), which best appreciates the development of the individual child.

Finally, not only must testing be disturbed, but assessment must be more than testing. Assessment "must be a continuous, dynamic, and often informal process" (p. 203), which best appreciates that children's achievement is tied to their sense of themselves and their sense of their place in the world.

REFERENCES

Gerdes, Paulus. "On Culture, Geometrical Thinking and Mathematics Education." *Educational Studies in Mathematics* 19 (1988): 137–62.

Katz, Lillian. "Impressions of Reggio Emilia Preschools." *Young Children* 45 (September 1990): 11–12.

National Council of Teachers of Mathematics, Commission on Standards for School Mathematics. *Curriculum and Evaluation Standards for School Mathematics.* Reston, Va.: The Council, 1989.

National Research Council. Mathematical Sciences Education Board. *Everybody Counts: A Report to the Nation on the Future of Mathematics Education.* Washington, D.C.: National Academy Press, 1989.

Thomas, Adele. "Ability and Achievement Expectations: Implications of Research for Classroom Practice." *Childhood Education* 65 (Summer 1989): 235–341.

Zaslavsky, Claudia. "Multicultural Mathe-matics Education for the Middle Grades." *Arithmetic Teacher* 38 (February 1991): 8–13.

THE MATHEMATICS TEST: A NEW ROLE FOR AN OLD FRIEND

Jon Rahn Manon

Most of us have, for many years, relied on timed teacher-designed mathematics tests to evaluate our students' progress in mathematics. We have often assessed the efficacy of our own instruction by the level of students' achievement on these same tests. Indeed, tests have come to bear the lion's share of the burden in determining whether we and our students have been successful in our respective roles of teaching and learning mathematics. Perhaps we have placed far too great an emphasis on our old friend, the mathematics test.

> *Perhaps we have placed too great an emphasis on the mathematics test.*

The NCTM's *Assessment Standards for School Mathematics* (1995) suggests that we instead rely on multiple sources of evidence in building a more complete picture of what individual students "know and are able to do." These sources might involve observation, communication, and an examination of various student products (NCTM 1995). We can, for example, observe our students as they work on challenging problems in groups, ask probing questions about their work on these problems, and collect the prod-

Jon Manon, 926 Devon Drive, Newark, DE 19711, is a doctoral candidate in the mathematics education department at the University of Delaware. He is currently studying the impact of students' informal mathematical experiences on their success in school mathematics.

ucts of this work in student portfolios for further review.

The mathematics test might be thought of, in this scheme, as a particular kind of student product. It must, in any case, be regarded as but one of many assessment alternatives. What part, then, should it come to play in our diagnostic repertoire? In what follows, suggestions are made for at least two important roles for the mathematics test in the future. Several cautions are also offered about the limitations of the teacher-produced test, a tired old friend that has borne a burden it was never really suited to bear.

CERTIFYING PROCEDURAL SKILLS

One highly efficient use of the teacher-designed test or quiz is to certify that our students have attained clearly specified procedural skills to a given criterion of performance. For example, we may believe that we need to demonstrate that every one of our students has mastered the techniques of organizing data into a stem-and-leaf diagram or a box-and-whiskers plot. This skill would be quite distinct, however, from using such plots for interpretation. The actual application of the data could only be assessed through an extended data-analysis project, but the creation of a data display might be quickly diagnosed with a paper-and-pencil quiz or test item. Such a procedural item need not be entirely pedestrian or completely constrained. It could be a problem such as the following:

> Create a data set having seven or more items and a mean of 85.

TESTS THAT INFORM OUR INSTRUCTION

When we evaluate our students' procedural knowledge, we are attempting to summarize one aspect of what individual students can do. This "summing up" is called a *summative* evaluation. Indirectly, of course, it carries with it information about how well our instructional strategies have succeeded. Sometimes, however, we would do well to design assessments that go more directly to such questions as "Where are we in relation to this subject as a class? What should we do next?" Such assessments are given not to evaluate individual progress as such but, rather, to give us information about the instructional process. Because they are used to inform our instructional decisions, they are often referred to as *formative* assessments. Tests can be used to sum up the current state of our students' procedural knowledge, but other, different tests can be designed to help us form or reform our instruction.

For example, when introducing the concept of the volume of a cylinder, one can take great care to stress that, as with prisms, the volume could be generated by translating the base through a third, orthogonal dimension. Students can then predict, with some fanfare, how the volume of a cone relates to that of a cylinder. Shortly thereafter, an item can be included on a test to illustrate this relationship (fig. 1).

An examination of students' work on this problem revealed that many students had not internalized the relationship that had been discussed rather thoroughly. At least half of them actually performed the

FIGURE 1

A movie theater decides to change the shape of its popcorn container from that of a cylindrical tub to a right-rectangular cone as pictured. The containers are of the same height, and the circular tops are of the same diameter. The price of a tub of popcorn was $4.50. How much should the theater management charge for the new cone of popcorn to keep the price proportional? Please show your work.

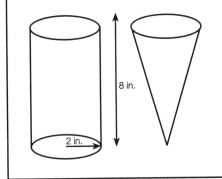

8 in.

2 in.

volume calculations before viewing the connection. These students had, apparently, learned about this relationship as a declarative, rather than an experienced, fact. Perhaps if students had actually constructed hollow cylinders and cones of like dimensions and experimented with their relative volumes, say, by pouring rice from one to another, they would have established the one-third relation as a real, rather than a declared, attribute.

> *Tests can be designed to help us form or reform instruction.*

The results on this test question—that many students had to revisit this relationship for themselves—suggested that the original instruction was not as successful as originally thought. This item is best used not as a measure of individual student achievement but rather to ascertain the effectiveness of instruction on the connection between the volumes of cylinders and cones. As such, the information gained from this question could be used to design another lesson rather than to yield a summative measure of individual students' understanding of conic volume.

A MORE MODEST ROLE

Tests may be used as an opportunity for students to exhibit routine procedural knowledge or as a quick estimate of the effectiveness of an aspect of an instructional program. We should not, however, expect our quizzes or tests to carry all the evaluative function. For example, this author was actually pleased when 25 percent of students were able to complete correctly all parts of the question in figure 2 as the tenth and final item on an hour-long examination. However, it was later realized that the students had not been given adequate time or resources to complete the problem.

FIGURE 2

Find the maximum number of points of intersection for the following figures. Assume that no two sides coincide. Please include the sketch from which you obtained each answer.

a) A triangle and a square
b) A triangle and a hexagon
c) A square and a pentagon
d) A 50-sided convex polygon and an 80-sided convex polygon
e) An n-gon and a p-gon, where n < p

Adapted from *Mathematics for Elementary Teachers: A Contemporary Approach* by Gary Musser (New York: Macmillan Publishing Co., 1991)

This problem should rightly have been posed as an extended exploration. It would certainly have provoked a rich interaction among students with competing hypotheses. A review of students' work suggests that at least three theories about the intersection of *n*- and *p*-gons arose. Students did not have the opportunity to discuss this problem until, for our intents and their purposes, it was too late. Conversations after high-stakes examinations inevitably center on whether one has gotten the item right or wrong and *not* on the mathematics itself. A potentially rich conversation was cut off at the pass (or fail).

This example brings up a related observation. All too often, we save our most creative questions for the test. Perhaps we are trying to impress colleagues with the difficulty of our examinations and, by implication, with the power of our own instruction. More probably, we believe that we must show that

our students have transferred their understanding from one context to another or from a simpler to a more complex situation. As we strengthen our own mathematical connections and consolidate our personal understanding by devising ever more clever questions, we ask our students to develop apace.

> *All too often we save our most creative questions for the test.*

This comment is not to suggest that we not give our students more complex problems. In fact, the current reform in mathematics education is defined in part by insisting that our students be challenged to think *more deeply* about important mathematical ideas and their connections. The question is, of course, under what circumstances will our students be able to make the most of these challenges?

Clearly, trying to crowd together several important problems into one fretful hour makes no sense at all. The *Assessment Standards for School Mathematics* (NCTM 1995) notes that mathematical work, as any other intellectual endeavor, proceeds in stages from rough draft to finished product. That our students ever complete a finished product on a timed mathematics test is indeed quite remarkable. Asking them to do their best work under such constraints is neither productive nor fair. Even the most accomplished of mathematicians would not wait until an hour before publication to begin work on *someone else's* hard problem.

Discovery on demand is a highly risky business. We squander opportunities for empowering insights, and we risk alienating our students from the joy and satisfaction that unfettered problem solving can bring. Who can bear to talk about an opportunity irrevocably missed? It is worse than yesterday's papers because the verdict is already in. Once an item has been graded wrong on a test, the concept it was meant to exemplify is forever consigned to the limbo of "I didn't understand it; I got it wrong."

TESTS AS PREPARATION FOR SENSE-MAKING

Once we acknowledge that we should not pose our consummate challenges in a testing situation, can test items ever be used to provoke sense-making, to encourage students to *begin* to construct meaning around important topics in the curriculum? Could we use the conventions and norms of the testing situation as a structured invitation to deliberation rather than as a grand summation? Perhaps a pretest can be used to draw our students' attention to ideas we think worthy of further consideration. We might take advantage of having our students' undivided attention during a test or quiz to *begin* important mathematical conversations.

For example, the item in figure 3 is meant to elicit higher-order thinking about rational numbers. It can be accessed and solved in a number of ways. It prompts preliminary exploration but does not ask for a full generalization of the concepts involved. Given this task, many students engage in an increasingly structured guess-and-check approach. Others realize immediately that the larger numbers are to be reserved for the numerators of the rationals but then must turn their attention to considering the relative sizes of the denominators. Number sense is clearly in evidence when a student reports that his or her final solution strategy was to form the "largest possible number of the largest pieces."

If most students are successful on this item, it can be used to prompt a dis-

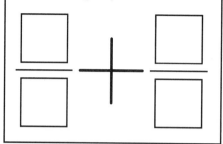

FIGURE 3

Use the digits 2, 3, 4, and 5 to fill in the boxes to make the largest possible sum of two rational numbers. Please explain why your sum is the largest possible sum.

cussion of the more general case in which *a* is less than *b* is less than *c* is less than *d*, which are integers to be used to construct the sum, difference, product, or quotient of two rational numbers. It does not seem, however, that we should "grade" such an item except to note the strengths and weaknesses of a work in progress.

We all have more to contribute to a conversation after we have given it some preliminary focused attention. No less should be required of our students if we expect them to enter into more profound mathematical deliberations. Asking our students to come to collaborative group work cold is probably not fair. We might even think of such a pretest as a way to level the playing field, as a device to get

everybody on the same page. If we are serious about striving for equity and excellence for all, then we need to find ways to prepare every one of our students to have a full voice in the mathematical conversation.

Does the mathematics test have a role to play in a more enlightened assessment scheme? It can be argued that it is still useful as a quick summative measure of procedural proficiency. Tests might also be used as periodic checks on our instructional practice: Have our students made the connections we had hoped for? How might we best proceed as we micromanage the instructional process?

Finally, pretests might be structured to provoke preliminary thinking on particular instances of more general problems. But whether summative, formative, or provocative, tests must no longer be expected to bear the burden of assessment all by themselves. Perhaps we should think of the test or quiz as a measurable point of departure rather than as the last word or ultimate destination.

REFERENCES

Musser, Gary. *Mathematics for Elementary Teachers: A Contemporary Approach.* New York: Macmillan Publishing Co., 1991.
National Council of Teachers of Mathematics. *Assessment Standards for School Mathematics.* Reston, Va.: The Council, 1995.

MORE THAN TESTING

Elizabeth Badger

The assessment of students' mathematical knowledge should yield information about their—

- ability to apply their knowledge to solve problems within mathematics and in other disciplines;
- ability to use mathematical language to communicate ideas;
- ability to reason and analyze;
- knowledge and understanding of concepts and procedures;
- disposition toward mathematics;
- understanding of the nature of mathematics.

Evaluation Standard 4: Mathematical Power, Curriculum and Evaluation Standards (NCTM 1989, p. 205)

To everyone's confusion, the terms *testing*, *assessment*, and *evaluation* are often used interchangeably. Nevertheless, they are not synonymous. We use *tests* in the process of *assessing* students' knowledge to make judgments, or *evaluations*. Evaluation depends on values. When we conclude that Sam or Alice is doing well or poorly in mathematics, we are referring consciously or unconsciously to their ability to perform the kinds of mathematics that we believe are important—that we value. Tests, however, are measuring instruments like thermometers and scales. They hold no value in themselves but are one of the many possible tools that we use to assess students' progress. Unfortunately, because

Elizabeth Badger is Director of Assessment, Massachusetts Department of Education, Quincy, MA 02169. She served on the evaluation working group for the NCTM's Curriculum and Evaluation Standards and is interested in the integration of assessment and instruction.

testing is the easiest of the three to think about and to do, we tend to focus on testing. Evaluation, however, is at the heart of teaching. Without evaluation, we would know neither what students understand nor how successfully we have taught them.

We tend to focus on tests rather than evaluation.

The purpose of this article is to explain a set of processes that teachers might use to structure their evaluations of students' learning so that they more closely reflect the *Curriculum and Evaluation Standards* (NCTM 1989). To illustrate the processes involved, we have chosen one area of mathematics, measurement, and a single task that could be used as a tool for assessing students' understanding. Although this particular task is neither special nor magical, the processes described are basic to all evaluations.

SETTING GOALS

Traditionally, evaluation starts with goals, which for many teachers may represent the first hurdle. Often these goals are defined too specifically (e.g., facility at double-digit multiplication) or too generally (e.g., adopting multiple approaches to problem solving) to reflect what mathematics is all about. Here we suggest a more fundamental approach, starting with the question "What is actually meant by knowing mathematics?"

The *Curriculum and Evaluation Standards* (1989) has profoundly influenced how we answer this question. Not too long ago we thought of learning as a set of building blocks—discrete skills that

had to be acquired in a fairly regular order. The role of the elementary school teacher was to lay the foundation, then succeeding teachers added new layers. We assumed that with enough blocks, the edifice of knowledge would eventually be strong enough to deal with "real" problems that required complex connections and applications. Only then could the student be said to "know mathematics."

The curriculum standards suggest a different metaphor. Instead of building blocks, they refer to networks, emphasizing the interconnections among skills, concepts, and contexts. When they define mathematical knowledge by listing different kinds of knowing, they are not suggesting a laundry list of discrete abilities but different facets of the same ability. For example, one doesn't understand concepts and *then* solve problems, one understands concepts *by* solving problems. One doesn't communicate mathematical ideas *as well as* reason about mathematics; rather, *through* communication one refines one's mathematical reasoning. This sense of wholeness reflects the general goal of mathematics education—what the curriculum standards refer to as "mathematical power."

DECIDING WHAT TO ASSESS

If we think of mathematics as a coherent set of knowledge, abilities, and dispositions, tests that focus on separate ideas or particular skills won't suffice. They can't tell us if students understand what they are doing or why they are doing it—whether they themselves see the connections among the ideas or the relevance of the skills. Without those connections, knowledge is inert. For this reason, it is important for teachers to think big, to consider the basic themes of elementary school mathematics and begin with them. Those big ideas include, but are not limited to, measurement, geometric ideas, numeration, patterns and functions, and fractions.

Evaluation should be the springboard for instruction.

Finding ways to assess students' understanding of these big ideas requires teachers to go beyond end-of-the-chapter questions and to think in terms of networks of related concepts and skills. For example, when we ask, What does it mean to say that a student understands measurement? we are intimating that understanding measurement involves much more than simply knowing how to measure in square inches or skill at converting square inches to square feet. Many other concepts and skills come into play. Some of them are listed here and in figure 1.

Numeration. All measurement requires an understanding of number. How are numbers related? How does the difference between 200 and 200 000 compare with that between 1/16 and 1/8? What does a really large number look like? What is the relationship of parts to a whole, such as one-third of a cup?

Ratio and proportion. Measurement gives a practical context to ratio and pro-

portion. As students convert from one measuring unit to another, they must recognize the relationship between units, whether they be inches and feet or equilateral triangles and hexagons. They must also understand the inverse relationship that exists between the size of a unit and the number needed to measure a given quantity.

Spatial thinking. Measurement is grounded in geometry. Often through using and comparing different shapes, students first become aware of size as an important attribute in describing objects, and it serves as an impetus for making measurements of area, perimeter, and volume.

Accuracy and precision. Although accuracy and error in measurement may be considered statistical ideas, the act of measuring supplies a practical demonstration that no measurement is completely accurate and that precision depends on the tools employed and the requirement of the task.

Estimation and reasonableness. In measurement, estimation is seen as more than just a process of rounding numbers or guessing; it is a way of judging reasonableness according to the size of the numbers involved.

Computation. Finally, measurement entails an understanding that formulas used for calculating are merely shortcuts for counting.

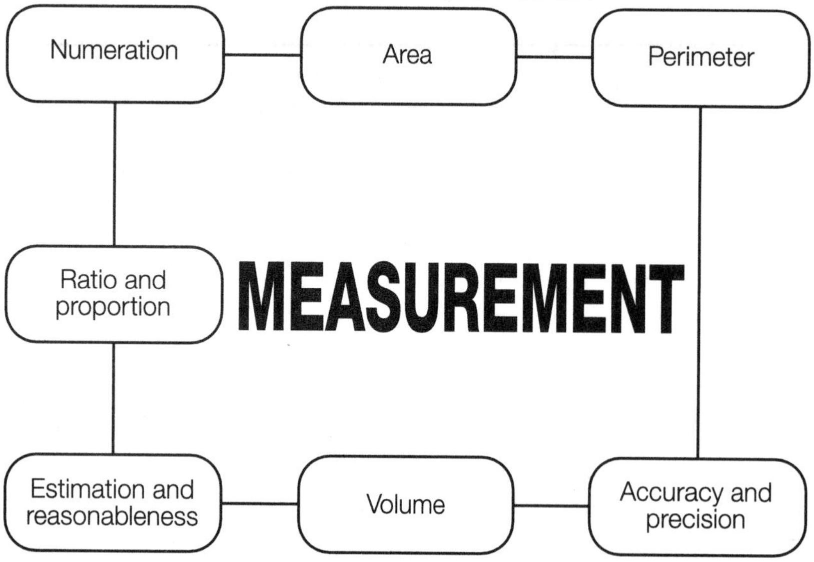

Although we may discriminate among them, all these concepts and procedures are connected and sometimes subsumed within each other. None are unique to measurement. All are part of any of the central themes of the elementary mathematics curriculum. Whatever themes we decide to assess, to the greatest extent possible our assessments should attempt to gain insight into students' understanding of this network.

GATHERING THE INFORMATION

A perfect test or a perfect task does not exist. Given the breadth of the goals, mathematical knowledge is too complex to be captured by a single instrument. Almost any task can be used, provided that we recognize what information we want to obtain from it. In fact, simple problems sometimes function better than elaborate ones in supplying the right kind of information. The one that follows is deceptively easy, but it incorporates most of the concepts about measurement that have been cited in the foregoing discussion. Equally important, it is open-ended, furnishing insight into how students understand a problem, as well as how they go about solving it and the kinds of evidence they consider to be sufficient. Finally, it engages students in a problem that is of interest to them. Similar situations can be found in many books. Two that are particularly useful for the lower elementary grades are *How Big Is the Moon?* (Baker, Semple, and Stead 1990) and *Living and Learning Mathematics* (Whitin, Mills, and O'Keefe 1990). Both books give practical discussions about evaluation as well as instruction.

Procedure. Students are given a set of small graduated containers, a large container full of popcorn kernels, and a balance with weights, but not a sufficient number to balance the kernels. They are asked to estimate the number of kernels in the large container and then to verify their estimate using any of or all the equipment. When they finish, they are given a container of dried lima beans and asked to estimate the number of beans.

This simple task has proved to be extremely challenging for most fourth graders, many eighth graders, and some adults. The lack of structure or explicit direction, the attraction of the balance,

FIGURE 1

What does it mean to say that a student understands measurement?

and such constraints as the insufficiency of weights contribute to its difficulty. It can, however, furnish a good context in which to gather information on students' understanding of many of the concepts described earlier.

In assessing students' ability, general impressions or final products are not sufficient. Although a wildly inaccurate final estimate or count is a sign that students do not understand the task, a correct one cannot be interpreted as a demonstration of understanding. Focused observations are needed before inferences can be made about what students know and understand. More specifically, the task can be used to observe and record the following:

Measuring skills. Does the student measure accurately? Use the correct unit for weight? Use the correct unit for volume? Keep track of the units used?

Proportional reasoning. Does the student relate equivalent measures? Keep ratios constant? Is the student able to use the number of kernels to calculate the number of lima beans without repeating the counting process?

Numeration. Does the student compute correctly? Use multiplication in place of repeated addition? Recognize the correct referent? Check for reasonableness? Distinguish between estimation and "rounding off"?

Planning and execution. Does the student ask for clarification when appropriate? Evaluate different approaches? Follow an orderly procedure? Make a written record? Check results?

Disposition. Does the student work with others or dominate? Exhibit confidence about completing the task? Use equipment competently? Remain engaged throughout the task?

Focused observations furnish greater insight into students' understanding and ability to "do mathematics" than written tests, but equally important, students should be given the opportunity to explain the reasoning behind their actions or to generalize from their findings. For example, after students complete the popcorn task, they might be asked to explore the following questions: What is similar or different about the var-

ious methods they used? What accounted for the discrepancies among the answers? What would be the most likely result if the same quantity of kernels had been given to everyone? Why? What are some similar problems? How could they be solved?

Discussions concerning the whys and wherefores of mathematics encourage students to act like mathematicians. In the act of explaining, they are forced to think again about what they did and why. They begin the habit of self-assessment, self-evaluation. Equally important, such discussions give teachers a window on their students' understanding.

USING THE RESULTS

Evaluation consists of more than observation. Basically, evaluation is a process of drawing inferences for which one needs evidence. Why does a teacher believe that Alice needs more experience with the relative size of numbers or that Sam is not yet capable of proportional reasoning? And equally important, how can that teacher communicate these assessments to Alice and Sam, their parents, or their next teachers?

Traditionally, such evaluations would be communicated simply in the form of a grade or percent of problems completed. Sam's understanding of proportions would be measured by a set of test problems in this form: If 10 pounds of potatoes cost $1.87, how much would 5 1/2 pounds cost? If Sam was unable to set up the correct relationships and calculate six out of the ten problems correctly, the teacher would judge that he could not yet reason proportionally. But what conclusions can be drawn when Sam then proceeds to count the number of kernels that balances fifty grams, find out how many fifty-gram lots the container holds, multiply the number of lots by the number of kernels in a single lot, and arrive at a reasonable answer? Here is contradictory evidence. Sam's test results do not tell the whole story. He has shown that he can "perform" by reasoning proportionally, but he may not see the connection between how he functions in the real world and what he is obliged to do in the more artificial context of "word problems." This kind of information not only is useful for the teacher's assessment of

Sam's knowledge, it forms the context for further instruction. Can Sam explain how he reasoned about the kernel problem? Can he make up some similar problems concerning weights, length, or money? Does doing so help him to see the connection between the word problems he has failed to complete and the problem he has just solved? Here the distinction between instruction and assessment begins to blur—as well it should. In promoting learning, evaluation should be used not only as a judgment of students' progress but also as a springboard for instruction. One follows the other in a logical progression.

> *Teachers can't evaluate and lecture simultaneously.*

DRAWING IT ALL TOGETHER

The most frequently voiced concern about this type of evaluation has to do with time. "If I am constantly evaluating, when do I find time for teaching?" Another concern refers to the amount of information that is collected. "How do I record all this material and how do I report it? Do I have to make a case study of each student?" Although different, these concerns are related; and no easy answers can be given, just a few guidelines.

Concerns about time. If instruction is defined primarily as "teacher talk," then alternative forms of evaluation are unquestionably intrusive and time-consuming because they have little to do with what is going on in the classroom. Teachers can't evaluate and lecture simultaneously. Neither can they really evaluate students' understanding by considering only the final product. They have to look at the thinking behind the product. Conversely, in more activity-oriented classrooms, no differentiation exists between the types of tasks that are used for instruction and those used for evaluation. Both should involve the same features. They should be interesting, challenging activities that reflect important themes in the mathematics curriculum. The difference occurs not in the kind of task but in the role of the teacher. Whereas in instruction the teacher plays the guide—sometimes structuring the situation to accommodate the needs of different students, sometimes detouring in response to students' concerns—in evaluation the role of the teacher is that of observer and recorder. However, the teacher need not play the same role for all students at the same time. What functions as an instructional task for some students can act as the means for evaluating others.

Concerns about collecting and recording information. If evaluations are to be more than opinions, evidence has to be recorded. The means one uses to collect and record data depend on the type of information collected. A wide variety of assessment tools can be used to obtain information, ranging from the highly structured short-answer question that demands a single correct answer to an extended investigation that may result in a number of conflicting, but correct, solutions. For enabling skills and factual knowledge, the former is most appropriate, but it is important not to stop there. To assess students' understanding, more open-ended questions are necessary, as well as discussions that extend the meaning of concepts beyond the obvious. Group investigations are also useful for revealing students' attitudes and dispositions, as well as their ability to connect and apply their knowledge. The use of one method of assessment is often suggested by the information gained from another. The more closely the match between the goals of evaluation and the tools that are used to assess them, the better our judgment will be.

A good deal of the recording can be done by the students themselves in the form of portfolios. Basically, portfolios are records of students' work—a type of elaborate grade book that contains not just scores, notes on progress, or percents of correct answers but also the work on which the scores and notes are based. In other words, portfolios are collections of primary data. They can contain tests, worksheets, notes from a journal, descriptions of investigations, solutions for problems—any written work that exemplifies the students' mathematical activities.

The advantage of a portfolio, as distinct from the individual work that it contains, is that it gives a more complete picture of the student's achievement in mathematics. For example, students invariably perform better on some tasks than others. Although Sam solves written problems with accuracy and competence, he finds it difficult to defend or explain his solutions. Alice, however, excels when challenged with an unusual problem but loses interest when required to carry through with details. A collection of work seen in its entirety allows teachers to appreciate the range of abilities possessed by each student. Such a perspective is less likely when individual pieces of work are viewed separately.

A second advantage of portfolios is the opportunity they afford for conversations about mathematics. Teachers can use them as prima facie evidence of what is going on in the classroom to communicate their goals and values to parents and others. For students, too, they can act as testaments to growth in skill and understanding.

Portfolios, however, are not a panacea. Their value is dependent on the kinds of mathematical activities that they contain. Essentially, they are a method of recording, not a way of teaching or assessing. Furthermore, portfolios show only the product, not the process. Students reveal their understanding in conversations with teachers, in class discussions, and in the give-and-take of group problem solving. They also reveal much about themselves in how they go about their work. Most thoughtful teachers make penetrating judgments about their students that are not necessarily reflected in the students' final products. These observations are also important records to be kept.

CONCLUSION

The NCTM's curriculum standards discuss two features that underlie all learning:

- The need to construct meaning for ourselves, to make concepts our own before we can really understand them
- The need to engage in resolving meaningful problems—either practical or theoretical

What is true of learning and teaching should also be true of evaluation. The tools we use to evaluate students' knowledge should be designed to engage and challenge students and allow them to display their understanding of mathematics. The worth of an evaluation, however, does not rest on a specific test or set of problems. The core issue consists of such questions as, What does it really mean to know mathematics? What evidence exists that my students have that knowledge? Such problems as the one described attempt to respond to these questions, but the problems in themselves do not make evaluation worthwhile. Their importance lies in what we learn about students' understanding.

REFERENCES

Baker, Dave, Cheryl Semple, and Tony Stead. *How Big Is the Moon?* Portsmouth, N.H.: Heinemann Educational Books, 1990.

National Council of Teachers of Mathematics. *Curriculum and Evaluation Standards for School Mathematics.* Reston, Va.: The Council, 1989.

Whitin, David J., Heidi Mills, and Timothy O'Keefe. *Living and Learning Mathematics.* Portsmouth, N.H.: Heinemann Educational Books, 1990.

GRADE ASSIGNMENT BASED ON PROGRESSIVE IMPROVEMENT

Warren W. Esty and Anne R. Teppo

The NCTM's *Curriculum and Evaluation Standards for School Mathematics* states, "Evaluation is a tool for implementing the *Standards* and effecting change systematically" (1989, p. 189). Tests are one facet of evaluation, and we maintain that mathematics classes are strongly affected by the way in which test scores are used to generate final course grades. In the traditional secondary school mathematics class, current grading practices tend to drive instruction by putting constraints on specific course content and its organization. In turn, content and its organization affect testing and therefore grading. The interaction of these factors is an aspect of assessment that is not specifically discussed by the NCTM's evaluation standards. The purpose of this article is to examine the impact of grading on mathematics instruction and on the implementation of the curriculum and evaluation standards.

Students' performance in today's secondary school mathematics curriculum is measured to a large extent by unit examinations administered on a regular basis. The numerical grades earned on these tests are averaged to help determine a final course grade. This article examines the logical consequences of this process

Warren Esty teaches at Montana State University, Bozeman, MT 59717. He does research in applied probability and is working on his second freshman-level textbook. Anne Teppo is a mathematics education consultant, 1611 Willow Way, Bozeman, MT 59715. She is involved in qualitative research investigating the development of mathematical concepts within the classroom environment.

of test-score averaging on the arrangement of course material, the nature of the tests themselves, and the learning emphasized. We believe that in each area, these consequences are negative. Furthermore, we believe that in line with the evaluation standards, test scores can be used to assign course grades in an objective and valid way that does not rely on averaging. An example of this type of grading will be described.

CONSEQUENCES OF AVERAGING

By the very nature of averages, examination scores earned early in the course are given equal weight with examination scores generated near the end. Thus, what students do not know early on in the course is given numerically equal weight with what they do not know at the end. Because early failures cannot be erased by subsequent learning, averaging also implies that specific learning must occur that we can test with a valid test after only a few weeks of the course.

Consider two examinations in a mathematics class, one given early on and the other given near the end of the term. Logically, the only way that they can be considered equal in assessing learning is if this learning is not regarded as cumulative. That is, each examination is truly a "unit" examination and the unit studied has no cumulative importance if it contributes nothing to subsequent concept development and if the procedures and concepts learned never reappear. These assumptions are false. The objections to averaging of test scores apply doubly to averaging of homework scores.

Yet mathematics teachers continue to assign final course grades on the basis of averaged scores.

Grade averaging has an impact on the arrangement of course material and the types of tests that are used. Material tends to be compartmentalized into small, discrete "digestible chunks," with related short examination problems that test specific and isolated skills. This approach allows teachers to demand immediate mastery of objectives with an accompanying 90-80-70-60 percent performance scale, yielding the grades they want to give.

Compartmentalizing course material severs connections between one topic and another. Concepts, which by definition must be abstracted from numerous examples in various contexts, are neglected in instruction because they cannot be mastered in small chunks at the 90-80-70-60 percent level during the short intervals between tests. Averaging of unit test scores forces teachers to compromise and write tests according to what the students can learn between tests, not according to what teachers really want the students to know.

For example, few students will fully grasp the difference between a function, f, and its image, $f(x)$, immediately after functions are introduced. The distinction between the rule itself and the number created by applying the rule to x is subtle but extremely important. Calculus students need to know what $f(x + h)$ is when $f(x) = x^2$, yet many do not distinguish it from $f(x) + h$ because they have not learned to isolate the rule, f ("square it"), from the image, x^2. After the term *function* is introduced in algebra, a unit test is, of course, given that explores some aspects of particular functions. But the *concept* of function will not have been fully developed through instruction and certainly not yet fully understood by the students. Thus the teacher can ask questions only at a low level of comprehension if he or she is designing a unit test that students can pass. Success on such a test, although it improves a student's chances for an acceptable final course grade, gives little indication of the student's progress toward understanding the essential concept of function.

> ## We need to assess concepts to emphasize their importance.

The evaluation standards recognize that tests "are one way of communicating what is important for students to know" (p. 189). Because students will not do well on conceptual questions, such as the distinction between f and $f(x)$, such questions are usually not asked. Because conceptual questions are not asked, students fail to recognize the importance of concepts. Then whatever misconceptions the students develop on their own persist. The pernicious effects of averaging carry through to higher-level courses.

Averaging and compartmentalizing reinforce one another. Without compartmentalizing averaging is inappropriate. With compartmentalizing averaging works. With averaging compartmentalizing seems necessary to justify the grading system. Therefore these two have settled in together. The compartmentalizing-averaging method of teaching and evaluating mathematics has come to be taken for granted. The vast majority of textbooks and courses depend on it. Teachers use it and it works—for material organized in compartments. But this type of organization is precisely what must be changed if mathematics courses are seriously to teach mathematical connections.

RECOMMENDATIONS OF THE CURRICULUM AND EVALUATION STANDARDS

The curriculum standards call for "a shift in emphasis from a curriculum dominated by memorization of isolated facts and procedures and by proficiency with paper-and-pencil skills to one that emphasizes conceptual understandings, multiple representations and connections, mathematical modeling, and mathematical problem solving" (p. 124). The averaging method currently employed in many mathematics classrooms inhibits the implementation of these recommendations.

The evaluation standards recognize that "students' grasp of mathematical concepts develops over time. Many concepts introduced in the early grades are later extended and studied in greater depth" (pp. 223–24). Clearly this type of development over time must happen throughout individual classes as well as from elementary to secondary grades. If we recognize that learning mathematics is cumulative and expect students to make connections among procedures and develop concepts over time, then we propose that it is acceptable—and completely expected—for students to be unable to demonstrate concept mastery until late in a course. The current practice of test-score averaging does not recognize these factors of time and complexity. The evaluation standards specifically assert that assessing what students do not know should receive decreased attention (p. 191), but averaging penalizes students for what they don't know during the progress of the course instead of rewarding them for what they do know at the end.

> ## Averaging penalizes students.

The evaluation standards call for us "to reassess the manner and methods by which we chart our students' progress" (p. 192). In terms of assigning students' grades, the evaluation standards assert that assessment should measure (a) how well the student has understood and integrated the material, (b) if the student can apply his or her learning in other contexts, and (c) if the student is prepared to proceed to the next grade or level (p. 200). These questions are best answered only at the end of a mathematics course. They imply that assessment for grade assignment should be based on long-term course goals. Using a scoring method other than averaging for assigning class grades can free existing instruction from its present constraints and make it possible to emphasize the learning of complex concepts and related multistage procedures.

GRADING BASED ON PROGRESSIVE IMPROVEMENT

We have developed and implemented a grading system based on progressive improvement that measures the types of student progress described by the evaluation standards' grading criteria. It is used for a ten-week course on the language and structure of mathematics offered to nonmathematically oriented students at Montana State University (Esty and Teppo 1991).

At the beginning of this class, students are informed that although they will be examined with diagnostic quizzes and tests throughout the course, only their performance in the final weeks of the class will be counted for assigning grades. They are told that what they learn will be cumulative and that at the end of the course they will be held responsible for *all* the material.

Daily homework is checked for accuracy but not scored. Early quizzes and examinations are scored but not counted toward the final grade. Class participation is required and supplies useful feedback for both the instructor and student. Thus, assessment during the first two-thirds of the class is used to inform students and instructor of individual progress, not to generate course grades, that is, assessment is diagnostic and furnishes instructional feedback.

Students' final grades are not penalized by averaging in test scores that measure incorrect or incomplete understanding that occurs in the early stages of the course. Course grades are assigned on the basis of knowledge and skills displayed in the final few weeks of the class using quizzes and cumulative examinations, which are written tests, and, to a much lesser extent, class answers, which are spoken—yielding quite different information.

Because this approach is so nontraditional, we have had to deal with students' fears that we don't mean it and that in the end we really will average in some poor early score. We repeatedly reassure the students that we are looking for improvement and eventual mastery, not for a chance to take points off. For instance, quiz scores, instead of being rated on a 90-80-70-60 percent scale, are classified as "already at the C (or A or B) level" or "soon to be C or better."

> ## Our grading scheme emphasized progressive improvement.

Students' performance is expected to improve throughout the course. By omitting the requirement of immediate mastery, students can be held to a higher standard and posed more challenging problems. For example, on the second test administered halfway through the autumn 1990 course, a performance of 50 percent was judged by the instructor to be what was expected, at that time, of an eventual C student. The instructor's comment to the students on this "low" test score was, "You will have another chance soon to demonstrate that you have mastered the exam material." This recognition that examination scores were acceptable even if they did not fit a 90-80-70-60 percent scale is to be distinguished from curving, which is sometimes necessary under an averaging sys tem according to which each score directly affects the student's final course grade.

Students' perceptions of the progressive grading system were obtained from interviews conducted as part of a qualitative study of the autumn 1990 course (Esty and Teppo 1991). Students remarked that this approach kept them working when they were not doing well on the diagnostic examinations and homework. "It keeps me feeling like I'm in the race," one student commented. Students knew they still had a chance to earn an acceptable final grade by continuing to improve throughout the course. As another student explained, "[You're given] a chance to make up the things you didn't understand [after] you've found a way to acquire the knowledge. You're rewarded for that, and I think it's really important."

This grading system acknowledges the reality that mathematics learning takes time. Instead of increasing anxiety early in the course for those who have not yet been able to grasp the material, this approach allows students the time actually required to put it all together and produces less negative reinforcement. Furthermore, less emphasis is placed on filing facts in short-term memory in cramming sessions just before unit examinations.

We have found that the students do not abuse this grading system—any more than they do any other grading system— by not working at the beginning of the course. As one interviewed student explained, "It isn't as though the teacher relieved us of the obligation or anything like that. He put all the students in a position where they could be confident in themselves." The students used the diagnostic quizzes to measure their performance as the course progressed. They understood that growth would occur and that they could realistically look forward to assimilating the material eventually. We have found that performance in the final weeks of the course accurately reflects this integration of knowledge throughout the course.

CONCLUSION

We maintain that the primary goal of instruction should be for students to master the material by the end of the course and that class grades should be assigned accordingly. We have found that the progressive-improvement grading system is a pedagogically effective way to assess and facilitate learning. By eliminating the artificial constraint on the material imposed by the test-score-averaging "instant mastery" requirement, the curriculum can be freed to include long-term learning of multistage procedures and broader mathematical concepts. Assessment changes are necessary if we are to implement the curriculum and evaluation standards.

REFERENCES

Esty, Warren W., and Anne R. Teppo. *A Study of a Conceptual Mathematics Course.* Technical Report 31891. Bozeman, Mont.: Montana State University, 1991.

National Council of Teachers of Mathematics. *Curriculum and Evaluation Standards for School Mathematics.* Reston, Va.: The Council, 1989.

AN ASSESSMENT EXAMPLE

Cathy G. Schloemer

I wanted to create a vehicle for assessing students' ability to communicate to the class their attempts at problem solving. In the past, homework problems had been presented at the chalkboard by volunteers, usually the same few students each day. To afford everyone the opportunity to participate and to allow students to prepare their problem solutions in advance, I selected homework problems that I judged to be most troublesome and assigned them for presentation by drawing the students' names from a hat.

I used the scoring rubric in table 1, which I shared with the students in advance, for this activity. I was surprised to find that the scoring rubric was, at first, difficult for me to use. For the first few problems I attempted to evaluate, the students' presentations seemed to go by in fast motion.

Cathy G. Schloemer is a teacher at Indiana Area Senior High School, Indiana, PA 15701.

The scoring rubric was hard to use at first.

More interesting than my role in the evaluation process, however, were the students' reactions to the activity. Even though the students knew that their presentations were being graded, quite a few of them waited until they arrived in class to get help with their problems. Furthermore, on an end-of-unit opinion questionnaire regarding this and other "unusual" assessment activities we had tried, all the students who wrote free-response comments at the end of the sheet mentioned in particular that they liked the assigning of specific problems that had to be presented on request: "It made me work harder on my problem than I normally would have"; "[It got] everyone to do a problem on the board,

instead of it always being the same people"; and "I know that some people hate it, but when you go to the front of the class, you remember it much better" were some comments.

In response to specific questions I asked on the questionnaire (table 2) to determine students' feelings about this new way of assessing homework, only two of seventeen respondents felt that the rubric was unfair. Sixteen liked knowing ahead of time what problem they would present in class, and only five objected to getting everyone to the chalkboard to present some problems. I was pleasantly surprised at the students' enthusiasm for this activity. It was rewarding to be able to get more effort and involvement from the students and to have them like it! Although these students were in a precalculus class, the idea would work for others as well.

TABLE 1	
My Scoring Rubric	
Points	*Criteria*
4	A suitable strategy was chosen and implemented. Any errors were of a minor nature—for example, copying, simple computation.
3	An apparently suitable strategy was selected, but some condition of the problem was ignored or misunderstood, leading to an incorrect solution, or a leap was made from the appropriate strategy to the correct answer without a clear explanation.
2	Some understanding of the problem was demonstrated, but— a) an inappropriate strategy led to a wrong answer; b) an appropriate strategy was presented without an answer; c) an appropriate strategy was incorrectly implemented.
1	A meaningful attempt was made to solve the problem beyond simply copying it, but the work stopped far short of a solution.
0	The work evidenced— a) only recopying of the original information; b) only a wrong answer; or c) no meaningful work.
Adapted from Charles, Lester, and O'Daffer (1987)	

TABLE 2
Students' Reactions to Assessment Activity

During the relations-and-functions unit, you presented assigned problems in class for a grade. For future planning, I would like to know your perceptions of the value of this activity. Please respond to the following statements. (Tally of students' responses appears in each column.)

	Responses				
Statement	Agree Strongly (5)	Agree (4)	Not Sure (3)	Disagree (2)	Disagree Strongly (1)
1. I thought the scoring rubric for oral problem solving was fair.	4	6	5	1	1
2. I liked knowing ahead of time which problem I had to present in class.	11	5			1
3. I liked having a method to get everyone to the board to present some problems.	3	5	4	4	1

Please use additional space to elaborate on any of the above or to make other comments regarding your perceptions of this "special" activity. Thank you for your help.

REFERENCE

Charles, Randall, Frank Lester, and Phares O'Daffer. *How to Evaluate Progress in Problem Solving*. Reston, Va.: National Council of Teachers of Mathematics, 1987.

GRADING COOPERATIVE PROBLEM SOLVING

Diana Lambdin Kroll, Joanna O. Masingila, and Sue Tinsley Mau

Do your students use cooperative-group work when they are involved in mathematical investigations and problem solving? Many teachers these days answer yes because they find that working together helps students become better problem solvers. Teachers who encourage their students to work problems cooperatively, however, frequently do not grade the results of those cooperative sessions, probably because using cooperative groups for classwork is a lot easier than assigning grades for that work.

However, the NCTM's *Curriculum and Evaluation Standards* (1989) stresses the importance of aligning assessment techniques with teaching methods. If students frequently work on problems in small groups, the teacher should also assess this work. Many ways are available to assess cooperative work: observing and questioning while students work cooperatively, keeping notes of whole-class discussions about cooperative work, commenting on individual students' write-ups of cooperatively solved problems, and assigning grades.

We note that assessment and grading are not synonymous. At least four reasons for assessing students' work can be cited:

Diana Kroll teaches at Indiana University. She is particularly interested in mathematical problem solving, alternative assessment techniques, and writing to learn mathematics. Joanna Masingila teaches at Syracuse University. Her special interest is in cooperative problem solving and mathematics practice in everyday situations. Sue Mau is on the faculty of the University of Notre Dame. She is interested in the mathematical attitudes and beliefs of college students.

(1) to make decisions about the content and methods of instruction, (2) to make decisions about classroom climate, (3) to help in communicating what is important, and (4) to assign grades (Lester and Kroll 1991). Although each of these reasons for assessing is important, our focus here is on assessment for the purpose of assigning grades. Although most teachers probably use a variety of data sources for assigning grades (e.g., individually performed quizzes and tests, individual classwork, homework, classroom observations, individual interviews, and student journals), this article describes how they can grade the cooperative-problem-solving efforts of their students. But before we can focus our attention on grading, we need first to consider exactly what we mean when we talk about cooperative learning and cooperative problem solving.

> *Assessment and grading are not synonymous.*

TWO TYPES OF COOPERATIVE LEARNING

When most people talk about cooperative learning, they usually envision students sharing ideas and working collaboratively to complete academic tasks. However, such a general definition overlooks the number of very different models for cooperative learning. The numerous models of cooperative learning can be broken down into two major types: peer-tutoring models and group-investigation models (Sharan 1980). The type of cooperative learning being used with students is important to know before deciding which type of grading scheme may be most appropriate for a class.

Peer Tutoring

In the peer-tutoring model of cooperative learning, students work together to help each other master tasks that generally emphasize acquisition of information or skills. As the name implies, more able students often serve as tutors for slower students. Many secondary school teachers use the peer-tutoring model frequently, for example, when they allow students to work together on class assignments or to begin their homework together. More structured peer-tutoring schemes are also very successful, for example, the various Student Team Learning methods developed by Robert Slavin: Student Teams–Achievement Division (STAD), Teams-Games-Tournament (TGT), Jigsaw II, and Team Assisted Individualization (TAI) (Slavin 1983). In each of these models, students study or play games together to learn new material or to master new skills and then demonstrate their skill individually, either on a test or in a game competition, with some sort of team average being used for group recognition and reward.

In other words, peer-tutoring models generally combine cooperation in learning with individual accountability and a group-reward structure. It is logical, and also appropriate, that peer-tutoring models use individual work to assess students' progress. If students were to work together to answer questions involving lower-level learning, for example, performing basic calculations, solving equations, writing definitions, or identifying figures, it would be extremely difficult to determine which students actually knew the answers or had the skills and which students did not.

Group Investigation

In the group-investigation model of cooperative learning, the types of tasks are generally different from those used in peer tutoring. In group investigation, students learn by cooperating on tasks that involve interpretation, synthesis, application of information, or problem solving. Although—as in the peer-tutoring model—more able students may help their peers, communication in the group-investigation model is more focused on interpretation and exchange of ideas. All members of the group struggle together to solve a problem that none of them has already mastered. Two of the most widely used group-investigation models are "learning together" (Johnson and Johnson 1987) and "group investigation" (Sharan 1980).

A group grade can encourage individuals to cooperate.

An example of a group-investigation problem might be a three- or four-day assignment to draft a proposal for a city park. Each group might be given a description of the task and a copy of a worksheet giving some basic information about the city, some important constraints (e.g., the park site has a stream, several trees, and two hills, and the overall cost must be less than $5000), and a list of the costs of a variety of possible materials and equipment. Students in each group might be assigned roles, for example, accountant—to make sure that everyone can do the calculations involved; architect—to ensure that all members help with layout and design; and elaborator—to relate the group's work to previous mathematics problems solved in class. The group is expected to work together to design a park, to specify what materials and equipment would be needed, to draw a picture of how the park would look, and to write a report describing and justifying their design.

Constructing model bridges using toothpicks to meet certain rules and specifications (Pollard 1985) is another example of a group-investigation problem that involves students' taking different roles as they work together toward a common goal. A less extensive group investigation might involve having students work collaboratively for ten to sixty minutes on a nonroutine mathematics word problem.

Assessment of group investigation is frequently done on a group basis; for example, the group's write-up of their problem's solution may represent their group effort. However, in many types of group investigation individuals are also ultimately accountable for being able to solve similar problems on their own.

ASSESSING COOPERATIVE PROBLEM SOLVING

Our focus is on grading cooperative problem solving—a specific instance of the group-investigation model of cooperative learning. However, before we consider how to grade cooperative-problem-solving efforts, some discussion explaining cooperative problem solving is needed. The defining feature of a "problem" situation is that students do not know at first how to proceed. Thus, in group problem solving, the group is confronted with a situation that challenges everyone, since no group member is able initially to solve the problem alone. Group members must work together to make sense of the problem; to plan an approach, or several; to try implementing their plan, often revising or replanning in the process; and eventually to verify that the solution they reach is appropriate for the problem situation.

Cooperative problem solving involves a group of students' working on a problem that is complex enough to require the students to (*a*) discuss the problem, (*b*) be systematic in keeping track of information, and (*c*) possibly assume different roles within the group, for example, recorder, calculator user, or skeptic. Another feature of cooperative problem solving is the monitoring of group members' thinking by other members of the group. In our classes we have heard group members monitor each other by comments such as, "Why do you think that?" "Is this going to get us anywhere?"

and "How did you come up with that?" We believe this monitoring feature is a key reason that cooperative problem solving is often more productive than individual problem solving.

One assessment scheme that can be used when students have been involved in cooperative mathematics problem solving includes both group and individual accountability. This scheme makes several assumptions:

1. The group being graded has experience in working together on problem-solving tasks.
2. The students have had previous practice in writing out their solutions to problems.
3. The students appreciate the importance of ensuring that everyone in their group participates in and understands their group's solution.

The assessment scheme consists of two phases. In phase 1, students work in small assigned groups to solve a problem and to write a single group solution. In phase 2, students work individually to answer questions about their group's solution and to solve several similar problems. Thus, individuals must be able on their own to answer questions about the group's solution and to solve extensions of the problem.

The grading of such problem-solving efforts is similarly divided into two phases, one corresponding to phase 1 (the group's work) and the other corresponding to phase 2 (each individual's effort). First, the teacher grades each group's solution. We recommend using some sort of analytic scoring scheme (see our example later in this article). Because all students in the group are assumed to have contributed to, and concurred in, the group's solution, all students in the group receive the same score on their group solution; for example, if a group's solution is awarded 14 of 15 possible points, each student receives 14 points.

Second, the teacher grades the individual papers. We have used three questions to assess individuals' work: a question for understanding, a problem parallel to the group's problem, and a problem that extends the group's problem. The individual papers allow the teacher to see which students are able to demonstrate a clear understanding of the problem, of their group's solution, and of extensions of the problem. Papers by different individuals may be awarded different scores; for example, if the questions are worth a total of 10 points, the four individual papers from a group might receive such scores as 8, 10, 5, and 9, depending on the degree of understanding demonstrated by each student.

One possible way to award individuals a grade for their cooperative-problem-solving effort is to total their group's score and their individual score. On the basis of this scheme, students in the same group may receive the same or different grades. For example, if a group's paper received 14 out of 15 points and individual students in the group received scores of 8, 10, 5, and 9 out of 10, their individual scores would be 22, 24, 19, and 23, respectively, from a total of 25 possible. Under this scheme, each student receives a grade based partly on the group's achievement and partly on his or her individual achievement.

Conversely, if all students in a group receive the same grade based on the achievement of the group as a whole, individuals often have more incentive to try to ensure that all group members understand the group's solution. Thus, another way to grade cooperative problem solving is to give all group members the same score. For example, each student could receive the sum of the group's solution score and the average of their individual scores. In the foregoing hypothetical example, all the students in the group would receive a score of 22 (14 + 8, where 8 is the average of the four individual scores: 8, 10, 5, and 9).

Selecting Problems

Careful thought is required to find or develop problems that are appropriate for grading cooperative work. In choosing a problem for grading, teachers need to consider several points. The problem should (a) involve the students in problem-solving behavior, that is, understanding the problem, making a plan for solving the problem, implementing the plan, and looking back; (b) interest the students and challenge their curiosity; and (c) present a new situation for which the students neither know an answer nor have a previously established procedure for finding an answer.

It is not necessary or wise to increase the level of mathematical difficulty when modifying for use in a group-problem-solving situation a problem originally intended for individual problem solving. However, the problem may need to be more complex for use with a group than with individuals. The problem should be complex enough to generate discussion among the group members and offer the possibility of several methods of solution. It should also require the use of more complex solution methods, such as listing, making a table, or approaching the problem systematically.

> ### Problems can be adapted in various ways for small-group work.

We offer, as examples, some problems that could be used in grading group-problem-solving efforts. Solutions to all problems discussed are given in the Appendix. For a geometry class, the triangular-arrangements problem might be appropriate for further exploration of the triangle inequality:

The three sides of a triangle have lengths a, b, and c. All three lengths are whole numbers, and $a \leq b \leq c$.

(a) Suppose that $c = 9$. Find the number of different triangles that are possible.
(b) For any given value of c, find a general law that expresses the number of possible triangles.

Other related problems can be made from this problem by—

1. changing the context or setting, for instance, fencing a plot of land with three sides of unknown length;
2. changing the numbers, for example, 8 instead of 9;
3. changing the number of conditions, for instance, specifying that the triangle is isosceles;
4. reversing given and wanted information, for example, given that twenty-five triangles are possible, find the value of c; and
5. changing some combination of context, numbers, conditions, and given and wanted information.

Adapting the basic problem in these five ways allows the teacher to give each group of students in the class a different problem without finding or creating entirely different problems.

Note that some types of modifications will leave the difficulty level of the problem essentially the same, whereas others will result in an easier or harder problem. The foregoing adaptations of the triangular-arrangements problem produce, respectively, the following effects on the original problem:

1. The difficulty level remains unchanged.
2. The problem becomes less complex, since fewer triangles must be tried.
3. The difficulty level is lowered by restricting the lengths of sides a and b.
4. The problem becomes more difficult by requiring the students to find the value of side c as well as consider the triangle inequality.

Teachers should choose their method of modification carefully to ensure that it produces a revised problem of the appropriate level of difficulty. We also advise exploring the problems thoroughly before having students work them. A minor modification can turn a ten-minute problem into a forty-five-minute problem. Exploring a problem before assigning it also allows teachers to make any such necessary corrections as rewording ambiguous phrases.

A problem more appropriate for an algebra class might be the mysterious-money problem (adapted from Thompson [1976, p. 104]) because it may involve the concept of solving for two unknowns:

An absent-minded bank teller switched the dollars and cents when he cashed a check for Jana, giving her dollars instead of cents and cents instead of dollars. After buying a five-cent stamp, Jana discovered that she had exactly twice as much left as the amount of her original check. What was the amount of the check?

Using the previously discussed five ways of adapting problems, the mysterious-money problem could be altered by—

1. changing the context to switching digits on a license plate, leaving the difficulty level unchanged;

2. changing the numbers from a five-cent stamp to a twenty-three-cent stamp, making the problem harder;

3. changing the number of conditions, for example, Jana buys something and also finds a coin on the sidewalk, thus increasing the complexity of the problem;

4. reversing given and wanted information, for example, given that Jana cashes a check for $31.63, the teller switches the dollars and cents, and Jana buys a five-cent stamp, find how much money Jana has left, thus making the problem much easier; and

5. changing some combination of context, numbers, conditions, and given and wanted information.

For a more thorough discussion of this process of adapting a problem, see *Teaching Problem Solving: What, Why and How* (Charles and Lester 1982). Here are some other examples of problems that could be used for cooperative-problem-solving efforts that will be graded. The hiking problem, a fraction application adapted from Adler and Adler (1978, p. 21), might be appropriate for an algebra or general-mathematics class:

> Moses was hiking from Harper to Belmont along the Winding Trail, which also passed through the town of Springfield. Forty minutes after he left Harper, Moses saw a sign reading, "From Harper to here is half as far as it is from here to Springfield." Moses hiked another 11 miles and saw a second sign reading, "From here to Belmont is half as far as it is from here to Springfield." Moses hiked for 1 more hour and reached Belmont. If he hiked at the same pace all the way, what is the length of the Winding Trail between Harper and Belmont?

Two appropriate modifications of the hiking problem might be (a) changing the numbers from 40 minutes to 20 minutes, one-half to one-third, 11 miles to 8 miles, and 1 hour to 30 minutes and (b) reversing given and wanted information so that the length of the trail is given and the number of miles between the first and second sign needs to be found. The first adaptation leaves the difficulty level of the problem unchanged; the second modification produces a slightly easier problem.

A problem that explores the relationship between perimeter and area and may be appropriate for general-mathematics, algebra, or geometry students is the don't-fence-me-in problem, adapted from Schroyer and Fitzgerald (1986, p. 19).

> Rebekah is planning her garden for the spring. She has ten square garden plots, each of the same size. One will be for carrots, one for lettuce, and so on. She wants to arrange the plots so each of them has at least one side in common with another garden plot. When she finishes arranging the plots she plans to put a rabbit-proof fence around the entire plot.

(a) How would Rebekah arrange her garden plots so that she would use the least amount of fencing? How would she arrange her plots to use the largest amount of fencing?

(b) In general, what happens to the smallest (largest) amount of fence as the number of garden plots increases? Justify your answer.

Assessment techniques should mirror teaching techniques.

Several ways to modify the don't-fence-me-in problem would be to (a) change the numbers from ten plots to twelve, (b) change the context to arranging square tables for a banquet, with one person required to sit at each exposed side of a table, and (c) reverse the given and wanted information by giving the amount of fence needed (perimeter of plot arrangement) and asking for the number of plots. The first and second adaptations leave the difficulty level of the problem unchanged, whereas the third modification makes the problem more difficult.

Grading Group and Individual Papers

Although devising problems that are appropriate for grading is not easy, an equally difficult task is deciding how to assess group solutions. We suggest using an analytic scoring scale like the one in table 1. To illustrate better how this scoring method might be used, we present in figures 1 and 2 two solutions for the triangular-arrangements problem.

Group A's work. Group A received 6 points for understanding because they demonstrated that they understood the relationship among the lengths of the triangle's sides (i.e., to have a triangle, $a + b$ must be greater than c). See figure 1. Their plan involved making an organized list of all possible triangles. The plan was clear and correctly implemented, so they received 6 points for planning. This group also found and correctly labeled the answer and generalization, so they received 3 points for their answer. Thus, our assessment of group A's work was U—6, P—6, A—3 (overall score—15).

Group B's work. Because group B understood that $a \leq b \leq c$ but they did not understand the relationship among the lengths when trying to form triangles, they received 3 points for understanding. See figure 2. This group had a clear, systematic plan, which they correctly implemented according to their understanding of the problem. Thus they received 6 points for planning. Both the answer (45 triangles) and the generalization were correct according to the group's plan. However, since they did not fully understand the problem, their answer and generalization were incorrect; as a result group B received 2 points for getting an answer. Their rating, then, was U—3, P—6, A—2 (overall score—11).

Phase 2 of the problem-solving work, the individual part, extends the group-problem-solving effort and assesses each group member's level of understanding of their group's solution. In this second phase, we recommend including three questions: one to assess each individual's basic understanding of the problem (question 1), a second giving a problem of similar difficulty to be solved (question 2), and a third giving an extension of the problem to be solved (question 3). Table 2 gives examples of the three types of follow-up questions for the triangular-arrangements problem and the mysterious-money problem. Individual follow-up questions for the hiking problem and the don't-fence-me-in problem are contained in table 3.

Work on the individual questions should be graded after the group's solution has been assigned point values.

TABLE 1		
Analytic Scoring Scale*		
Understanding the problem	0:	Complete misunderstanding of the problem
	3:	Misunderstanding or misinterpreting part of the problem
	6:	Complete understanding of the problem
Planning a solution	0:	No attempt or totally inappropriate plan
	3:	Partially correct plan based on part of the problem's being interpreted correctly
	6:	Plan that leads or could have led to a correct solution if implemented properly
Getting an answer	0:	No answer or wrong answer based on an inappropriate plan
	1:	Copying error, computational error, or partial answer for a problem with multiple answers
	2:	Incorrect answer following from an incorrect plan that was implemented properly
	3:	Correct answer and correct label for the answer

*Adapted from Charles, Lester, and O'Daffer (1987, p. 30)

Since the individual questions are to assess each group member's understanding of what their group did, each individual's work must be graded in

> *Assess using cooperative problem solving only if you teach this way.*

light of the group's understanding of the original problem. For example, if a group did not recognize the need to use the triangle inequality, group members will likely make the same error in answering their individual questions. Since points have already been deducted on the group's solution for this mis-

take, points for this same misunderstanding should not be deducted again on the individual questions.

Tips for Grading Cooperative Problem Solving

Plan ahead. It is impossible to say too much about the need for planning, and, of course, no matter how carefully thought out, some plans will not work quite as expected. Here is a list of several things to consider:

1. From where will appropriate problems for grading come? From the textbook? From another teacher? From the district's resource person? It may be useful to start a card file or database of interesting problems. Often teachers can jot

down ideas for modifying problems that they find in textbooks or problems they have previously used in class. The *Mathematics Teacher* calendar is an excellent source of problems! Several other good sources of problems are listed in the Annotated Bibliography.

2. If the work of the entire class is to be graded on the same day, five to eight groups will probably be working at the same time. Will different statements or modifications of the same problem be used for all groups, or will different problems be chosen? If restatements of the same problem are used, will groups' overhearing each other's ideas present a problem?

3. If the work of all algebra, or geometry, classes is graded on the same day, will it be necessary to have different sets of questions for each class? High school students are particularly generous in sharing information with one another between classes, and as a result, the problem may not actually be a problem for classes that meet later in the day.

4. What about the usual time constraints of secondary school teaching? Will students be able to complete the task during the time allotted? What should be done if they don't finish?

5. What about the room layout? Do students have sufficient space to work without interfering with other groups? Are materials (calculators, manipulatives, etc.) sufficient for small-group problem solving? If not, can the necessary materi-

FIGURE 1	**FIGURE 2**
A Correct Group Solution to the Triangular-Arrangements Problem	A Partially Correct Group Solution to the Triangular-Arrangements Problem

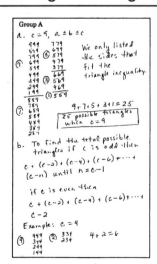

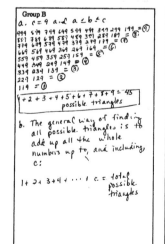

Emphasis on Assessment

als be made or acquired from another teacher?

6. How will points be distributed? Our guidelines can be adapted to fit particular needs, or teachers may want to create their own grading scheme. In either situation, teachers should plan the point distribution ahead of time and give students some indication of the grading plans. Waiting until after the problems have been graded can lead to frustration for both teacher and students.

> *The overall plan should motivate students and give teachers feedback.*

Our most important piece of advice is, Do not assess this way unless you teach this way. Students do not automatically work cooperatively, especially if they have previously experienced years of instruction focused on individual accomplishment. Students need time to adjust to group work and to each other. Give each group at least several class periods to work together before grading their work. Teachers may even want to "practice grade" the work of cooperative groups once or twice before they actually assign grades for group work to give them a chance to hone their grading procedures and ensure that students understand what type of work they are expecting. For more ideas on using cooperative learning in the mathematics class, consult Artzt and Newman (1990) or Davidson (1990).

THE OVERALL ASSESSMENT PLAN

The overall assessment plan needs to accomplish several goals: (*a*) to motivate students to learn as much as they can (participating in a group-solution effort is quite helpful in this regard), (*b*) to give the teacher relevant feedback about individual students' understanding (accomplished by the individual portion of the group solution), and (*c*) to generate data from which the teacher can assign grades (the combination of the two parts of the cooperative-problem-solving test can generate such data). However, to assure that the grades assigned to individuals are

valid, teachers will want to assess each student on a variety of tasks, many of which are individual and a few of which are cooperative. We have had success with designing tests worth 100 points: 25 points for a group-individual problem-solving effort, such as the one we've described in this article, and 75 points for a totally individual, more traditional portion of the test. In a marking period, we obtain other grades from various sources, such as homework, classwork (individual and cooperative), quizzes, individual journals, and group projects.

Assigning grades for cooperative work is just one example of how teaching according to the *Curriculum and Evaluation Standards* (1989) involves changes in how students are assessed, as well as changes in content and instruction. We've offered some tips for grading cooperative groups on challenging problems—problems that truly require insight, understanding, and problem-solving skills. The benefits to be gained outweigh the difficulties this new approach may seem to present.

TABLE 2
Individual Follow-up Questions for the Triangular-Arrangements Problem and the Mysterious-Money Problem

The triangular-arrangements problem

1. (2 points) In the problem your group just solved, would $c = 9$, $b = 5$, and $a = 4$ be possible values for c, b, and a? Justify your answer.
2. (4 points) If $c = 4$, how many triangles would be possible?
3. (4 points) If the number of possible triangles is 36, what is the value of c?

The mysterious-money problem

1. (2 points) If Jana's check was for $5.43, how much money did the teller give Jana when cashing her check?
2. (4 points) Suppose that the teller cashed Jana's check in the same manner as in the original problem. After buying a 68-cent pen, Jana discovered that she had exactly twice as much left as the amount of the check she had cashed. What was the amount of the check?
3. (4 points) Suppose that the bank teller cashed Jana's check for $11.16 in the same manner as in the original problem. After finding $0.63 in her purse, does Jana have more than twice as much as the amount of her original check? Justify your answer.

TABLE 3
Individual Follow-up Questions for the Hiking Problem and the Don't-Fence-Me-In Problem

The hiking problem

1. (2 points) How long did Moses take to hike to Springfield?
2. (4 points) Joni hiked from Bloomington to Nashville along the Hilly Trail, passing by Knight's Korner Grocery Store. Thirty minutes after she left Bloomington, she saw a sign reading, "If you came from Bloomington, you have come one-fourth of the way to Knight's Korner!" She hiked another 11 miles and saw a second sign reading, "From here to Knight's Korner is half as far as it is from here to Nashville." Joni hiked for another two hours and reached Nashville. If she hiked at the same pace all the way, what is the length of the Hilly Trail between Bloomington and Nashville?
3. (4 points) If the Winding Trail in the original problem had been 13 miles long and Moses had walked 90 minutes from the second sign to Belmont, what would be the distance between the two signs? Note: All other information is the same as in the original problem.

The don't fence-me-in problem

1. (2 points) Can the garden plots be arranged in more than one way using the least amount of fencing? Explain your answer.
2. (4 points) If Rebekah had 4 garden plots of the same size, how would she arrange them so that she would use the greatest amount of fencing?
3. (4 points) If Rebekah had 18 garden plots of the same size, how would she arrange them so that she would use the least amount of fencing?

APPENDIX

Solution to Triangular-Arrangements Problem

Group problem

1. Twenty-five triangles are possible. See group A's solution for a more detailed explanation.

2. If c is odd, the total number of possible triangles is the sum of the positive odd integers less than or equal to c. If c is even, the total number of possible triangles is the sum of the positive even integers less than or equal to c.

Follow-up questions

1. No, $c = 9$, $b = 5$, and $a = 4$ are not values that can form a triangle because $a + b \not> c$.

2. If $c = 4$, then $4 + 2 = 6$, so six triangles are possible.

3. Since for $c = 9$ twenty-five triangles are possible and $36 - 25 = 11$, then c must be odd and $c = 11$ because $11 + 9 + 7 + 5 + 3 + 1 = 36$.

> *The benefits outweigh the difficulties of this new approach.*

Solution to Mysterious-Money Problem

Group problem

Use an equation such as $100c + d - 5 = 2(100d + c)$, where d = number of dollars and c = number of cents, and simplify to $c = (199d + 5) \div 98$. Then using an organized list to find possible solutions will yield $31.63 as the amount of Jana's check.

Follow-up questions

1. If we switch the dollars and cents, the teller gave her $43.05.

2. Using a solution process like the one used in the group problem yields $10.21 as the amount of the check.

3. The teller gave Jana $16.11; adding $0.63 gives a total of $16.74, which is 1.5 times as much as the original check of $11.16.

Solution to Hiking Problem

Group problem

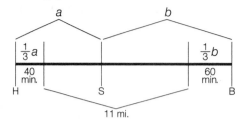

From H to S took 120 minutes; from S to B took 180. Thus Moses walked a total of 300 minutes.

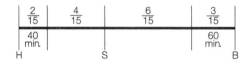

Let x be the total distance from H to B:

$$\left(\frac{4}{15} + \frac{6}{15}\right)x = 11$$

$$x = \frac{33}{2}$$

$$x = 16.5$$

The winding trail is 16.5 miles long between Harper and Belmont.

Follow-up questions

1. Moses hiked for 300 minutes, or 5 hours.

2. Using a method similar to the one in the group problem yields an answer of 22 miles for the length of the Hilly Trail between Bloomington and Nashville.

3. The distance between the two signs is $8 \frac{2}{3}$ miles, which can be found by using the method illustrated in the foregoing.

Solution to Don't-Fence-Me-In Problem

Group problem

1. The least amount of fencing would be used for the most compact arrangement, that is, the one closest to a square. For ten plots the most compact would be either a $3 \times 3 + 1$ arrangement or a 2×5 arrangement. The greatest amount of fencing would be used for the least compact arrangement. For ten plots the least compact would be a 1×10 arrangement.

2. In general, as the number of plots increases by 1, the amount of fencing increases by two sides of a fence. This

generalization is always true for the least compact arrangements. For the most compact arrangements, using the least amount of fencing, the amount of fencing increases by 2 for the first plot added to a rectangular arrangement but remains at this amount through the next rectangular arrangement. For example, for nine plots the smallest amount of fencing is used by a 3×3 arrangement with a perimeter of 12. For ten plots in a $3 \times 3 + 1$ arrangement, the perimeter is 14. For eleven plots in a $3 \times 3 + 2$ arrangement, the perimeter is also 14, as is the amount of fencing for twelve plots in a 3×4 arrangement. Then for thirteen plots in a $3 \times 4 + 1$ arrangement, the perimeter increases to 16.

Follow-up questions

1. Yes. It could be a 2×5 or $3 \times 3 + 1$ arrangement.

2. A 1×4 arrangement would require the most fencing.

3. A 3×6 arrangement would require the least amount of fencing.

ANNOTATED BIBLIOGRAPHY

Gardner, Martin. *Mathematical Puzzles of Sam Loyd.* New York: Dover Publications, 1959.
———. *More Mathematical Puzzles of Sam Loyd.* New York: Dover Publications, 1960.
———. *Perplexing Puzzles and Tantalizing Teasers.* New York: Dover Publications, 1969.
———. *Aha! Insight.* San Francisco: W. H. Freeman & Co., 1978.
———. *Aha! Gotcha: Paradoxes to Puzzle and Delight.* New York: W. H. Freeman & Co., 1982.
———. *Wheels, Life and Other Mathematical Amusements.* New York: W. H. Freeman & Co., 1983.
———. *Penrose Tiles to Trapdoor Ciphers.* New York: W. H. Freeman & Co., 1989.

The foregoing books by Martin Gardner are available in paperback and contain problems of various types and levels.

Jacobs, Harold R. *Elementary Algebra.* San Francisco: W. H. Freeman & Co., 1979.
———. *Mathematics: A Human Endeavor.* New York: W. H. Freeman & Co., 1982.
———. *Geometry.* New York: W. H. Freeman & Co., 1987.

All three of Jacobs's books contain excellent, motivating problems for secondary school students.

Krulik, Stephen, and Jesse A. Rudnick. *A Sourcebook for Teaching Problem Solving.* Boston: Allyn & Bacon, 1984.

————. *Problem Solving: A Handbook for Teachers.* 2d ed. Boston: Allyn & Bacon, 1987.

Each of these two books contains problems for all grades, along with notes about teaching problem solving.

Mayer, Carol, and Tom Sallee. *Make It Simpler: A Practical Guide to Problem Solving in Mathematics.* Menlo Park, Calif.: Addison-Wesley Publishing Co., 1983.

This book of black-line masters has problems for middle-grade students accompanied by suggestions for the teacher on using cooperative problem solving in the classroom.

REFERENCES

Adler, Peggy, and Irving Adler. *Math Puzzles.* New York: Franklin Watts, 1978.

Artzt, Alice F., and Claire M. Newman. *How to Use Cooperative Learning in the Mathematics Classroom.* Reston, Va.: National Council of Teachers of Mathematics, 1990.

Charles, Randall, and Frank K. Lester, Jr. *Teaching Problem Solving: What, Why and How.* Palo Alto, Calif.: Dale Seymour Publications, 1982.

Charles, Randall, Frank Lester, and Phares O'Daffer. *How to Evaluate Progress in Problem Solving.* Reston, Va.: National Council of Teachers of Mathematics, 1987.

Davidson, Neil, ed. *Cooperative Learning in Mathematics: A Handbook for Teachers.* New York: Addison-Wesley Publishing Co., 1990.

Johnson, David W., and Roger Johnson. *Learning Together and Alone: Cooperation, Competition and Individualistic Learning.* 2d ed. Englewood Cliffs, N.J.: Prentice-Hall, 1987.

Lester, Frank K., Jr., and Diana Lambdin Kroll. "Evaluation: A New Vision." *Mathematics Teacher* 84 (April 1991): 276–84.

National Council of Teachers of Mathematics. *Curriculum and Evaluation Standards for School Mathematics.* Reston, Va.: The Council, 1989.

Pollard, Jeanne. *Building Toothpick Bridges.* Palo Alto, Calif.: Dale Seymour Publications, 1985.

Sharan, Shlomo. "Cooperative Learning in Small Groups: Recent Methods and Effects on Achievement, Attitudes, and Ethnic Relations." *Review of Educational Research* 50 (Summer 1980): 241–71.

Shroyer, Janet, and William Fitzgerald. *Mouse and Elephant: Measuring Growth.* Menlo Park, Calif.: Addison-Wesley Publishing Co., 1986.

Slavin, Robert E. *Cooperative Learning.* New York: Longman, 1983.

Thompson, Maynard. *Number Theory.* Bloomington, Ind.: Indiana University Mathematics Education Development Center; Menlo Park, Calif.: Addison-Wesley Publishing Co., 1976.

MIRROR, MIRROR ON THE WALL ... TEACHING SELF-ASSESSMENT TO STUDENTS

Julianna E. Csongor

Students need to learn about themselves. A knowledge of self facilitates security, self-reliance, and self-confidence. Adolescents must be taught to assess their own performance realistically with respect to given standards and to use this knowledge for optimal learning. What better place to do so than in the mathematics classroom?

We can place more responsibility on students' shoulders for the evaluation of their own performance, attitude, and behavior. For example, when students know the time and content of the next test, they should not have to wait until after they fail the test to find out that they did not know the material. They should be able to judge their own preparedness on review exercises, get extra help, do extra work, and so on, *before* the test.

> **Test anxiety can be reduced.**

Some people have a natural ability for self-assessment and others do not. However, I believe that this skill, just like many other skills, can be developed in students. Accuracy in self-assessment in my classes is an important element of the overall assessment of each student.

Within five minutes of the end of the allotted time for the test, I instruct students to stop working, to think back

Julianna E. Csongor is a teacher at Saint Maria Gosetti High School, Philadelphia, PA 19148.

about how they felt during the test, and to estimate their grade problem by problem by using the criteria given at the beginning of the year (see table 1).

The following incentives for correct estimates are offered: three extra points on the test if the student accurately predicts her or his grade, two extra points if the student's estimate is within ± 1 percent, and one extra point if the estimate is within ± 3 percent. Some students put almost as much effort into estimating their grade as they do solving the problems on the test! For some reason they seem to want those "free" extra points. They do not mind the process of self-evaluation any more. As a matter of fact, most students continue to put their estimated grade on tests even when I forget to remind them.

To make self-assessment a success, teachers have to earn the students' confidence and cooperation by overcoming their natural fear of being wrong and by

making the process enjoyable and worthwhile. At first, some students find it difficult to look and realize that the test they have just worked on for forty-five minutes is worth possibly only a 50 percent score. Others are unduly worried or have no self-confidence at all and will estimate a score of 10 percent, or worse yet, of 0 percent. For others wishful thinking takes over that will materialize in a guess of 100 percent, even when the student has left out several items. Following the procedures outlined here, by the middle of the year at least half the class can come within 3 percent of their actual earned grade on a given test. Further, no one is way off—they are all in the ballpark.

A tremendous by-product of this process has been that many students perform self-evaluation without being prompted. They go back and double-check their work because they cannot decide how to evaluate a particular ques-

---

TABLE 1

1. I understood the problem, knew the appropriate method for solving it, and am confident my answer is correct. (Full credit)

2. I understood the problem and knew the appropriate method for solving it, but my answer looks and feels "funny." I probably made a stupid mistake. (3/4 credit)

3. I understood the problem, was not sure of what method to use, but think I got the correct answer. (1/2 credit)

4. I did not quite understand the question, but I thought I remembered a similar one, so I improvised a method and guessed the answer. (1/2 credit)

5. I had no idea what the question was all about. (No credit)

When the estimate is a failing grade, students are required to write a few words of explanation for their failure and to state their reasons for not seeking extra help before a test.

---

tion for purposes of estimating their grade. Many times this process results in revisions that yield a correct solution. In all my classes, I have observed a gradual, but marked, reduction in test anxiety. Surprisingly, this process seems to work best with my classes of slow learners. On a recent test, four such students out of thirty-eight produced perfect papers for a 103 percent score; having correctly estimated their score to be 100 percent, each of them earned an extra 3 percent.

Assessment of students' attitudes and dispositions can be just as important as assessment of their specific mathematical skills. My students look at themselves periodically with the aid of a form adapted from one used by our guidance department for college recommendations (see table 2). In the beginning of the marking period we have a general discussion about the meaning of each category and my expectations. Occasionally I put the form on the overhead projector to remind students to think about how they are doing at present. Each quarter they are required to complete one of these self-evaluation forms to indicate how they see themselves in relation to their classmates. My basic instruction on handing out the forms to them is, "Compared to your classmates, how would you rate yourself in terms of academic skills, attitudes, and class behavior?" I try to return the forms promptly with my evaluation and schedule an interview with each student to discuss any discrepancies and suggestions for improvement.

Many educators are concerned about teaching students self-esteem. I believe that self-esteem has to be developed, not learned! Even though we cannot teach self-esteem nor give it, we can and should foster a nurturing atmosphere and an environment rich with opportunities for students to be able to develop it.

Students are remarkably adept at discovering where they stand with respect to other students, in understanding their own special skills, and in recognizing their shortcomings. Through guidance, we can take advantage of this ability and help students take more responsibility for their own learning.

BIBLIOGRAPHY

Lester, Frank K., Jr., and Diana Lambdin Kroll. "Evaluation: A New Vision." *Mathematics Teacher* 84 (April 1991): 276–83.

Levy, Jerre. "Children Think with Whole Brains: Myth and Reality." In *Student Learning Styles and Brain Behavior: Programs, Instrumentation, Research,* pp. 173–84. Reston, Va.: National Association of Secondary School Principals, 1982.

National Council of Teachers of Mathematics. *Curriculum and Evaluation Standards for School Mathematics.* Reston, Va.: The Council, 1989.

Pogrow, S. "Challenging At-Risk Students: Findings from the HOTS Program." *Phi Delta Kappan* 5 (January 1990): 389–97.

TABLE 2

Self-Evaluation Guide	Poor	Average	Good	Very Good	Excellent	Top 3
Creative, original thought						
Motivation						
Independence, initiative						
Intellectual curiosity						
Academic achievement						
Written expression of ideas						
Effective class discussion						
Disciplined work habits						
Potential for growth						
Class behavior						
SUMMARY EVALUATION						

SECTION III

Looking at
Alternative Assessment
Options

One of the most important themes of the current reform in assessment is the need for teachers to use multiple forms of assessment to be able to make valid inferences about students' progress. Portfolios, journals, performance assessments, interviews, writing, presentations, extended projects, discussions, and partner quizzes are among the alternatives to testing that are frequently recommended.

Each article in this section focuses attention on one or more alternative forms of assessment. The techniques range considerably in scope and emphasis (for example, from having students do free writing during the first five minutes of class to building portfolios for documenting students' growth over the course of an entire year). Some assessments are intended for nongrading purposes; others include grading schemes. Some articles deal with high school examples, whereas others concentrate more on the middle school or elementary grades. Not all forms of alternative assessment are represented in this section of readings, although we made an effort to include as wide a range as possible.

In "Assessing Mathematics Learning for Students with Learning Differences," Lee Cross and Michael Hynes give an overview of a wide array of alternative assessment techniques, all of which can actually be useful with any students. Cross and Hynes briefly consider observation, interviewing, holistic scoring, checklists, and journals. Because they furnish a survey of so many different techniques, their paper seems useful as an introduction to the notion of alternative assessment.

Of the six Assessment Standards presented in NCTM's *Assessment Standards for School Mathematics*, mathematics is the first. In other words, it is essential that we identify the important mathematics in any assessment we undertake. Yet how does one define, or even recognize, important mathematics? In "Quality Mathematics: How Can We Tell?" David Clarke addresses this issue head on. Clarke maintains that it is important to involve students in identifying characteristics of quality mathematics as well as in developing rubrics for assessing mathematical performance. He describes a process teachers can use to get students involved. Sharing responsibility with students

seems to be a new, but important, expectation in the assessment process.

Linda Wilson argues in "What Gets Graded Is What Gets Valued" that alternative forms of assessment often are ineffective if they are not incorporated into a teacher's grading scheme. Teachers trying to move toward the use of more diverse sources of information (such as those discussed in other articles in this section) must find ways to show that they value these new sources or students will continue to believe that traditional methods of assessment (e.g., homework, quizzes, and tests) are all that really matters.

In "Aligning Assessment with the NCTM's Curriculum Standards," Cathy Schloemer describes eight alternative assessments that she used in a unit on functions and relations. The assessments involved students in writing, giving real-life examples, sketching graphs, and demonstrating with manipulatives. For the tasks that were graded, a rubric is provided.

Diane Miller encourages teachers to use the first five minutes of class to have students write about such diverse topics as their understanding of a concept or their feelings about mathematics. In "Begin Mathematics Class with Writing," Miller argues that it is efficient to have students share their thoughts while the teacher performs administrative duties and that such an exercise provides students with an opportunity to reflect on mathematical ideas and relationships in a nongraded format.

Karen Norwood and Glenda Carter also recommend having students write during the beginning of class because journal writing helps bring "to light thoughts and understandings that typical classroom interactions or tests do not elucidate." "Journal Writing: An Insight into Students' Understanding" includes ten tips for getting started with journal writing, as well as seventeen sample journal prompts.

"Pic-Jour Math: Pictorial Journal Writing in Mathematics" proposes the use of multimodal journals to assist students in communicating the mathematics they have learned. Andi Stix enumerates reasons for using a multimodal approach that enables students to link verbal knowledge, visual imagery, and personal experience through writing, pictures, numbers, symbols, and manipulatives. Stix furnishes an assessment form and four examples of students' work.

Alice Artzt writes about improving mathematical communication in "Integrating Writing and Cooperative Learning in the Mathematics Class." She used students' journal responses to assess the effectiveness of group formation and to make appropriate changes. Students also worked in groups to discuss what they had done incorrectly on tests and then submitted a written explanation along with their reworked problems.

Diana Lambdin and Vicki Walker write about three years of experience with portfolios in Walker's sixth-grade classroom in an article entitled "Planning for Classroom Portfolio Assessment." They have learned three primary lessons from portfolio use: (1) the importance of having a reason for assigning portfolios, (2) the importance of establishing workable routines for managing them, and (3) the importance of giving students clear guidance. Included in the article are tips for getting started with portfolios and a method for evaluating them.

In "Student Mathematics Portfolio: More than a Display Case," Mary Crowley echoes many of the points made by Lambdin and Walker as well as suggests a variety of assignments appropriate for use in portfolios. These include not only adaptations of previously completed assignments (e.g., homework with errors debugged and corrected, or papers chosen as favorites by the student or by the teacher) but also new assignments to be produced specifically for portfolio inclusion.

Madeleine Long and Meir Ben-Hur are proponents of using interviews as an alternative assessment technique. In "Informing Learning through the Clinical Interview," Long and Ben-Hur maintain that interviews where students work mathematical tasks as well as answer questions can be effective diagnostic tools, can provide insight into one's teaching, and can also serve as a form of instruction.

Denise Spangler argues in "Assessing Students' Beliefs about Mathematics" that the affective domain (attitudes and beliefs) is just as important an area for student assessment as the cognitive domain. Helping students become aware of their beliefs about mathematics through open-ended questions is the focus of her article. Spangler gives suggestions for presenting such questions in a number of different formats and offers a variety of questions that are useful for prompting student discussion and debate about beliefs.

Doug Clarke and Linda Wilson's article, "Valuing What We See," points out how frequently teachers observe and hear things during class that can furnish important information to guide their teaching. Unfortunately, informal teacher observations are often forgotten in the frenzy of teaching. Maintaining that documenting observations is important, Clarke and Wilson provide practical suggestions for capturing these assessment data, including when to document observations, what to look for, how to observe and document, and how to use observational information once it has been collected.

ASSESSING MATHEMATICS LEARNING FOR STUDENTS WITH LEARNING DIFFERENCES

Lee Cross and Michael C. Hynes

The *Curriculum and Evaluation Standards for School Mathematics* (NCTM 1989) advocates the alignment of the mathematics curriculum with instructional practices and assessment techniques. The authors clearly understood that this alignment would not occur without expanding the notion of assessment and making the process of assessment more meaningful for all students. Consequently, the guidelines for the evaluation of mathematics became a significant part of the curriculum standards and stated the following:

- Student assessment must be integral to instruction.
- Multiple means of assessment should be used.
- All aspects of mathematical knowledge and its connections should be assessed.

Teachers should be paying more attention to assessing what students know about mathematics and spending less time determining what they do not know. This attention is especially true for

Lee Cross and Mike Hynes work at the University of Central Florida, Orlando, FL 32816-1250. Cross teaches assessment and methods classes for preservice teachers of students with disabilities. Hynes is director of the Martin Marietta/UCF Academy for Mathematics and Science Education. Alternative assessment is a key component in the academy's program to develop K–8 building-level mathematics leaders.

students who have experienced difficulty in learning mathematics. Constant reminders of failure only lead to low self-esteem, which can lead to lower achievement. Perhaps this downward spiral can be stopped by changing the emphasis of assessment from checking only for the correct answer to recording what students *know*, how they *think* about mathematics, and how they *apply* mathematics to real-world problems.

Many students in our schools have learning problems in the area of mathematics. Many of these students are labeled handicapped and at risk for school failure. These students may exhibit deficits in computational skills, spatial awareness, understanding of mathematical concepts, problem solving, and memory of procedures and strategies. A larger and larger percent of these students are being taught in regular classrooms for all or most of the school day. Educators (Gartner and Lipsky 1987; Lilly 1988; Reynolds, Wang, and Walberg 1987; Stainback and Stainback 1987; Wang, Reynolds, and Walberg 1986) have advocated that adaptive instructional strategies be used to help these students succeed in regular classrooms. More recently, researchers have proposed that educators working with disabled students must adapt instruction in mathematics to that proposed by the curriculum standards (Cawley, Baker-Kroczynski, and Urban 1992). However, adapting instruction alone is not sufficient. The methods of assessment must be adapted as well.

These disabled students are penalized most by traditional paper-and-pencil tests, particularly when their performance is being compared with that of typical children at a particular grade or age. Clearly, if children learn mathematics with difficulty or use different methods of learning, standard paper-and-pencil assessments will not be sufficient to document learning and students' progress. Using alternative forms of assessment is essential to describe what a student has learned, how he or she learns best, under what conditions he or she learns, and his or her understanding of mathematical processes.

Some alternative-assessment forms appropriate for students with handicaps are observation, interviews, holistic scoring, checklists, portfolios, and journals, as well as paper-and-pencil forms of assessment.

ASSESSING THROUGH OBSERVATION

Many teachers have made observation an integral part of evaluation. They practice targeting one or two students at each lesson for observation. To record observations, sticky notes or computer labels are used. Names of students targeted for the lesson are written on one or two sticky notes. Blanks are available for writing spontaneous observations about other students. These observations are then pasted on a specific sheet for each student in a class notebook. Figure 1 illustrates how observations can be used to assess students' understanding of mathematics effectively.

For students with disabilities, using observation as an assessment technique gives the teacher a window to obtain student-performance information that cannot be gleaned from paper-and-pencil tests. Teachers can unobtrusively gain insight into the approach to the task as well as the persistence in completing the task. Additionally, information can be obtained about how students are constructing meaning from concrete manipulations, as in the illustration with James. All observation should be systematically recorded. The record can document achievement and communicate a student's success with mathematics to the student and others. These documented observations, when linked to paper-and-pencil test results, the results of interviews, the record of achievement on a checklist, and other assessment data, will give a more complete picture of a student's success in mathematics.

INTERVIEWING

Students with disabilities often have difficulty in problem solving because their lack of fluency in reading can cause a misunderstanding of mathematical concepts, poor computational skills, or poor dispositions toward learning mathematics. Alternative-assessment techniques should be used to determine the areas of problem solving in which the student has strengths as well as weaknesses. One alternative technique for assessing problem-solving abilities is interviewing students while they are in a problem-solving situation. Teachers can interview students informally in conversation while monitoring seatwork, or the teacher may plan a more structured, individual interview to survey the understanding of several students. Figure 2 illustrates assessing with an interview.

HOLISTIC SCORING

Relying on observation or interview techniques to assess problem solving is not always effective. Interviews may be too time-consuming to use for an entire class or even with targeted students. An alternative to interviews is using a holistic-scoring technique. (See fig. 3 [Hynes 1990].) Three types of holistic scoring are generally recognized for evaluating mathematics learning: ana

lytic scoring, focused holistic scoring, and general-impression scoring. (More information on holistic scoring can be found in *How to Evaluate Progress in Problem Solving* [Charles, Lester, and O'Daffer 1987].) The focus of holistic scoring is on the process rather than on the correct answer. Students are given some credit for employing all or part of the correct steps in the problem, even if they get the wrong answer. Of course, if the student executes an appropriate process and also gets the correct answer, more points are awarded. In short, students are given credit for what they know. In implementing holistic-scoring techniques, it becomes imperative that students show all written work and record the thinking processes they used to solve the problem. Since writing problem solutions is often difficult for students with disabilities, these students may need to work in pairs or cooperative groups, have an adult assist in recording their work, or act out the solutions while showing the abstract solutions. Figure 4 presents a solution to a problem by two students, and the teacher's assessment and recommendations are shown in figure 5.

FIGURE 1

Using Observation to Assess James's Understanding of Area and Factors

Mr. Mir has been working on geometry and measurement in his class and wants to assess students' understanding of calculating the area of rectangles. He is concerned about how to assess James, a student with learning disabilities who has difficulty making transitions from the concrete to the abstract. Mr. Mir was concerned that James might not be able to distinguish perimeter from area or apply a rudimentary formula to calculate the area. Previously, James had done poorly on written tests on area. Mr. Mir believes that the written tests do not reflect James's understanding of the mathematical concepts because James shows more insight during class presentations and discussions. Mr. Mir decides to assess James's understanding of area by observing him working with manipulatives while the rest of the class works at the abstract level.

Mr. Mir requests, "Class, make a rectangle that is 4 units by 6 units. Record the area of this rectangle and the dimensions of all rectangles that have the same area as the first rectangle, using only whole-number dimensions."

Mr. Mir observes James using square tiles to make his 4-by-6 rectangle. James makes the rectangle and records that the area of the rectangle is 20. Mr. Mir notes that James added 4 + 6 + 4 + 6 to get 20. As James tries to respond to Mr. Mir's direction to make more rectangles, he seems confused. Mr. Mir asks the class to take time out. "Each member of the class can ask someone sitting nearby two questions about the problem." James interacts with the student in front of him in an acceptable manner and asks how the other student got 24. After the class returns to work, Mr. Mir notes that James has erased his first answer and written the correct answer.

As James makes other rectangles with an area of 24, Mr. Mir writes that he seems to have grasped a concrete understanding of area but failed to show all the possible rectangles with an area of 24.

Teacher assessment. James demonstrated some understanding of area and the ability to find the area of the rectangle using concrete materials. He is also able to represent the area of a rectangle symbolically when allowed to use concrete materials.

Recommendations. James seemed to benefit from using manipulatives. He could make the described rectangles, but he seems to confuse area and perimeter. Continued use of the manipulatives will be necessary to help him make this distinction. Since James was not able to make all the rectangles for an area of 24, he may need more work on the factors of 24. He may know the factors and not be able to connect this problem and the factors of a number. More observation is needed. The written work given James was assigned to help determine if he is progressing in relating abstract number sentences to models and pictures. If time allows, interviewing James about his understanding might be helpful.

Emphasis on Assessment

FIGURE 2

Using Interviewing to Assess José's Ability to Solve Two-Step Problems

Since José has reading difficulties, Ms. Ryerson presents the following problem to him orally while pointing to the important facts.

> You and your dad go fishing. Your dad catches 4 fish and throws back 2 because the fish were too small. You catch 6 good-sized eating fish. Late in the afternoon you and your dad go home and give your mom the fish to cook for supper. How many fish did your mom have to cook for supper?

The first step for Ms. Ryerson was to ask José to tell her about the problem. By explaining the problem, he completes the first step in problem solving—understanding the problem. José's response indicates that he is supposed to tell how many fish were cooked for supper. The teacher then continues the interview process by asking José how he would find out how many fish should be cooked. José's response will indicate whether he can select the correct operations and plan the solution. This question will probably lead to calculating the answer or solving the problem. José explains that he will add 4 and 2 and 6. At this point, the teacher suggested that Jose could use some fish counters to retell the story of the fishing trip. The teacher gives José a red paper labeled "dad" and a green paper labeled "José." José is asked to retell the story, placing the fish counters on the appropriate paper. As José retells the story with the manipulatives, he takes the correct action to indicate he understands the meaning of throwing back fish. In continuing the abstract solution of the problem, he adds 4, 2, and 6 correctly.

Teacher assessment. When given two-step problems, José is able to identify the question the problem is asking. Initially, he does recognize one of the correct operations; however, José does not appear to comprehend the problem. In the retelling procedure, the teacher observes that José appears to comprehend the problem, but he is unable to transfer this comprehension and the physical action to the mathematical operations.

Recommendations. José needs more experience with two-step problem-solving exercises. He appears to profit from acting out the problem. His experiences should include working with another student to share their understanding of problems and creating his own two-step problems. He also needs to improve his conceptual understanding of operations. This student needs to experience real-world situations that indicate the operations needed. He needs to experience many models of subtraction: how many more, subset, and comparison, as well as the take-away model.

FIGURE 3

A Sample Focused Holistic-Scoring Scale for a Problem-Solving Assignment

0 points
1. Problem is not attempted or the answer sheet is blank.
2. The data copied are erroneous and no attempt has been made to use these data.
3. An incorrect answer is written and no work is shown.

1 point
1. The data in the problem are recopied but nothing is done.
2. A correct strategy is indicated but not applied to the problem.
3. The student tries to reach a subgoal but never does.

2 points
1. An inappropriate method is indicated and some work is done, but the correct answer is not reached.
2. A correct strategy is followed but the student does not pursue the work sufficiently to get the solution.
3. The correct answer is written but the work either is not intelligible or is not shown.

3 points
1. The student follows a correct strategy but commits a computational error in the middle, which leads to an incorrect solution.
2. The student uses a correct strategy but ignores or misunderstands some conditions and never reaches a solution.
3. The correct answer is given and the work gives some evidence that an appropriate method was used. However, the implementation of the strategy is not clear.

4 points
1. The student uses an appropriate method and implements it correctly but commits a computational error toward the end and obtains an incorrect answer.
2. The student follows a correct method and performs the necessary work but toward the end loses sight of the answer or does not label the answer appropriately.
3. The student makes an error in copying. Except for this error, the work shows complete understanding of the method and implementation, even though an incorrect answer is reached.

5 points
1. The student has followed a correct method, performed appropriate computations, and labeled answers correctly.

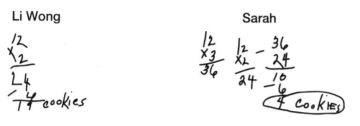
CHECKLIST

When assessing progress in learning, teachers should be primarily concerned with the content of mathematics. Another dimension of learning mathematics, however, should also be assessed. Students' dispositions toward learning mathematics are important, too. Students' confidence during mathematics learning, their willingness to persevere in mathematical tasks, and their inclination to monitor their own thinking and performance all are important in the evaluation process (NCTM 1989). These dispositions are usually assessed as students engage in instructional activities in the classroom. For example, as they work in cooperative groups, teachers should note the ability of students to function properly during the instructional activity.

Mrs. Locklear has been using cooperative groups in her mathematics class two to three times a week for several weeks. Groups in her class solve problems, build models, practice with activities, and study for weekly tests. She has seen increases in achievement in some of the slower students in her class. Mrs. Locklear has worked with her students on such social skills necessary for cooperative-group work as negotiating, complimenting one another, and accepting criticism. Although she thinks that most groups are working well together, she is concerned that a few individuals and their groups might not be responding well to this strategy. She has noticed that some of the students with learning problems may not be actively involved in their groups. A month ago, Mrs. Locklear developed a checklist to assess students while they worked in cooperative groups (fig. 6). Figure 7 highlights an assessment and recommendation of the checklist.

A checklist supplies a strategy to record data systematically. Whereas the checklist in this example is used to assess students who are working in cooperative groups, checklists have many potential uses in assessment. These devices are excellent assessment tools to support teacher observation (Charles, Lester, and O'Daffer 1987). In cooperative learning, group members can use a checklist to rate their peers in the group. Checklists can also be used for self-appraisal.

Filling out a checklist every day on every student is not necessary; however, a teacher who chooses to use checklists to assess students should use them periodically to assess students' progress on the attainment of concepts and skills as well as dispositions. Repeated observation using checklists will make patterns of behavior more apparent.

JOURNALS

Mathematics instruction should furnish opportunities for students to communicate their understanding of mathematics. Journal writing is a communication format that allows students to reach agreement among themselves about the use of mathematical terms and to recog-

---

FIGURE 5

Teacher's Assessment of Student Work

Teacher assessment. Although Li Wong did not get the correct answer to the problem, he did convert 2 dozen to the exact number of cookies. He then subtracted 6, the number of cookies given to the children after school, to determine the number of cookies left for dinner, but he made a computational error. However, Li Wong forgot to consider the total number of cookies. Mother made 36 cookies. The teacher made a decision to give Li Wong 2 points because he used an inappropriate method, did complete the problem, and reached an incorrect answer.

Using the focused holistic-scoring scale, the teacher gave Sarah 4 points. She used the correct strategy but near the end committed a computational error, which caused an incorrect answer.

Li Wong and Sarah received some points for their solutions even though they failed to obtain the correct answer. Both students attempted to apply the correct strategies in solving the problem. Thus, their ability to use the correct problem-solving processes were recognized. Analyzing the processes both students used was fairly easy, since they showed a great deal of their work.

Recommendations. Both Li Wong and Sarah may benefit from problem-solving experiences in pairs or cooperative groups. Computational errors are a barrier to completing the problem correctly for both students. By working together or with other students, Li Wong and Sarah may detect and correct these errors. Likewise, the discussion of a group may have allowed Li Wong to see another step in the problem. Additionally, both students need some practice with the algorithms for operations. If these students work on problem solving independently, they should be encouraged to use a calculator so that their computational skills do not interfere with the problem-solving process.

Emphasis on Assessment

FIGURE 6
Cooperative-Learning Checklist

Skills	NAMES					
Followed directions	❑	❑	❑	❑	❑	❑
Stayed on task	❑	❑	❑	❑	❑	❑
Explained ideas clearly to others	❑	❑	❑	❑	❑	❑
Supported ideas of others	❑	❑	❑	❑	❑	❑
Developed a plan	❑	❑	❑	❑	❑	❑
Engaged in constructive criticism	❑	❑	❑	❑	❑	❑
Persisted in completing the assignment	❑	❑	❑	❑	❑	❑
Performed the following roles:						
Checker	❑	❑	❑	❑	❑	❑
Recorder	❑	❑	❑	❑	❑	❑
Leader	❑	❑	❑	❑	❑	❑
Summarizer	❑	❑	❑	❑	❑	❑

nize the importance of shared understanding of mathematical ideas. Writing about mathematics helps students clarify their understanding and gives teachers valuable information from which instructional decisions can be made (NCTM 1989). Figure 8 describes one use of journal writing to improve understanding of mathematical ideas.

Journals are an excellent means of self-assessment. Students with disabilities often have difficulty expressing themselves in writing. With structure and guidance they can, and should, develop reflective skills. Often students with mild handicaps are so accustomed to receiving feedback from others, particularly negative feedback, that they fail to take responsibility for their own understanding of content. Journals help develop this important skill.

Journals should be kept on a consistent basis. Ideally, daily entries should be made in the journal. Teachers of self-contained classrooms can have students keep one journal for all subjects.

Students can write in a special mathematics section or communicate in a special color. If journals are used as part of the assessment program, they should be continually monitored by the teacher to identify any instructional needs of the student. Systematically gathering and analyzing information from the students' journals is necessary. Some teachers collect three or four different journals each day to read and then respond to the students' entries. In addition to the three or four targeted students, teachers may allow one or two students voluntarily to submit their journals if they have something they want the teacher to read and respond to quickly.

Teachers who function in a departmental situation can collect two or three journals from each class. This tactic requires that the teacher do no more "grading" than if one whole class turned in an assignment for grading. When students with learning differences are in the mathematics class, monitoring the journals of these children more often than those of other students may be necessary.

ADAPTING ASSESSMENT TECHNIQUES

Table 1 lists characteristics that impede progress in mathematics for students with mild handicaps, along with suggested alternative-assessment procedures for these students. Even these procedures may need some adaptation to be appropriate for students with disabilities. Some suggestions for adaptations appear in the third column. As students with learning problems become more proficient in mathematics, many of the adaptations may be phased out, or less obtrusive methods may be selected.

FIGURE 7
Using a Checklist to Assess a Student's Disposition Toward Learning Mathematics

While students are working in groups of four, Mrs. Locklear walks from group to group and uses the checklist to assess the individual students in the group. She has had an opportunity to assess each group two or three times.

Teacher assessment. Mrs. Locklear notes that Tyrone, a low achiever, is not really participating in his group. He is slow to get on task and seems to be easily frustrated. He rarely supports others and does not share his ideas in the group. Although he was assigned the role of checker, he rarely assumes the responsibility. In contrast, Latesha, a student with mild mental retardation, seems to function well in her cooperative group. Latesha gets on task quickly and supports other group members. She has also assumed the role of checker, but her resource teacher had practiced that role with her.

Recommendations. Mrs. Locklear feels that Tyrone would benefit from the group experience but is not taking advantage of the opportunity. She decides that tomorrow she will take aside all the students who are checkers and do some role-playing with them to give some strategies for the checker role. Asking one of the members of Tyrone's group to encourage him to participate might be helpful. Perhaps Tyrone would do better in another group. Latesha needs no adjustment at this time, only continued support and encouragement.

FIGURE 8

Using Journals to Assess Students' Ability to Communicate Mathematical Ideas

Miss Brant, a fifth-grade teacher, has been having her students write in their mathematics journals daily as a form of self-assessment. In the initial journal-writing experiences, Miss Brant instructed her students to write about what they had learned and what was difficult for them. While reading the students' journals, she realized that many were having difficulty expressing themselves in writing. For those students who needed more structure, she decided to begin the daily journal assignment using the questions that follow. Miss Brant suggested to Donny and Enrico, two students who attend the special-education resource class, that they may want to copy the problem down to answer questions 1 and 2. Miss Brant told them not to worry about spelling every word correctly. She stressed how important it was to get their ideas in writing.

1. What did you find easy in this lesson?
2. What was most difficult for you today?
3. What new thing did you learn today?

Teacher assessment. In reviewing Donny and Enrico's journals, Miss Brant discovered that both boys were having difficulty with equivalent fractions. On Tuesday and Wednesday, both boys said that "3/4 = ?/8" was the most difficult equation for them to solve. Enrico's response to the third question was, "I hate fractions!" Donny's response to it was "Nothin'." However, when Miss Brant asked Donny to write a sentence about what he learned that day, he responded, "The bigger the bottom number the smaller the piece."

Recommendations. Miss Brant realizes that she can gain some insight into both boys' progress by continuing to monitor their journals carefully. At the same time, she wants the boys to use the journals as a way to describe their own progress. She decided that she will spend time with some of the students in extending their journal-writing skills. Miss Brant decided that she will also begin charting the areas that students frequently identify as difficult. Miss Brant views the students' journals as valuable information about students' progress and the need for further instruction.

These assessment procedures should not be viewed as alternatives but rather as examples of appropriate assessment procedures for the student who learns mathematics differently. These assessment techniques should be used systematically if sound decisions are to be made about instructing children with disabilities.

SUMMARY

To determine the progress of, and make appropriate educational decisions for, students with disabilities or at-risk students, teachers should use assessment techniques that accurately determine the students' progress *in spite of their learning differences.* Alternative-assessment procedures not only are for students with disabilities but are appropriate for *all students.* However, given the learning characteristics of many students who are challenged in one way or another, it is imperative that alternative-assessment procedures be used.

The authors are not suggesting that paper-and-pencil assessments be abandoned. Information gained from each assessment may be useful to the overall assessment of the student with disabilities. The information gained from pencil-and-paper assessments, however, is not sufficient to assess the mathematics learning for these students.

An assortment of appropriately applied assessment strategies should be used to gain a comprehensive view of the abilities of students with disabilities.

REFERENCES

Cawley, John F., Susan Baker-Kroczynski, and Annie Urban. "Seeking Excellence in Mathematics Education for Students with Mild Disabilities." *Teaching Exceptional Children* 24 (Winter 1992): 40–43.

Charles, Randall, Frank Lester, and Phares O'Daffer. *How to Evaluate Progress in Problem Solving.* Reston, Va.: National Council of Teachers of Mathematics, 1987.

Gartner, Alan, and Dorothy K. Lipsky. "Beyond Special Education: Toward a Quality System for All Students." *Harvard Educational Review* 57 (November 1987): 367–85.

Hynes, Michael C. *Alternative Assessment in Mathematics: A Workshop Leader Handbook.* D. D. Eisenhower Grant Report. Orlando, Fla.: University of Central Florida, 1990.

Lilly, M. S. "The Regular Education Initiative: A Force for Change in General and Special Education." *Education and Training in Mental Retardation* 23 (November 1988): 253–60.

National Council of Teachers of Mathematics. *Curriculum and Evaluation Standards for School Mathematics.* Reston, Va.: The Council, 1989.

Reynolds, M. C., M. C. Wang, and H. J. Walberg. "The Necessary Restructuring of Special and Regular Education." *Exceptional Children* 53 (February 1987): 391–98.

Stainback, Susan, and William Stainback. "Integration versus Cooperation: A Commentary on Educating Children with Learning Problems: A Shared Responsibility." *Exceptional Children* 54 (September 1987): 66–68.

Wang, M. C., M. C. Reynolds, and H. J. Walberg. "Rethinking Special Education." *Educational Leadership* 44 (September 1986): 26–31.

TABLE 1
Adopting Assessment Techniques for Students with Learning Difficulties

Examples of learning difficulties	Alternative-assessment procedures	Examples of assessment adaptations
Reading difficulty	Interview	Students use pictures or manipulatives.
	Observation and questioning	Teacher presents problems orally.
	Journals	Students dictate journal entries to an aide who records the information.
		Students respond by acting out interpretations of problems or solutions.
Computational difficulty	Interview	Students use manipulatives in skill-development activities.
	Observation	Students use calculators in problem solving.
	Journals	Teacher provides positive feedback about progress.
Difficulty translating concrete understanding to abstract level	Interview	Students use manipulatives to create an abstract solution.
	Checklists	Teacher records repeated successes at the abstract level before verifying mastery
	Journals	Students' entries use pictures. Teacher has students explain pictures orally.

Learns more slowly	Holistic scoring	Teacher to—
		    provide mnemonics for steps during assessment;
		    give fewer questions or problems on tests;
		    test in pairs or in cooperative groups;
		    allow students to complete graded assignments at home.

Difficulty remembering procedural steps	Interview	Teacher to— color code steps on tests;
	Observation	remind students of self-monitoring strategies;
	Holistic scoring	provide mnemonics for steps during assessment.
Fear of failure	Observation	Teacher to— remind students to use stress-reduction techniques;
	Self-appraisal checklist	remind students to use "self-talk" techniques;
	Interview	ask easy questions initially to build up students' confidence.
Lack of such number-sense concepts as "more than," "less than," or the value of multidigit numbers	Interview	Teacher to— encourage the use of manipulatives;
	Holistic scoring	give partial credit in estimation exercises;
	Observation	color code to focus attention on place value;
	Journals	encourage expressions about numbers.

QUALITY MATHEMATICS: HOW CAN WE TELL?

David Clarke

The motivation for this article comes from a conversation that occurred in my home recently.

Daughter: Dad, what do I do?

Dad (this author): Huh?

Daughter: My teacher says if I do everything required in this math assignment, the best he will give me is a C.

Dad: Run that past me again.

Daughter: He says that in order to get an A, we have to go beyond what's required in the assignment. If we only do what it says in the assignment, the best we can get is a C.

As the conversation continued, I realized that my daughter and her classmates were confused about what would be considered a good performance. The teacher's intentions were reasonably clear: he was trying to stimulate quality mathematics by leaving the specific task requirements as open as possible. Unfortunately, his class had little idea of the characteristics of quality mathematics.

A second conversation is also relevant here. I was presenting an assessment workshop for some teachers near San Francisco. During the discussion about different types of tasks, one teacher raised her hand and made this comment:

> David, I think my problem is that my kids aren't clear on what good mathematics looks like, and, to be honest, I don't think I'm all that clear on it either.

Well, I can put 2 and 2 together with the best of them. We seem to have a seri-

Prepared by David Clarke
University of Melbourne
Parkville, Victoria, Australia

ous issue here. What do we mean by quality mathematics in school, and how can we bring our students to share our vision of a quality mathematics performance?

What constitutes quality mathematics?

RENEGOTIATING THE DIDACTIC CONTRACT

In part, the problems stem from the recent commitment to task diversity:

- Diversity of context—from abstract academic problems to elaborately contextualized story problems
- Diversity of types of tasks—from closed, routine, and procedural tasks to open-ended, novel, investigative projects
- Diversity of communicative modes—from written short answers to practical demonstrations of particular mathematical performances

This commitment to diversity has as one of its goals the comprehensive modeling of mathematical activity. The difficulty for teachers and students is that the tenets of quality have become blurred.

Consider the response to the following task:

> Fred's apartment has five rooms and a total area of 60 square meters. Draw a possible plan of Fred's apartment. Label all rooms and show the dimensions—length and width—of each room.

Alan's response follows (Clarke and Helme 1994):

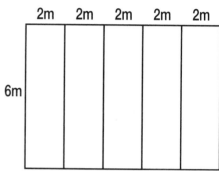

How should Alan's teacher respond? Does the mathematical consistency of Alan's solution outweigh the contextual inconsistency? Clearly, no one would design a real apartment in which moving from the kitchen to the living room meant going through the bathroom and two bedrooms. But if the teacher's purpose was to assess Alan's understanding of *area*, perhaps this answer is satisfactory. If, however, the teacher expected a more sophisticated plan and, as a consequence, a less trivial partitioning of the sixty square meters of area, then he or she might decide to penalize Alan for the triviality of his solution or for its contextual inconsistency.

The difficulty is that Alan may recognize the practical inadequacy of his design. It may be that he just did not believe that practicality was a relevant criterion in a mathematics class. In fact, when asked about his solution, Alan responded in these words (Clarke and Helme 1994):

> I was just thinking of the maths involved. I guess that probably comes from the way you learn maths, just doing calculations and learning calculations. But if I was

planning an extension for the house … I wouldn't think in that kind of way.

Alan's response may not indicate an inadequacy to contextualize mathematics successfully, only a lack of recognition of any need to do so.

Alan has a particular understanding of the "didactic contract" in the mathematics classroom (Brousseau 1986). The didactic contract is that set of shared understandings by which the teacher and the class know what is expected: what questions the teacher can reasonably ask, what assistance the students can reasonably expect, and what form of response will be considered satisfactory. Alan's response conformed to his understanding of the didactic contract as it operated in mathematics classrooms. Other classrooms might operate under different didactic contracts.

Many of the new tasks finding their place in the mathematics classrooms of today challenge the existing didactic contract. For example, consider the question "Which is the better fit: a square peg in a round hole or a round peg in a square hole?" (Schoenfeld 1985). Many students believe that such a task makes unreasonable demands, many are confused about what is required, and many teachers are unsure how to assess the diverse responses that such a task produces. Such tasks stimulate rich and complex mathematical activity and offer significant insight into students' ability to use the mathematical skills they possess. However, introducing such tasks into a classroom requires renegotiating the didactic contract. Essentially, teachers establish a consensus within their classrooms about what constitutes quality mathematics. One approach to developing classroom criteria for quality mathematics follows.

QUALITY MATHEMATICS PERFORMANCE: CLASSROOM CRITERIA

Constructive assessment seeks to optimize students' involvement in the assessment process. Such involvement will develop in students an understanding of the characteristics of quality mathematical performance, at their existing level of competence; a familiarity and feeling of ownership related to the purposes and practices of assessment; and a critical facility enabling them to judge the quality of their own mathematical performances and those of others. Consistent with this goal is the strategy of involving students in identifying the characteristics of quality mathematics and developing rubrics for assessing mathematical performance. In the scenario that follows, this goal is achieved

> ## Students must share the vision of a quality performance.

through discussing samples of other students' work on a task.

An assessment scenario

Clusters of schools, educational regions, state educational authorities, or curriculum developers collect a variety of tasks consistent with the new emphasis on task diversity, together with sample students' responses to each task. Ideally, these sample responses should include one good response, one poor response, and one response of average quality. Banks of tasks and corresponding students' responses are made available to schools.

From the bank of available tasks, the teacher selects a type of task similar to those within the students' related classroom experience. This task is distributed in class, and students are given an appropriate amount of time to attempt the task. At this point, the teacher must stress that this task is a new sort of mathematical task; the purpose of the exercise is to familiarize everyone with the new type of task. All students should be encouraged to do their best. Some students will find the new tasks quite threatening, and the use of small groups is recommended. The teaching strategy "think, pair, share" may be useful. In this strategy students first work alone to clarify their understanding of the task and to identify relevant facts and skills, then work in pairs to solve the problem. The pairs combine into groups of four to share their solutions and attempt to reach consensus before a whole-class discussion of the task.

After a brief discussion of the task, the teacher distributes to each group copies of samples of other students' attempts at the task. These copies include one good, one poor, and one average sample, but none are labeled or graded in any way that might indicate their relative merit. No sample is from a student known to the class. Students are asked to select the responses that they believe are best and worst. They must justify their choices by identifying what particular qualities of the responses distinguished the good response from the poor response. The teacher should record these response attributes, which will become the reference points for future discussions of class responses to this type of task.

Teachers with an obligation to grade students' performance may choose to implement the additional step of leading the class in determining a rubric, based on the previous discussion, that will then become the basis for grading future attempts at tasks of this type. Students can be encouraged to apply the new rubric to their own responses, with the acknowledgment by the teacher that this lesson was intended to familiarize them with the task. The students' grades will not be included in any significant assessment.

> ## Think, pair, share.

In Australia, the foregoing procedure has been used with success for a variety of tasks. In addition to the two examples given in this article, tasks such as "How many piano tuners are there in Chicago?" (see Lovitt and Clarke [1988]) or "The average of five numbers is 17.2; what might the numbers be?" (see Sullivan and Clarke [1991]) challenge students' assumptions about the content of school mathematics and the characteristics of a quality response. The use of such tasks in mathematics classrooms for instruction or assessment requires the explicit renegotiation of the terms of the didactic contract. Through this renegotiation, teachers and students come to share an image of what constitutes quality mathematics. This process can be reduced to the simple step-by-step procedure shown in figure 1.

The resultant assessment or grading scheme not only has the endorsement of all students and the teacher but is far more likely to be used and interpreted with understanding. The process of negotiating the assessment scheme will likely be educationally valuable for the students, requiring that they think carefully about the characteristics of quality mathematical performance.

MODELING, MONITORING, AND INFORMING QUALITY PERFORMANCE

It should be possible to identify from this assessment the characteristics of quality school mathematics. Assessment has three basic functions:

To model

To monitor

To inform

This article has focused predominantly on the function of modeling. The obligation placed on teachers and those responsible for developing mathematics curriculum is to ensure that mathematics assessment accurately reflects what they consider to be quality school mathematics. This goal does not appear to have been true of mathematics assessment in the recent past. This article has presented guidelines for a simple classroom procedure whereby teachers and students can reach a common understanding of what is meant by quality mathematics performance in classrooms.

REFERENCES

Brousseau, Guy. "Fondements et méthodes de la didactique des mathématiques." *Recherches en didactique des mathématiques* 7 (1986): 33–115.

Clarke, David J., and Sue Helme. "Context as Construct." *In Contexts in Mathematics Education: Panel Discussion Papers*, edited by B. Atweh, pp. 1-10. Kelvin Grove, Queensland: Mathematics Education Research Group of Australasia (MERGA), 1994.

Lovitt, Charles J., and Doug M. Clarke. *Mathematics Curriculum and Teaching Project: Activity Bank.* Vol. 1. Carlton, Victoria: Curriculum Corp., 1988.

Schoenfeld, Alan. *Mathematical Problem Solving.* London: Academic Press, 1985.

Sullivan, Peter, and David Clarke. "Catering to All Abilities through 'Good' Questions." *Arithmetic Teacher* 39 (October 1991): 14–18.

WHAT GETS GRADED
IS WHAT GETS VALUED

Linda Wilson

In countless high schools across the United States and Canada, mathematics teachers are struggling to make sense of and to implement the reforms advocated by the National Council of Teachers of Mathematics. The fall 1993 publication of the working draft of the NCTM's *Assessment Standards for School Mathematics* has placed assessment practices at the forefront of reform. Particularly in high schools, where grades have an elevated importance, changing the way we assess what our students know is a daunting challenge. I would like to relate one story of a teacher who believes very strongly in reform but whose efforts were largely thwarted by her grading system. This fictionalized story is based on a case-study research project conducted by the author during three months in spring 1992.

Ms. League teaches second-year algebra, along with geometry and general mathematics, in a middle-class school that has made a public, districtwide commitment to substantial reforms, using assessment as its cornerstone. Ms. League, a teacher at the school for five years, considers herself a maverick in the mathematics department. She fought to keep mathematics occupying a central part of her district's new vision and to change to a less traditional mathematics textbook series. She serves on two important reform committees and publicly endorses their work.

Linda Wilson teaches at the University of Delaware, Newark, DE 19716. She is interested in assessment issues in the mathematics classroom and is assistant project director of the NCTM's Assessment Standards for School Mathematics.

A "MAVERICK" TEACHER IN ACTION

An average day in algebra class found Ms. League asking her students about their homework assignments. A few responded with questions about particular textbook problems.

Self-assessment is a central part of authentic assessment.

Ms. League demonstrated solutions to the linear and quadratic systems of equations for about twenty minutes. She then assigned a problem for the students to try in their teaching pairs, which are the prearranged small groups or pairs that work together on various assignments. Members of these groups sat together to work. The problem was more abstract and complicated than those that the students had completed for homework. Ms. League suggested that they work on it by sketching a graph and making decisions from the graph.

As students worked on the problem, Ms. League gave help when needed. At one point she paused and interrupted their work by saying, "If you're having trouble with this, you need to write down, 'I need to study how to graph hyperbolas.' Be sure to write that down."

Before she demonstrated the solution, she said, "When I was walking around, I saw all levels of thinking. Some of you were struggling with the graph. Others had trouble with the procedures. Remember that the test is on Friday, and although some of you did okay working

together today, remember that on the test you will have to work alone. Be sure you know how much you can do alone before the test on Friday."

Students continued working on problems in pairs until the end of class, when Ms. League gave them their homework assignment for the next day—six more problems from the textbook similar to the ones done in class. She added, "Your other assignment is to look at what you wrote down today about what you need to do, for example, 'I need to review parabolas.' So do that tonight also."

Two aspects of this classroom are especially interesting from an assessment perspective. The first is that Ms. League routinely observed and interviewed her students as they worked in their teaching pairs, and the second is that she also emphasized ways students could assess their own work. She learned what her students knew and could do in mathematics by interviewing and observing their work in pairs. She knew her students well and could discuss their strengths and weaknesses at length.

VALUING CONCEPTUAL KNOWLEDGE

As with so many good teachers, Ms. League held a vast store of informal knowledge about her students in her head. It was also central to her theory about teaching. She believed that knowing her students individually was fundamental to her teaching. She viewed observing and interviewing her students as they work as one of the more authentic aspects of her assessment method.

Ms. League asked her students to remind themselves of their strengths and weaknesses as learners. She frequently asked them to write comments to themselves about the concepts or procedures that needed more work or practice. Indeed, the NCTM's *Assessment Standards* draft endorses self-evaluation as a central aspect of authentic assessment and advocates that students keep journals noting their progress or that teachers invite students to be active participants in assessing their learning.

Ms. League would often ask students to respond to higher-order-thinking questions that went beyond the procedural aspects of a lesson. In the first lesson on logarithms, for example, she asked students to ponder why a log of a negative number is not possible. She clearly stated that she expected students to write individual explanations. These higher-order explanations were sometimes to be finished in class and sometimes part of a regular homework assignment that included textbook problems. It was evident, from frequent use of this type of assignment, that Ms. League valued her students' conceptual knowledge, not solely their ability to complete algebraic procedures.

Ms. League used several authentic assessment practices, including observing, interviewing, and asking students to write about mathematical concepts and their knowledge of them. One would expect her students to understand that talking and writing about mathematics were just as valued as completing routine procedures or algorithms. On the contrary, however, when students were interviewed, this perception was not evident, as the following excerpt suggests.

I: Have you ever had to write anything in mathematics class? Write a paragraph or explain something?
S: Yes, a report. I did a report once. That was for extra credit, though.
I: For what class was that?
S: Algebra 1. That was a while ago.

I: So you never had a situation where a teacher said, "Here's a problem. Tell me what the answer is. Now explain how you did it."
S: Yes. I have had that on a couple of tests before, too.
I: In this class?
S: Well, not in this class.

> *Students avoided activities that did not count toward their grade.*

AN IMPORTANT LESSON TO BE LEARNED

Why is it that Ms. League's students did not recognize that they routinely were given writing assignments? The answer appears to rest in her grading system. At the end of the quarter, students received traditional A, B, C, D, or F grades, based on quizzes, tests, and examinations taken during that quarter. Homework was checked occasionally and points were given for its completion. Homework checks, however, did not include the extra assignments designed to foster self-assessment or higher-order thinking. Thus the extra assignments did not count toward the grade.

The tests and quizzes written by Ms. League were based on textbook problems and were identical to those assigned for homework, with the numbers having been changed. The tests determined whether students could complete the procedures or algorithms they had been doing in class for the previous week or ten days. They did not include the higher-order-thinking or self-evaluation questions. Students had to work individually and were not allowed to collaborate on the tests and quizzes.

The techniques described earlier as components of an authentic assessment system were not part of the grading system. Students, for the most part, avoided any activities that did not count toward

their grade. On any given day, approximately half of them did not complete their homework. When Ms. League asked them to complete writing assignments in class or for homework, most of them ignored her. They did not do the self-evaluations, nor did they answer the higher-order-thinking questions. In fact, they did not recognize that writing was part of their algebra work.

The students, like most other high school students, were savvy about budgeting their energies. Only those tasks or activities that were reviewed and then recorded in the grade book received any effort or recognition. They paid little attention to any assessment activities other than quizzes, tests, examinations, and an occasional homework assignment. Because these activities were graded, they were valued by the students.

In the students' eyes, what counted as mathematical knowledge was the correct solution of decontextualized problems, such as a system of equations. Ms. League had a different notion of what counted as doing mathematics, which is illustrated by her higher-order questions and her exhortations to students to think, write, and work collaboratively. The nontraditional activities used reasoning, reflecting, and communicating more than routine procedures. But since the nontraditional activities were not graded, they were not valued by students.

An important lesson can be learned from this story. What do our students perceive as being of value in our classrooms? Many high school mathematics teachers are convinced, as Ms. League was, that using multiple sources of information about their students can lead to more valid inferences about what they know. Translating those beliefs into grading practices, though exceedingly more complicated, must be done or all our good efforts may be for naught. Our students know only too well to value only those items that get graded.

ALIGNING ASSESSMENT WITH THE NCTM'S CURRICULUM STANDARDS

Cathy G. Schloemer

I recently found myself in the ideal situation of wanting to integrate the NCTM's *Curriculum and Evaluation Standards for School Mathematics* (1989) more fully into my teaching and, at the same time, being enrolled in a class that required me to research some aspect of assessment and then engage in a practical assessment project. As a result, I decided to find out more about standards-aligned assessment and then see if I could use it with my high school precalculus students.

I discovered that devising, or even using, standards-aligned assessment tools wasn't as straightforward for me as the writers of the document must have intended it to seem. Only after considerable study did I realize that the focus of assessment according to the standards was improved communication. This focus meant I had to find ways to get my students to let me know how and what they were thinking about mathematics and not just test them on their working of routine problems. Another concern was that I wanted to choose methods that could realistically be implemented again at any time. For me, for example, that constraint meant that portfolios and journals were not a practical consideration. The nature of my schedule just did not allow me the time required to implement this type of assessment tool.

With these thoughts in mind, I decided to seek ways to get my students communicating. I wanted them to talk more—both to me and to one another, I wanted them to act out mathematics in whatever ways I could devise for them, and I wanted them to write about mathematics. The writing tasks would have to be brief enough for me to review on a daily basis, so I elected to deal with focused writing tasks. In such tasks, the teacher poses a question or situation and allows perhaps five minutes for an in-class response or possibly one page of handwriting for an out-of-class response.

> **I wanted to develop methods that could be used at any time.**

This article highlights some of the activities and outcomes that occurred in my precalculus class of twenty-two students during an otherwise ordinary unit on functions and relations. As will be indicated, some of the activities were a part of ongoing informal assessment, and others were a part of a unit test. For problems requiring grading, the technique of scoring is included. Activities are described chronologically so that the reader can more easily see the interplay between assessment and instruction.

PROJECTS FOR UNIT ON FUNCTIONS AND RELATIONS

Project activity 1

I reviewed the meaning of function and relation with the class and presented several real-world examples of functions (e.g., the pairing of items in a market with their prices or the pairing of pieces of flatware with their assigned compartments in a drawer) as well as relations that are not functions. A portion of the out-of-class assignment was the following writing activity:

> Explain in your own words the difference between *relation* and *function*. Use an original real-world example to illustrate your explanation.

Because of absences the day before, initially only nineteen students responded. Just five gave clear, correct, or nearly correct responses. Interestingly, when I began to read the best-written example to the class the next day, the students quickly objected, stating that this "original" example was a favorite illustration used by one of their former teachers! The students apparently had a great deal of difficulty creating their own examples and explaining the concepts of relation and function.

I discovered that it takes practice to read and write responses quickly to this type of homework. Others have suggested that checking a set of such papers requires only five to ten minutes, but I needed thirty minutes on my first try. Realizing that the students needed another chance to show that they could clearly explain *relation* and *function*, I returned the papers to them the next day and asked them to write a response back to me. Nearly all the students corrected their original answers to my satisfaction. Some of the other interesting replies included, "It was a good idea to do this type of thing because it is easy to simply use equations, but to explain it is hard" and "I liked the exercise, but coming up with an example is kind of hard."

Cathy Schloemer teaches at Indiana Area Senior High School, Indiana, PA 15701. She is interested in ways to help students build connections between everyday experiences and mathematical concepts.

I again wrote brief responses to the students and passed their papers back the next day. I was disappointed that the students either wrote back nothing at all or stated, "Oh, I understand." I had hoped they would write more. I decided to delay any further evaluation of students' comprehension of this topic until the unit test.

Project activity 2

I reviewed the greatest-integer function in particular and discussed step functions in general. I gave several real-world examples of step functions (e.g., the classic postage-stamp function) before assigning the following out-of-class writing activity:

Describe a real-world example of a step function, and then sketch a graph that will demonstrate that it is a step function.

Nineteen students responded. The quality of the responses was much higher than for activity 1—ten papers were so outstanding that I felt moved to display them in a prominent location where many students could view them. Both the originality of the examples and the clarity of the explanations showed great improvement. One student showed how his water company charges customers in increments based on any fraction of a ten-gallon unit in water use. Another student showed how young children are assigned to a certain basketball league (prebeginner, beginner, advanced beginner, and so on) solely on the basis of age; players are automatically advanced to the next level on their birthday. I did read and respond to this set of papers in only about fifteen minutes. I showed my responses to the students.

Project activity 3

I demonstrated both algebraic and geometric representations of even and odd functions. A function is *even* if $f(-x) = f(x)$ and odd if $f(-x) = -f(x)$. Many examples were given. Part of the students' assignment was the following:

Sketch graphs of two even functions not discussed in class or in your text. Explain how you know they are even.

Sketch graphs of two odd functions not discussed in class or in your text. Explain how you know they are odd.

Eighteen students responded. Although the responses were mostly correct, originality was nearly nonexistent. Interestingly, seven students mistakenly thought that a relation symmetric about the *x*-axis would be an even function. I explained to the class why this relation was neither even nor a function and gave several additional examples. I also returned their papers so that they could read the individual comments I had written. I decided to construct an item for the unit test to determine whether the students had subsequently corrected their geometric model of even functions.

> *It takes practice for students to write what they are thinking.*

Project activity 4

I explained the concept of composition of functions, using both real-world and purely algebraic examples. I demonstrated how everyday items could be used to illustrate the composition of functions. (For example, a pencil could perform a writing function on a piece of paper. Then a paper clip could perform a clipping function on the penciled paper.) I assigned students to get an item from home that evening that performed a (G-rated—suitable for general audiences) function. The next day the students assembled in their cooperative groups and attempted to create a function that was a composition of the functions brought to class by the group members. An individual group member demonstrated each group's creation. This entire activity, from the gathering of the groups to the final presentation, took only about five minutes. I made no attempt at any formal assessment but decided to include a problem of this nature on the unit test.

Project activity 5

On the unit test, I included a performance assessment like the in-class composition-of-functions activity. While a student teacher proctored the written part of the examination, each student met with me individually at a desk behind a screen and responded to the following instruction:

Use any of the items provided to illustrate the composition of at least two functions.

The items supplied were index cards, a pencil, a clothespin, a pencil eraser, a toy person, two Duplo blocks, and a box with a lid.

Of twenty students present on the day of the test, seventeen had no difficulty with the activity. Most of the students produced an example similar to the sample activity described in project activity 4. One student used an index card to put wings on the toy person (depicting a "winging" function) and then put the toy into the box (thus performing the "boxing" function). I found, however, that I had trouble avoiding teaching the students during the testing. Even students who were working correctly watched my face for visual reassurance. I was relieved to be merely marking the responses right or wrong.

Apparently my demonstration on the day before the groups' composing of functions was not sufficient for students to master the function-modeling activity. The three students who were present for my demonstration but absent for the cooperative activity all found this test question very difficult and could not produce a clear example of a composition.

Project activity 6

I gave the students these unit-test questions to assess their understanding of function and relation concepts:

On the floor of my closet, there are four pairs of dress shoes: my husband's brown and black pairs and my navy and cordovan pairs.

a. Write a function relating the shoes and their owners. How do you know this is a function?

b. Write a relation (which is not a function) relating the shoes and their owners. How do you know this relation is not a function?

A five-point scale (0–4) was used to evaluate students' performance on each of these two problems. Ten of twenty students responding earned full credit by giving complete and correct responses to each problem. The following scoring rubric was used for less adequate answers:

3 points: Example or explanation was only partially correct or contained minor errors. Remaining work was correct.

(*Sample response, part (b)*: "((husband, brown), (husband, black), (Mrs. S., navy), (Mrs. S., cordovan)) A function is a set of ordered pairs.") [Student did not state why the relation was not a function.]

2 points: Only the example was incorrect, or only the explanation was incorrect, or both the example and explanation were only partially correct or contained minor errors.

(*Sample response, part (a)*: "((husband, brown), (husband, black), (wife, navy), (wife, cordovan)) For every x there is exactly 1 y.")

1 point: Only the example was partially correct, or only the explanation was partially correct.

0 points: No correct work was shown.

Project activity 7

I gave this question on the unit test to determine students' understanding of even functions:

Last night when you were reviewing for your precalculus test, you fell asleep and had a weird dream in which you walked into a different mathematics class where

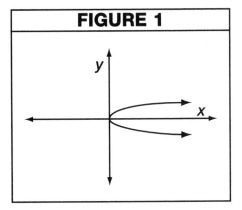

FIGURE 1

two students, Pat and Chris, were having an argument about the graph in figure 1. Pat said that it *was* an example of an even function, and Chris insisted it was *not*. Who was right? Please give your most convincing argument for your answer.

> *The writing activities helped students realize that they did not understand a concept.*

I realized too late that I needed to ask students to discuss both the evenness or oddness of the relation and whether it was a function. Eleven of twenty students responding were awarded full credit because they gave correct answers, but ten of these students explained simply that the relation was not a function so Chris was right. Four students produced completely wrong responses or blank papers for no credit. The remaining five students gave nearly correct responses containing a single incorrect statement or phrase, so they were awarded two points of three possible.

Project activity 8

I surveyed the students to determine their feelings about the unusual assessment activities included in this unit. See table 1, which summarizes the students' responses.

Apparently most of the students found that the writing activities helped to clarify those concepts they did not understand and that my written comments to them were helpful. They were less enthusiastic, however, about including essay questions on the unit test. Most of the students also felt that building the composition-of-functions models helped them to understand composition better and that the activity was not excessively elementary. I found these results reassuring because I was concerned that the students might be insulted by being asked to use manipulatives.

PERSONAL REACTION TO PROJECT

Participating in these kinds of assessment activities gave me a view of my students' thinking that I would otherwise not have seen. I hope that my experience will save others some legwork in their beginning attempts at standards-aligned assessment and might help them feel more confident in trying new techniques. The results are bound to be enlightening and occasionally surprising!

REFERENCE

National Council of Teachers of Mathematics. *Curriculum and Evaluation Standards for School Mathematics*. Reston, Va.: The Council, 1989.

TABLE 1

Students' Reactions to Assessment Activities

During the relations and functions unit, you participated in the following unusual activities:

1. Writing assessments about
    a) the meaning of function and relation;
    b) step functions;
    c) even and odd functions.

2. Composing real-world functions (in-class group work and test problem)

For future planning, I would like to know your perceptions of the value of these activities. Please respond to the following statements. (Tally of student responses appears in parentheses.)

	Agree strongly 5	Agree 4	Not sure 3	Disagree 2	Disagree strongly 1
1. I found the writing activities interesting.	(0	8	5	4	0)
2. The writing activities helped me develop a better understanding of some of the concepts in this unit.	(0	9	6	1	1)
3. The writing activities helped me to become aware of what I did not understand.	(2	8	3	2	1)
4. I found it helpful for my teacher to write notes to me in response to my writings.	(3	8	4	1	1)
5. I felt uncomfortable trying to write about mathematics.	(1	5	2	6	3)
6. I don't think we should have to write about mathematics.	(2	2	4	8	1)
7. I think the group activity in which we formed the composition of real-world functions helped me understand composition of functions better.	(3	7	5	1	0)
8. The writing and function-composition activities helped me connect math ideas to the real world.	(3	6	5	2	1)
9. I thought that building function-composition models was too elementary for us.	(0	5	4	4	3)
10. I thought it was a good idea to include writing activities on the unit test.	(1	2	8	4	2)
11. I thought it was a good idea to include the function-composition problem on the unit test.	(3	3	8	2	1)

Please use this space to elaborate on any of the above or to make other comments regarding your perceptions of the "special" activities included with this unit. Thank you for your help.

BEGIN MATHEMATICS CLASS WITH WRITING

L. Diane Miller

First impressions often influence the development of our attitudes toward, and decisions about, people, places, and things. The same can be said about the beginning of a mathematics class. The first few minutes of a class often influence the success of the class.

The beginning secondary school teacher is faced with making the physical and mental transition from one class to another during a three-to-five-minute interval. Once students enter the classroom, the roll must be checked, papers must be returned, questions must be answered, books must be loaned, chalkboards must be erased, and the overhead projector must be positioned as students' social chatter gets louder and louder. How can this generally nonproductive period of class be turned into a constructive time for learning?

Exemplary teachers do not waste class time. They begin class as soon as students enter the room by engaging them in a constructive activity. One activity that has proved highly successful for some secondary school teachers is the use of writing prompts during the first five minutes of class. Prompts elicit from students a written response to a specific question or problem. One prompt may ask students to produce a clear expression of their understanding of mathematical content; another may ask about students' feelings toward their mathematics class specifically or their attitudes toward mathematics generally. Students must

L. Diane Miller
Curtin University of Technology
Perth, Western Australia 6001

read the prompt and formulate and write their responses within five minutes. Prompts can be produced on a sheet of paper, distributed to the class, and collected at the end of the five minutes. Or they can be displayed on an overhead projector with students' responses written on notebook paper for collection at the end of the writing period or in a journal for collection at the end of a week.

> *"Writing helps me make the transition to math class."*

Secondary school teachers who have implemented this practice in their instructional routine say that a set of twenty-five to thirty papers can be read in five to ten minutes because they do not read the responses with the same analytical eye used when evaluating a problem or a proof. I suggest not grading the writings for content, spelling, or grammatical errors. The prompts offer students a nonthreatening opportunity to write about their understanding of the subject matter. Improving the quality of students' writing is not the primary objective, although it can be a side benefit over a period of time. Some teachers choose to write comments on the papers and return them to the students. Others choose not to respond in writing but to say something to students, in private, about what they have written. Sometimes a set of writings will initiate a comment by the teacher to the whole class. The teacher should be careful not to single out individual students but instead to make general com-

ments to the class, such as, "I learned from your writings...."

Writing prompts should not ask students to recite formulas or complete routine computations. Instead, they should ask students to express their conceptual understanding of a topic. The following three examples have been used by practicing teachers:

General mathematics. You have studied the commutative property for addition and multiplication of real numbers. Not all operations are commutative. If you were asked to explain to a friend why division is not commutative, what would you say?

Algebra. Suppose a friend asks you to check the answers to some homework problems. Would you mark the following problem correct or incorrect? Explain why it is correct or incorrect.

$$(a + b)^2 = a^2 + b^2$$

Geometry. Suppose your younger sister or brother was working some problems that applied the Pythagorean theorem, that is, $a^2 + b^2 = c^2$ After working a few problems (s)he asked you, "How do we know that the sum of the squares of the legs of a right triangle equals the square of the hypotenuse?" What would you say?

The benefits of writing in the mathematics classroom are numerous. Writing is an active process that promotes students' procedural and conceptual understanding of mathematics. Students often find out what they think when they write. Writing about mathematics gives students an opportunity to reflect on, and clarify their thinking about, mathematical ideas and relationships, an activity suggested in the *Curriculum and Evaluation Standards for School Mathematics* (NCTM 1989). It can also serve as an informal assessment of understanding, allowing individual students to ask questions or express their "nonunderstanding" in private to the teacher. It establishes an open channel of communication between teacher and students that promotes good rapport and a positive classroom environment.

Both teachers and students have testified to the benefits of beginning class with a writing prompt. An experienced teacher wrote in his journal, "Another thought often expressed by the students was that writing at the beginning of the hour [class] got them in an algebra thinking mode." A second-year teacher said, "It helps both me and the students to get organized for class. While they are writing, I can check roll, return papers, and collect my thoughts for the lesson." A second-year-algebra student wrote, "I think it [writing] lets us clear our minds and express our thoughts. It also helps me make the transition from English class to math class."

Every teacher wants the beginning of each class to be productive. Writing during the first five minutes of class engages students in an activity that benefits both the teacher and the students and gives the teacher a few extra minutes to accomplish routine classroom details.

BIBLIOGRAPHY

Bell, Elizabeth S., and Ronald N. Bell. "Writing and Mathematical Problem Solving: Arguments in Favor of Synthesis." *School Science and Mathematics* 85 (March 1985): 210–21.

Johnson, Marvin L. "Writing in Mathematics Classes: A Valuable Tool for Learning." *Mathematics Teacher* 83 (February 1983): 117–19.

Miller, L. Diane. "When Students Write in Algebra Class." *Australian Mathematics Teacher* 46 (July 1990): 4–7.

———. "Writing to Learn Mathematics." *Mathematics Teacher* 84 (October 1991): 516–21.

Miller, L. Diane, and David A. England. Writing to Learn Algebra." *School Science and Mathematics* 89 (April 1989): 299–312.

Nahrgang, Cynthia L., and Bruce T. Petersen. "Using Writing to Learn Mathematics." *Mathematics Teacher* 79 (September 1986): 461–65.

National Council of Teachers of Mathematics. *Curriculum and Evaluation Standards for School Mathematics*. Reston, Va.: The Council, 1989.

JOURNAL WRITING: AN INSIGHT INTO STUDENTS' UNDERSTANDING

Karen S. Norwood and Glenda Carter

During the first ten minutes of our fifth-grade mathematics class, students are busily writing in their journals. We use journal writing to focus students on a review or to assess their ideas about a topic before its introduction. We have also used this activity to assess how well students understand a topic in progress. We find that journal writing often brings to light thoughts and understandings that typical classroom interactions or tests do not elucidate. An example of this type of journal writing is illustrated in figure 1. As is evident from the product of the writing task, this student can do a multiplication problem algorithmically but lacks a conceptual understanding of the operation. This student's lack of understanding can be further explored by other journal writings or by a direct interview to find out where the student has gotten off track. Journal writing enables us to recognize that this student needs remediation.

Because we have experienced some roadblocks in incorporating journal writing into the classroom, we would like to offer the following suggestions:

1. Since students are often more resistant to new processes and procedures once the school year has started, we recommend introducing journal writing at the beginning of the school year. Let students know that journal writing is an expected activity for mathematics class that can give them a greater understanding of mathematics and give the teacher a better understanding of their knowledge of mathematics. Explain the reasons for asking them to write.
2. Prepare a special booklet journal in which students can take pride and over which they can have ownership. Suggest that they submit drawings for the cover of the journal. Duplicate the cover on colored paper, fold the cover, and insert plain white pages. A sample cover, such as the one in figure 2, serves to illustrate to the students that this product is special and is to be used only for their thoughts about mathematics.
3. Decide how long to allow students to write; set an egg timer to go off when time has expired.
4. Since students tend to write more if they are instructed to address their comments to a friend or family member, have them write to someone specific.

Karen Norwood teaches at North Carolina State University, Raleigh, NC 27695. She has written supplementary materials for alternative assessment for several textbook companies. Glenda Carter is the associate director of the Center for Research in Mathematics and Science Education at the same university. Her research focuses on alternative assessment.

FIGURE 1

Student's Journal Writing on Multiplication

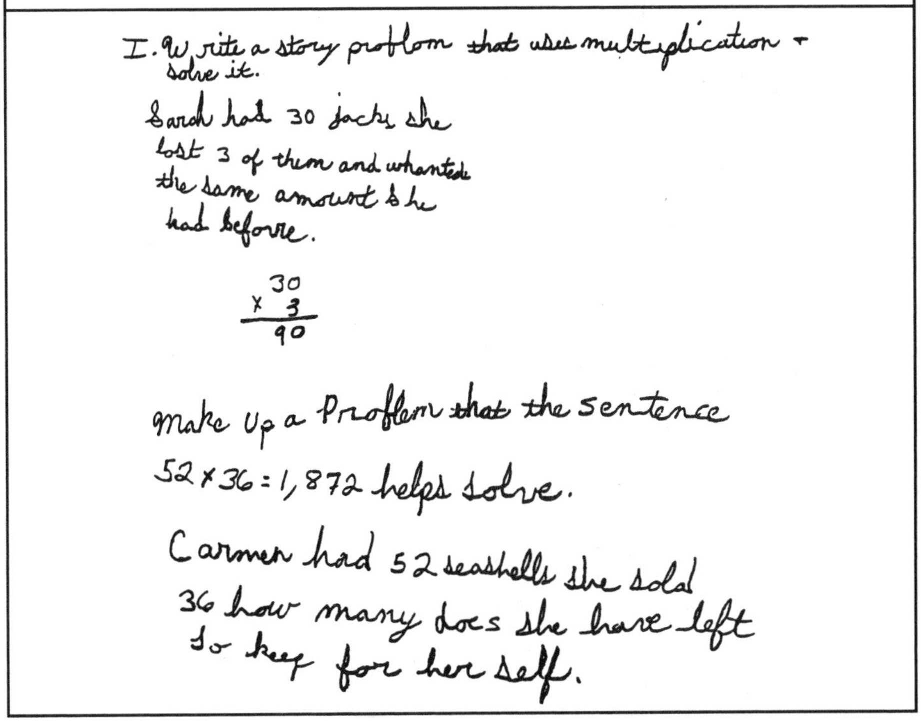
I. Write a story problom that uses multiplication + solve it.

Sarah had 30 jacks she lost 3 of them and whanted the same amount she had beforre.

30 × 3 = 90

make Up a Problem that the sentence 52×36=1,872 helps solve.

Carmen had 52 seashells she sold 36 how many does she have left to keep for her self.

FIGURE 2
Sample Journal Cover

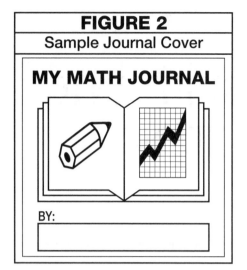

MY MATH JOURNAL

BY:

5. Clearly explain your expectations to your students, and give them details concerning how their writing will be evaluated.

6. Introduce journal writing by using exercises that are affective in nature (see fig. 3). For instance, students are able to respond more easily to a question such as "How did taking the math test make you feel?" than to a cognitive question such as "Explain how to subtract l/5 from 1/2."

7. Respond to the students' writings on a frequent basis. Let the students know that what they write is indeed being read. Reading five journals a night is a realistic goal. The wealth of information that can be gained from the journal is worth the time it takes to read and respond to students.

8. Don't give up. Be patient. Students who are unaccustomed to writing in mathematics class may become frustrated. It will take time for students to understand their teacher's expectations for them.

9. Join the students in writing. Address the topic from a teacher's point of view. Share your writings with your students.

10. Exhibit, with students' permission, those writings that most closely illustrate desirable characteristics, such as clear, concise explanations and creative word problems.

Like most worthwhile endeavors, helping students produce journal writing that will affect their understanding of mathematics and illustrate their feelings and knowledge of mathematics will require time and patience. It will also require practice on the students' part. The following prompts might help students start their journal writing. The topics in parentheses can be changed to reflect curriculum content in a given classroom.

1. Write a "mathematics autobiography." Describe your earliest experiences in mathematics both in and outside of school.

2. Explain in your own words the meaning of (*area, perimeter, ratio*).

3. Explain what is most important to understand about (adding fractions with unlike denominators; multiplying decimals).

4. Describe any places you became stuck when solving a problem, and tell what you did to get unstuck.

FIGURE 3
Student's feelings about mathematics

What math is to me

Adding, subtracting dividing and multiplying are parts of math. Geometry, time, money and fractions are parts of math also. When I learn math I can work at stores and resturants. Subtracting helps me to take something away from something. Multiplying is a quick way of adding. Math is fun sometimes. Sometimes it is hard. Math is my favorite subject. When I pay attention in class I can learn fractions to know how to cook. Math is an important part of my life. There are four operations.

What Math Is To me

Math is not so good to me. Sometimes it gets on my nerus I dont like the example If the teacher explains how we do it at the top of the page and we work it out we dont need examples Math is so easy it horable. When we have math test is plain oh borring Math is a lesson we should cut down on. If we had math once a six weeks and do math all day I would love it! Math is dull. Math is not so fun.

Emphasis on Assessment

5. What I like most (or least) about mathematics is _____
_____
_____
_____.

6. Write a letter to a student who will be taking this class next year, giving some advice about this class.

7. Something I'd really like to know about mathematics is _____
_____
_____
_____.

8. The most important thing I learned about mathematics this week is ___
_____
_____
_____
_____.

Sometimes teachers may wish to have students do expository writing. The following examples are the types of questions to which students can be asked to respond in their journals.

1. Write a story problem that can be solved by using $12 \times 7 = 84$.

2. Find a graph in a newspaper or magazine. Write a paragraph about what the graph represents and why the graph is drawn the way it is.

3. Please draw a picture, a diagram, or a model to illustrate ($1/3 \times 1/2$; the difference between area and perimeter).

4. Your best friend was absent from school today. Write a letter to him or her to explain what you learned in mathematics class.

5. Explain to your cousin how multiplication is like addition. You may use pictures or graphs.

6. Explain to your cousin how division is like subtraction. You may use pictures or graphs.

7. Explain to your sister or brother in fourth grade how to add 1/2 and 1/3. Be specific. You may use pictures or graphs.

8. How do you use fractions in your life?

9. How are fractions and decimals alike? Different?

The NCTM's *Curriculum and Evaluation Standards for School Mathematics* (1989) calls for teaching students to communicate mathematically. Journal writing in the mathematics classroom offers students that opportunity. It enables students to use the skills of reading, listening, viewing, and questioning to interpret and evaluate mathematical ideas. Journal writing can also be designed to allow students to explore connections within mathematics and between mathematics and other subjects. When journal writing occurs regularly, students learn to value the opportunity to reflect on their new learning and relate their new learning to what they already know.

A better understanding of students' thinking in mathematics is needed if mathematics education is to be improved. Research has indicated that many traditional tests are not giving a clear enough picture of students' conceptual development in mathematics to assess their progress or misunderstandings. Journal writing is a simple, inexpensive tool for alternatively evaluating students' progress.

BIBLIOGRAPHY

McIntosh, Margaret E. "No Time for Writing in Your Class?" *Mathematics Teacher* 84 (September 1991): 423–33.

National Council of Teachers of Mathematics. *Curriculum and Evaluation Standards for School Mathematics.* Reston, Va.: The Council, 1989.

Stenmark, Jean. *Alternative Assessments in Mathematics.* Berkeley, Calif.: University of California, 1989.

PIC-JOUR MATH: PICTORIAL JOURNAL WRITING IN MATHEMATICS

Andi Stix

Come every fall, teachers of mathematics are confronted with oversized classes filled with students who vary in both their learning style and their way of communicating what they have learned. Teachers are challenged to recognize and exploit those differences—or risk bored or confused students who lack any true mathematical understanding and may end up manipulating numerical symbols and equations by rote.

Both experience and research in the past twenty years have demonstrated the clear effectiveness of using a multimodal, interactive approach to teaching basic mathematics concepts. Multimodal teaching gives each student the opportunity to focus on his or her own best, innate style of communication and learning.

Most multimodal approaches have emphasized the combined use of numbers, manipulatives, and pictures in teaching students and assessing their level of comprehension. This article will focus on another essential element of multimodal teaching: journal writing. Although writing about mathematics has received relatively less attention than writing in language arts or social studies, this activity can open an important new avenue to the teacher seeking to reach every student effectively.

Pic-Jour Math uses journal writing, including pictures, numbers, symbols, and manipulatives, to help students in grades 3 through 8 understand mathematics concepts—and make them truly

their own. The results are a better understanding and retention of mathematics, a decrease in "math anxiety," and a heightened confidence level among students who have really made a lesson "their own" (Stix 1992). At the same time, writing about mathematics offers a flexible assessment tool for teachers and parents to review and analyze students' thinking, reasoning, and learning styles.

SUPPORT FOR MULTIMODAL APPROACHES

Historical evidence abounds that people naturally integrate information in

Andi Stix teaches at Pace University, New York, NY 10038. She is a consultant in mathematics, active learning, and interdisciplinary studies.

FIGURE 1
Assessment Form

Name: _____   Topic: _____

Evaluator: _____   Date: _____

A. Application	Words	Pictures	Numbers
1._____	_____	_____	_____
2._____	_____	_____	_____
3._____	_____	_____	_____
4._____	_____	_____	_____
5._____	_____	_____	_____
6._____	_____	_____	_____
7._____	_____	_____	_____

B. Central idea	Nonexistent	Marginal	Adequate	Above average	High
1. Offers logical evidence to support every major point: *Clear logical order *Good sequence ability *Smooth transition between steps	1	2	3	4	5
2. Manipulates diagrams or materials	1	2	3	4	5
3. Coordinates pictures, numbers, or words	1	2	3	4	5
4. Exhibits a level of understanding	1	2	3	4	5

C. Comments

D. Overall rating

Nonexistent	Marginal	Adequate	Above average	Excellent
1	2	3	4	5

many different ways. Despite various approaches over the years to structuring classroom presentations, however, Cuban (1983) contends that teaching in this century has retained a predominantly passive, symbol-oriented mode that relies on a question-and-answer format. Baum (1990) states that most schools still have a distinct tendency to reward only verbal proficiency.

One problem inherent in a lecture-driven, rote form of teaching is the difficulty in assessing students' actual level of comprehension. As an example, suppose pi is introduced in a typical, lecture-style presentation. Following such a lesson, many students will remember that the circumference of any circle may be obtained by multiplying its diameter by pi. They may remember the formula long enough to recixte it on their next test and may even be able to employ pi successfully in later calculations. That most of these youngsters really *understand* what pi means or could clearly explain the concept to others is highly questionable.

Are the circumference and diameter of all circles related in some way?

In contrast, the multimodal approach to teaching conveys a deeper and truer understanding of mathematics. Presmeg (1985), Gagne and White (1978), and Clements and Del Campo (1989) agree that a multimodal approach can enable students to link verbal knowledge, visual imagery, and personal experience. Verbalization can be used to move the individual to a deeper level of understanding (Phillips 1987). At the same time, visualizing mathematical ideas, especially during the middle grades, offers students a way to bridge concrete and abstract modes of thinking (Ben-Chaim, Lappan, and Houang 1989).

In practice, a multimodal approach to teaching gives students the opportunity to discover mathematical truths on their own, in their own natural learning style. The difference can be seen by revisiting the lesson on pi, this time using a multi-modal approach.

The teacher starts off by asking, not telling, the students if they think the rela-

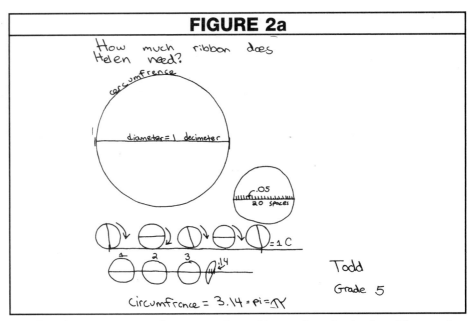

FIGURE 2a

tionship between circumference and diameter should be the same for any circle. Most of the students aren't sure, so the teacher suggests an experiment in which students are to decorate the edge of a lamp shade in their bedroom with a ribbon in the school colors. They need to find out the shade's circumference to know how much ribbon to use. They know that the diameter of the shade is one decimeter. "Using the diameter alone," the teacher asks, "can you figure

FIGURE 2b
Assessment Form

Name: _Nate_   Topic: _Pi_

Evaluator: _Bordin_   Date: _3/15/92_

A. Application

	Words	Pictures	Numbers
1. diameter = decimeter	✓		
2. string = circumference	✓		
3. rolled hat to check circumference	✓		
4. measured with picture pi	✓		
5. answer = 3.14	✓		✓
6.			
7.			

B. Central idea

	Nonexistent	Marginal	Adequate	Above average	High

1. Offers logical evidence to support every major point:
  *Clear logical order
  *Good sequence ability
  *Smooth transition between steps
	1	2	3	(4)	5

2. Manipulates diagrams or materials	(1)	2	3	4	5
3. Coordinates pictures, numbers, or words	1	2	(3)	4	5
4. Exhibits a level of understanding	1	2	3	(4)	5

C. Comments

I like how you described measuring the circumference in two ways, with a string and rolling the picture pi as if it were the hat. I would like a bit more of an explanation, however, of how you used the picture pi to determine that the answer equals 3.14.

D. Overall rating

Nonexistent	Marginal	Adequate	Above average	Excellent
1	2	3	4	5

FIGURE 3a

First we took a plastic circle with a black line running its diameter. The black line had small vertical lines through it that each represented 20 mm of the diameter of the circle. Then we drew a straight line on a large piece of paper. We rolled the circle along the line one full circle and we marked where it stopped. Then we used the line across the circle measured how many times the line would fit up to the mark of the full rotation. It fit 3.14 times. That number represents pie which is the relationship between the diameter and the circumference.

Here's a picture that summarizes what we did

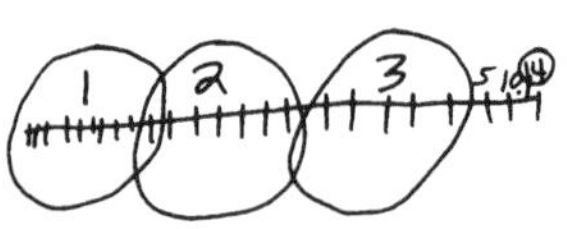

Howie
Grade 6

out how much ribbon you need?" The students agree that they can—if the relationship between diameter and circumference really is constant.

Each student is then handed Picture Pi, a flat, clear acrylic disc manufactured by The Interactive Classroom (1993) (plastic lids from tennis-ball cans or coffee cans could also work well) and asked to measure its diameter and circumference. The diameter is easy to measure with a ruler; the edge of the circle requires more invention. Here is where differ-

FIGURE 3b

Assessment Form

Name: Todd   Topic: Pi

Evaluator: Sue   Date: 4/12/92

A. Application

	Words	Pictures	Numbers
1. diameter = 1 decimeter		✓	
2. each of 20 sections = .05		✓	✓
3. rolled circumference = 1 rotation		✓	✓
4. finds 3 whole diameters		✓	✓
5. finds .14		✓	✓
6. answer 3.14 = pi		✓	✓
7.			

B. Central idea

	Nonexistent	Marginal	Adequate	Above average	High
1. Offers logical evidence to support every major point: *Clear logical order *Good sequence ability *Smooth transition between steps	1	2	3	(4)	5
2. Manipulates diagrams or materials	1	2	3	4	(5)
3. Coordinates pictures, numbers, or words	1	2	3	4	(5)
4. Exhibits a level of understanding	1	2	3	(4)	5

C. Comments

Student relies on pictures & numbers to express concepts. Uses words only as labels. Needs more of an explanation of relationship the circumference does not equal pi. Ask student for verbal & written clarification to insure integration of concept.

D. Overall rating

Nonexistent	Marginal	Adequate	Above average	Excellent
1	2	3	(4+)	5

ences in strategies will start to appear. Some students will use a string to measure the circumference, some will wrap a strip of paper around the edge, and some will rotate the disc along a sheet of paper and measure the line segment created. Again, no one way is "right"; the student is encouraged to use the method with which she or he feels most comfortable.

The teacher then suggests that the students think of the diameter of the disc as being worth a dollar, or 100 cents. Most students agree that the circumference of the disc can fit three whole diameters, worth three dollars, with a small amount left over. The diameter of the disc, worth 100 cents, is then divided into twenty equal segments. Each will be worth five cents. Measuring this "left over" amount along the diameter makes it clear that the remainder equals a little less than three of the five-cent sections of the diameter, or 14 cents, or about 14/100. That "measurement" can be read as about $3.14, or simply 3.14—a close approximation of pi.

"But," the teacher continues, "will other circles necessarily have the same relationship between their circumference and diameter?" The teacher shows students a smaller disc from the Picture Pi set. Most students guess that the relationship will be smaller than the approximately 3.14 value arrived at earlier, reasoning that as a circle decreases in size, the relationship also should decrease. They decide to test their theory by repeating the process with the smaller disc.

Surprise! The students discover for themselves that pi is a constant regardless of the size of the circle. To figure out how much school ribbon is needed for the lamp shade, they realize that they can multiply the diameter (one decimeter) by 3.14, the approximation of pi, to find out that they need 3.14 decimeters of ribbon—plus, the teacher adds with a smile, a bit extra for an overlap of the ribbon.

The student has now solved the pi problem both spatially, using hands-on manipulatives, and numerically. But a student may tend to see manipulatives in isolation, without bridging them to symbolic representations or numbers. This gap is where writing enters the picture.

Next the teacher asks the students, perhaps as homework, to describe—in writing, pictures, and numbers—the process each of them used to determine pi. Proper grammar and artistic style are not of concern; the very process of explaining and showing how she or he used the discs will enable each student to link his or her manipulative experience to the numbers.

THE JOURNAL-WRITING MODE

Vacca and Vacca (1966) concluded that the most effective method of using writing to teach mathematics is through a journal, which acts as an essential vehicle to record and assess the verbalization and visualization processes that are simultaneously at work in the learning process. Journal writing also offers an interactive way for students to communicate *back* what they have learned, so that teaching is not a one-way street. Journal writing encourages students to sort out logically, construct, and make concepts meaningful for themselves. Initially, the writing serves to help students sort the information for themselves; later, they are better able to communicate those ideas to others.

> *Evaluation of portfolios can replace a test.*

In addition, Selfe, Petersen, and Nahrgang (1986) found that although the initial journal entries may be unfocused, the jottings will progress to more concrete writing as students examine their thoughts and as their perceptions of a solution begin to solidify. Unlike memorization, expressive writing can expose misconceptions that otherwise might go unnoticed and allow students to clarify issues for themselves and the teacher. Evans (1984) found that students remembered and retained information better after the information was discussed in a journal entry.

Research (Stix 1992) with preservice teachers suggests that Pic-Jour Math, "a pictorial journal process" using pictures, words, and numbers, also enhances the student's ability to define concepts and to present a clear, logical solution to a given task. With more modes of expression available, students have more evidence to prove their points. Additionally, students who were exposed to a multimodal approach that included journal writing reported that their mathematics anxiety decreased (Stix 1992).

ALTERNATIVE ASSESSMENT FOR PORTFOLIO EVALUATION

Informally reviewing the class's journal writing is an excellent way for teachers to assess students' acquisition of a particular concept. Formal evalua-

FIGURE 4a

How much ribbon does Helen need?

Helen has a teddy bear with a black hat. She wants to buy a pink ribbon for the hat.

She knows the diameter of the hat, which equals one decimeter. To find out the circumfrence she did two things. First she measured it with string. To make sure that her awnser was right, she took the top part of the hat (which was where she wanted to put the ribon) and made a starting marck on a long piece of paper. Then she roled the hat along the piece of paper and made a marck when she finished roling. She used a picture pie to measure the distance.

The awnser was: 3.14 decimeters.

Note

FIGURE 4b

Assessment Form

Name: Howie   Topic: Pi

Evaluator: Diane   Date: 2/12/92

A. Application	Words	Pictures	Numbers
1. diameter → into 20 parts	✓		
2. rolled out circumference	✓	✓	
3. measured amount of diameters	✓	✓	✓
4. answer = 3.14	✓	✓	✓
5. 3.14 = relationship of d & c	✓		
6.			
7.			

B. Central idea	Nonexistent	Marginal	Adequate	Above average	High
1. Offers logical evidence to support every major point: *Clear logical order *Good sequence ability *Smooth transition between steps	1	2	3	4	(5)
2. Manipulates diagrams or materials	1	2	3	(4)	5
3. Coordinates pictures, numbers, or words	1	2	3	(4+)	5
4. Exhibits a level of understanding	1	2	3	4	(5)

C. Comments

The written explanation is clear and easy to follow. In the number/picture section, Howie uses an arrow to prove .14. I needed to refer to the diagrams to recognize that Howie knew that each 20th of the diameter equalled .05.

D. Overall rating				
Nonexistent	Marginal	Adequate	Above average	Excellent
1	2	3	4	(5)

FIGURE 5a

The first thing that Dwayne will do is find out the circumference of Pookey's hat. He needs to do this so that he will know how much ribbon to buy. The first step for Dwayne is to Draw a line across 2 sheets of paper. He will then take his picture pie and roll it across the line. At each point he will draw a point (.) such as this. [diagram]. Each point that Dwayne comes to he will mark it. He will then roll the picture pie a second time, he will mark it a second time [diagram]. He now has two sections that can be considered as whole sections. Now Dwayne will look at his paper. He will roll the picture pie [diagram] a third time. [diagram]. Dwayne now has 3 whole sections with some room left over. Dwayne has 3 sections with more room left. Dwayne will look at his picture pie and count the remaining lines (iiiii) that are left. Dwayne has come to the conclusion that he needs to buy close to 3.14 yards of ribbon for Pookey's hat. He is therefore figuring out using π to figure out how much ribbon he needs to buy   3.14

tion of a section of the students' journals every week or two, or after a particular unit, can also substitute for a traditional test if a proper assessment technique is used.

A suggested format for evaluating students' journals (fig. 1) begins with an assessment of a student's flow of thought: how often he or she employed words, pictures, and numbers at each step of his or her discovery process. This procedure clarifies which mode or combination of modes the student favors.

FIGURE 5b
Assessment Form

Name: Martha   Topic: Pi

Evaluator: Joanne   Date: 4-28-93

A. Application

	Words	Pictures	Numbers
1. Rolls circumference	✓	✓	
2. Rolls circumference 2nd time	✓	✓	
3. Two whole sections	✓		
4. Rolls disk 3rd time	✓	✓	✓
5. Left over—ribbon = 3.14?	✓		✓
6.			
7.			

B. Central idea

	Nonexistent	Marginal	Adequate	Above average	High
1. Offers logical evidence to support every major point: *Clear logical order *Good sequence ability *Smooth transition between steps	1	②—	3	4	5
2. Manipulates diagrams or materials	1	②—	3	4	5
3. Coordinates pictures, numbers, or words	1	②—	3	4	5
4. Exhibits a level of understanding	1	②—	3	4	5

C. Comments

Martha appears confused. Ask her whether or not she meant placing the picture pi across the circumference to determine how many diameters can fit on the line. It might be helpful for Martha to perform it again & to ask her to verbalize the task.

D. Overall rating

Nonexistent	Marginal	Adequate	Above average	Excellent
1	②—	3	4	5

Next, using a scale of 1 through 5 (for ratings of nonexistent, marginal, adequate, above average, and excellent), the teacher rates the student's handling of the central ideas of the lesson: first, whether the student offers logical evidence to support his or her major points; second, whether he or she manipulates diagrams appropriately, using good spatial sense; third, how he or she coordinates pictures, words, or numbers for each step; and fourth, whether she or he exhibits an overall level of understanding. Sometimes the student has an immediate sense of the task. At other times, the process itself becomes a catalyst and the understanding crystallizes at the end.

The evaluation form also includes a section for comments, including positive feedback to the student, points of suggestion, and a final overall rating of his or her understanding of the lesson. The evaluation form thereby furnishes a written record of the student's work and an assessment of his or her level of understanding as perceived by the teacher, the parent, and the student himself or herself.

Student journal entries from an actual multimodal lesson in pi (figs. 2 and 3) demonstrate that students vary tremendously in the way they choose to recount a lesson, depending on what mode they prefer. In figure 2a, as his teacher notes in the assessment form (fig. 2b), the student relies almost exclusively—and very effectively—on pictures and numbers to express himself, using words only as labels. In contrast, the student who made the journal entry in figure 3a is extremely verbal. Significantly, both students received high ratings from their teachers—4+ and 5−, respectively—for coordinating pictures, words, or numbers. They were not penalized for preferring to use one mode over another because both students expressed themselves effectively. Other examples of students' work are included in figures 4 and 5 to show the diversity of responses and thus the diversity of evaluation.

CONCLUSION

Teachers need to respect that students come to the classroom with eclectic processes for integrating information. Furthermore, they need to acknowledge the evidence that children have distinct modes of self-expression. A multimodal approach to instruction and assessment appears to be a logical alternative to current instructional strategies. Moreover, an integrated approach, including pictorial journal writing or note-taking, takes advantage of students' strengths, deepens their understanding, and teaches them to communicate their ideas to others effectively.

Anxiety and enthusiasm are equally contagious. If teachers gain confidence in better identifying and nurturing potential talent through the recognition of differences in learning, we may see an increase in the percent of students who go on to major in mathematics at the college level. At the least, youngsters will become active participants in their own learning, problem solvers who discover that fun, interest, and even excitement are to be found in learning mathematics.

REFERENCES

Baum, Susan. *Gifted but Learning Disabled: A Puzzling Paradox*. Reston, Va.: Council for Exceptional Children, 1990. ERIC Document Reproduction Service no. ED 479 90.

Ben-Chaim, David, Glenda Lappan, and Richard T. Houang. "The Role of Visualization in the Middle School Mathematics Curriculum." *Focus on Learning Problems in Mathematics* 11 (1989): 49–60.

Clements, M. A., and G. Del Campo. "Linking Verbal Knowledge, Visual Images, and Episodes for Mathematical Learnings." *Focus on Learning Problems in Mathematics* 11 (1989): 25–33.

Cuban, Larry. "How Did Teachers Teach, 1890–1980?" *Theory into Practice* 22 (1983): 159–68.

Evans, C. S. "Writing to Learn in Math." *Language Arts* 61 (1984): 825–35.

Gagne, Robert M., and R. T. White. "Memory Structures and Learning Outcomes." *Review of Educational Research* 48 (1978): 187–222.

The Interactive Classroom. *Picture Pi*. Manipulative. New Rochelle, N.Y.: Author, 1993.

Phillips, E. *Algebra*. Edited by V Pedwaydon. Proceedings of Honors Teachers: Workshop of Middle Grade Mathematics. ERIC Document Reproduction Service no. ED 295 792. 1987.

Presmeg, Norma C. *The Role of Visually Mediated Processes in High School Mathematics: A Classroom Investigation*. Ph.D. diss., University of Cambridge, Cambridge, England, 1985.

Selfe, C. L., Bruce T. Petersen, and Cynthia L. Nahrgang. "Journal Writing in Mathematics." In *Writing across the Disciplines: Research into Practice*, edited by Art Young and Tony Fulwiler. Montclair, N.J.: Boynton/Cooks, 1986.

Stix, Andi. "The Development and Field Testing of a Multimodal Method for Teaching Mathematical Concepts to Preservice Teachers by Utilizing Pictorial Journal Writing." Ph.D. diss, Columbia University Teachers College, 1992. *Abstracts International*, Pub. #92-18719.

Vacca, R. T., and J. Vacca. *Content Area Reading*. Boston: Little, Brown Co., 1986.

INTEGRATING WRITING
AND COOPERATIVE LEARNING
IN THE MATHEMATICS CLASS

Alice F. Artzt

As teachers have recognized the importance of giving students opportunities to communicate their ideas about mathematics, they have begun to implement writing activities and cooperative-learning strategies in their classrooms (e.g., Abel and Abel [1988]; Artzt [1979]; Havens [1989]; LeGere [1991]; McIntosh [1991]; Nahrgang and Petersen [1986]; Sutton [1992]).

When integrating the use of both strategies, the author has been excited to see how each strategy enhances the effectiveness of the other. That is, the information gained from the thoughts and feelings expressed by the students in their journal writing facilitates more accurate monitoring and regulation of the within-group interactions. Becoming closely informed about the quality of the discourse taking place within the groups aids in arranging more effective group formations. Similarly, when using the cooperative-learning environment as a setting for students' writing, more natural prompts can be devised for students to discuss mathematics. Finally, the combined use of writing and cooperative learning can enhance assessment techniques.

This article describes ways in which writing activities and cooperative-learning strategies can be integrated to orches-

Alice Artzt teaches at Queens College of the City University of New York, Flushing, NY 11367. She has used cooperative-learning and writing techniques in the classroom and is engaged in research that examines students' behaviors during cooperative-learning activities.

trate and promote the type of classroom discourse in which the students have increased opportunities to communicate their mathematical ideas. Although all the experiences described occurred in teacher-preparation classes, the techniques are adaptable to other mathematics courses and grade levels.

> I thought that six
> of the seven groups
> were working well.

WRITING TO ENHANCE COOPERATIVE LEARNING

Initial group assignments. One essential ingredient in the effectiveness of cooperative-learning groups is group formation (Artzt and Armour-Thomas 1992). Strategies ranging from random assignments to assignments based on such factors as ability and student-requested friendship choices have been recommended (Artzt and Newman 1990a, 1990b; Johnson, Johnson, and Holubec 1986; Slavin 1990). At the beginning of the semester, the students are informed that part of the classroom activities will require that they work in groups of three or four. To maximize opportunities for mathematical communication and giving and receiving help, the students are asked to help the teacher form groups of heterogeneous ability. By asking students to write about their past experiences in mathematics, their attitudes toward mathematics, and

their perceptions of their own mathematical ability, the teacher is able to create groups that will meet the needs of the students. The students are told that the first group arrangements will be based on their responses. They are encouraged to be as honest with themselves as possible in deciding what their needs would be in a group. (See table 1 for excerpts from students' responses.)

Making adjustments to group arrangements

When students are dissatisfied with fellow group members, they will be less likely to express and explore ideas freely, activities that are essential for small-group problem solving. The teacher, therefore, should keep well informed about the attitudes and behaviors of each group member. One way is by overseeing students' interactions as they work together. Unfortunately, as the author has discovered, what meets the eye may be very deceiving. For example, in one class, the author was under the impression that six of the seven groups were working well. Within these six groups, all the students appeared to be satisfied and to be engaging in a high degree of quality communication about mathematics. The students had worked in their groups for approximately three weeks. The day before their unit test, the students were told that after the test some changes might be made in the groups. The students were asked to communicate their feelings about this matter in their jour-

TABLE 1
Excerpts from Students' Mathematics-Ability Descriptions

"I love math when I understand what I'm doing, otherwise I'm *very apprehensive* about the subject. I would appreciate being placed in a group that could help me."

"I like math when I have a teacher who is clear and when I feel free to ask questions if I need help. I think I could be average in math but I need help and a review of math (BIG review)—maybe I'm below average."

"I had trouble with math in the past and feel very intimidated by it. However, when I had a good teacher, I enjoyed math and did fairly well. I need help but I'm fairly average."

"I'm not a good math student, and it always made me feel unconfident. It was always a struggle for me. I need help."

"I have always enjoyed math class, but on exams I tend not to do very well, and that makes me very afraid of any math class. I'm sort of average."

"I was always good at math so I always loved it."

"I always loved math and did very well in the classes."

nals. They had the assurance, of course, that their comments would be kept confidential. Many of their comments were unexpected, which was one of the inspirations for writing this article.

Discussed here are three of the most interesting groups, two that seemed to be functioning well and one that appeared to be deficient in student interaction (referred to as group I, II, and III, respectively). Group I had the most surprising situation. From outward appearances, this group appeared to be functioning the best. All the students seemed highly involved and committed to helping each other. The responses of three of the four members reflected the positive feelings that were anticipated. For example, one said, "I have enjoyed working with the people in my group. It has been helpful to share my math anxieties with others, and to have them help me with them. I think that we have worked well together and would like to remain with this group." Surprisingly, however, the weakest student in the group (student A), who appeared to be receiving a great deal of assistance, wrote, "Regarding the question of changing groups: I personally would very much like to try working with another group." Her reasons for wishing to change were not revealed until the subsequent writing assignment in which the students were asked to write about their feelings in their new groups. She said, "It really is a difference when you are in a group that doesn't make you feel that you are slow."

In group II, which also appeared to be working well together, the student of highest ability (student B) expressed dissatisfaction. She complained about the other members of her group. She claimed that one group member had no interest in improving and that the other member did not share enough of her ideas. She said, "I wouldn't mind working with a new group. If I were in the same group as the ones who care, it would be more advantageous to me and the group. I could have more practice in explaining and they could understand more." When she was switched to a new group, she said, "Now that I can help people, I feel great about it."

The students in group III were obviously not sufficiently interactive. One student expressed this lack of interaction positively. She said, "We don't have disagreements—the experience has been pleasant." She showed that she was aware that there was something wrong when she said, "One problem that I do see is that we don't seem to be doing as well as the other groups and I'm not sure why. Besides that, I think the four of us work well together." Another student (student C) recognized that the lack of disagreements was a negative factor. She said, "All of us seem to understand everything the same; there is no controversy. Since we seem to always agree on answers, we never go over them in detail. I wouldn't mind working in another group." After she was switched to a new group, she said, "I feel very good about how the group helps each other. We really get to talk and discuss each problem until everyone in the group understands."

What lesson can be learned? It is really an old lesson of which we are only beginning to take heed. The more students are given the means to communicate with the teacher and with each other, the better the quality of instruction. Had the avenues of communication not been opened, student A would never have revealed that the others in group I were making her feel inferior by the way in which they were giving her help. Student B would never have disclosed that she had a real craving to help others and therefore would have been overlooked as a great resource for the weakest student in the class. Student C would never have divulged that she was not just a very shy person but someone with the ability and desire to communicate with others about mathematics.

> *"Now that I can help people, I feel great about it."*

Another important discovery was that, as important as it may be to rearrange groups, it is equally important to be sensitive to those students whose needs would be best served by not changing their groups. One of the most mathematics-anxious students in the class (student D) wrote the following:

> I am really glad that you had asked us to write our reaction to working with a new group because I was going to mention it. My reaction was almost like running into a brick wall but maybe not that dramatic. I would deal with a new group but I feel somewhat uneasy about it. When you first put us into groups at the beginning I was amazed that you grouped me with my friend. Never did I think we would be together. This made me feel comfortable because I am very used to her, and I feel she understands me a lot. When I have a problem with the homework, everyone really helps me and takes the time to explain it. So I feel very comfortable in going to them with a problem, and my group has the patience to explain it to me even if I do not get it the first time.

As another means of keeping track of the effectiveness of each group formation, students were asked to write general comments about the help they gave to, or received from, their group members.

TABLE 2
Excerpts from Students' Group Descriptions

"Last time we met I came out feeling good because two people in my group had promised to go over a problem that I still did not understand. That felt good that they were willing to help me. When I feel that I can help them it makes me feel better to ask for it. Sometimes I don't want to ask for help because I feel that I am the only one doing most of the asking, then I really don't want to. My group is usually very helpful and all do try to take the extra time to explain it to me. Lots of times I don't get it the first time and my group is patient about it. They're getting used to it. And it's a great feeling not to pretend you know something when you don't."

"It makes me feel so good to give input into my group. It makes me feel like I know what I'm doing. This has been a good thing for me, because I never thought of myself as being smart in math, or able to help my peers. I love getting help, although I tend to sometimes not ask for it because I am sometimes embarrassed to ask. But I think I'm getting over that. Getting help shows me different ways of doing things."

"The help which I have given within my group seems to be useful. Sometimes my input helps one of the other members in the group see a procedure clearer than before. This gives me a better understanding of the material and a really good feeling of accomplishment. The help which I have received is countless. I have seen different methods of attacking problems and different perspectives of certain problems. I believe my group has compatible strengths and weaknesses. Where one understands the material, someone else is lacking. We help each other in order to get the most out of the material. I even see some members of the group out of class. Even then, we discuss certain problems with homework and help each other out. The group has helped me a lot. I hope to have made the same impression upon them."

"The main reason I enjoy working with my group is that we seem to always have at least one person that's strong on a particular topic that's being discussed in class."

This assignment turned out to be another effective means of monitoring the intragroup relationships. Some comments were made that were most revealing and very unexpected. Several students expressed their reluctance to ask questions within their groups. Other students revealed the importance of having equitable helping relationships within the group. (See table 2.)

A most interesting and unexpected comment came from a high-ability student who was fearful that her helpfulness could actually be harmful. She said, "Sometimes as I'm explaining something I feel I'm confusing her even more. What's scary is that I even confuse myself. Sometimes when I'm figuring out an answer I make a mistake, cross it out, and start over. If she follows along with me and then I tell her I was wrong, then the next time she sees the problem, she'll be confused about which method to use. So maybe my 'help' is more confusing than helpful."

Human interaction is indeed complex; contrary to what many believe, the small group may not be a safe environment for asking questions. Students need to feel deserving of help. They need to believe that they have worth as a contributor, as well. They must also feel sufficiently comfortable with their fellow group members so that they are not fearful of revealing their weaknesses. In fact, in some situations, helping the students learn problem-solving techniques and effective ways to work with others is more advantageous than changing the students' groups on the basis of perceived needs.

USING COOPERATIVE LEARNING TO ENHANCE WRITING ABOUT MATHEMATICS

Within the cooperative-learning setting, asking students to write about the specific help they gave to, or received from, their group is natural. This prompt seems to elicit very rich written communication about mathematics. For example, consider these selected responses when students were asked to describe their experience in finding a median to create a box-and-whiskers plot. One student said, "We all were having trouble finding the median—we were unsure what to do if it was odd or even. We tried to help each other out and I think we did. I understand now that if there are an odd amount of numbers, you take the middle number

$$(x \quad x \quad x \quad \textcircled{x} \quad x \quad x \quad x)$$

and you take the average of the two middle numbers if there are an even amount of numbers

$$(x \quad x \quad x \quad \boxed{x \quad x} \quad x \quad x \quad x)$$

Interestingly, this student latched on to a very concrete method of finding the median. In contrast, a student from a different group chose a more abstract, algorithmic approach:

> Today I had a lot of trouble with understanding exactly how to get the median. Thanks to the girls in my group I now understand. In order to get the median, you take the middle number from the numbers arranged from lowest to highest. If there is an even number of scores, then you take half of that number and the number that follows. For example, if you have 4 scores you take half, which is 2 and then 3, or the second and third number and take their average to equal the median. However, this changes if the number of scores are odd. If this is the case, then you take half the number of scores and round it to the next highest number. For example, if there are 3 scores, half of 3 is 1 1/2, so I'd round this number to 2 and then take the second number in position to represent the median. If it weren't for my group, I would have never clarified this confusion. Thanks to the group I don't feel frustrated about math anymore, because I know that help is there when I need it.

The value of having students give these detailed mathematical descriptions has been well documented (e.g., Davison and Pearce [1988]; Johnson [1983]; Meyers [1986]; Miller [1991]; Nahrgang and Petersen [1986]) and was recognized during this class. Comparing the variety of approaches described by each group was interesting for the class. In fact, after the students wrote about their techniques, each approach was explained by representatives of the different groups. Furthermore, the students were asked to share their writing in the group to check that they had indeed explained the mathematical procedures correctly.

USING COOPERATIVE LEARNING AND WRITING TO ENHANCE ASSESSMENT

One of the main purposes of assessment is to help students learn. By integrating writing activities and cooperative-learning strategies within the context of assessment, teachers can ensure that these learning goals are more readily achieved. The following discussion describes how the author implemented this technique when trying to assess students' understanding of combinatorics and probability.

One of Slavin's approaches, Student Teams Achievement Divisions (STAD), was used to inspire the students to work together and help one another (1990). In this approach, students' test scores are compared with their own past averages, and points are awarded on the basis of the degree to which students meet or exceed their own earlier performances. The students were highly motivated to contribute points to their group. The tests were graded and returned to the students, who subsequently had the chance to meet with group members to go over any errors. The students were then allowed to redo the incorrect problems provided that they did three things.

> ## Since we agree on answers, we never go over them in detail.

First, they had to give a written explanation of the thought processes they used to arrive at their incorrect solution. Second, they had to do the problem correctly. Third, they had to give a written explanation justifying that their new answer made sense. Students were only given full credit if their explanations were suitable. The tests were regraded, and final grades were formed by taking a weighted average of the first and second test grades. Because my goal was to give an accurate assessment of what they knew at the end of the process while not discounting their original performance, the second test grade counted two-thirds of the average.

The students' explanations were most revealing. On one problem, the students were required to complete a chart that listed the number of ways of getting indicated sums on the roll of two dice (see table 3). One student continued the chart with the following numbers: 4, 5, 6, 7, 8, 9, 10, 11. He was therefore claiming that eleven ways would exist to roll a sum

TABLE 3	
The Number of Ways to Get a Sum on a Roll of Two Dice	
Sum	Ways
2	1
3	2
4	3
5	
6	
7	
8	
9	
10	
11	
12	

of 12. His explanation of his thought processes was as follows: "I can't believe I did this! I thought at that time of a pattern 2/1, 3/2, 4/3, ... Therefore I jumped in hurriedly, assuming it keeps going, without giving much thought (nervous). I shouldn't have rushed. I could have used a dot diagram or, just by reasoning it out in my head there is only one combination: 6 on one die and 6 on the other die to add to twelve." Another example of a correct response was on a related question in which the students had to find the probability of rolling a sum that is a prime number. One student wrote, "My answer was 18/36. First I looked for all the prime numbers, forgetting 2 and by mistake including 9. Then I added all the ways each number could be rolled. The correct prime numbers are (2, 3, 5, 7, 11), and the number of ways are then added, being 1 + 2 + 4 + 6 + 2 = 15. So the prob-

ability is 15/36, or 15 ways out of a total of 36 possible outcomes." See table 4 for other general comments students made.

The majority of students' errors did not result from a lack of understanding of the concepts being examined but rather from carelessness, rushing, failure to read the problem correctly, and anxiety that interrupted the process of rational thought. For this reason, most of the students had little difficulty in correcting their errors. When they lacked understanding, the students turned to their group members for help. Twenty-four students took the test. Of the twenty-one students who did not get 100 percent on the first test, only ten received 100 percent on the corrected examination, as the criteria for the pointedness of the explanations were very demanding. The revised solutions were usually correct.

The author believes that this was a good strategy in assessment. Reactions in their journals indicate that students agreed.

> ## Some students are better served by not changing groups.

In writing about the benefits of retaking the test, some students tried to analyze why their performance did not reflect their understanding. Most students said that their errors were caused by rushing, which led to carelessness; anxiety; improper reading of the problem; and failure to look back after they had finished. Some students marveled about what happened in their minds as they

TABLE 4
Excerpts from Students' Explanations of Errors
"This was pure stupidity, and not checking my answer over. I cannot believe what I wrote, forgetting the third number. I think, I thought it was simple, so I just rushed through it."
"The reason I got this wrong is because I couldn't comprehend what they were asking."
"This was a careless mistake. I was looking at the tan marbles and not the yellow ones."
"The way I see I got this question wrong is that I did not read it properly or it didn't compute in my head. What I gave for my answer does not make any sense."
"I guess I must have been rushing and wrote one toss twice. I must have just been making sure there weren't any heads on the second toss and overlooked the repeat. I understood the problem, I was just rushing. If I would have looked back I would have seen that I wrote (HTT) twice. What is important is that I fully understand the problem, the mistake was just plain *careless*!"

took a test. One said, "As I was redoing the test, I was thinking of how I did not think during the test. Every single one of those problems I knew." Perhaps their recognition and verbalization of their test-taking deficiencies will help them in the future. Many said it would.

On the problems that were done incorrectly because of a lack of understanding, the students consulted other group members. One said, "I wanted to go on without really looking at my mistakes but finally a person in my group helped me and explained it. It was so simple and I just blew it out of proportion. I'm glad I understand it now. I feel much better about it. The other stuff was careless mistakes and I learned that I should not, no matter what, rush taking a test." Another said, "It also helped me see different ways of approaching the problems by asking other people how they got their correct answers."

CONCLUDING REMARKS

The advantages of using writing in the mathematics class in combination with cooperative-learning groups are numerous. We can open the doors of communication to reveal the inside story of students' cooperative-learning groups. This approach will enable us to improve group formations and thus group functioning to make cooperative-learning activities work more effectively for both students and teachers. The cooperative-learning environment is a fruitful setting within which students can write descriptions of the help they have given and received. The students can review one another's work and thereby check the understanding of their group members.

Within this setting, assessment techniques can be improved as well. The group structure makes it convenient for students to help one another prepare to take tests. By having students examine their errors and write about the thoughts that led to those errors, teachers can engage students in real learning after the test has been returned. Students can receive help from their group members to correct their errors and gain the understanding that will allow them to explain in writing the justifications for the revised solutions. As students are given increased opportunities to communicate with the teacher and with other students about mathematics and about their feelings about what transpires in the mathematics classroom, the more likely it is that students' individual needs will be met and that meaningful learning will occur.

REFERENCES

Abel, Jean P., and Frederic J. Abel. "Writing in the Mathematics Classroom." *The Clearing House* 62 (December 1989): 155–58.

Artzt, Alice F. "Student Teams in Mathematics Class." *Mathematics Teacher* 72 (October 1979): 5–8.

Artzt, Alice F., and Claire M. Newman. "Cooperative Learning." *Mathematics Teacher* 83 (September 1990a): 448–52.

———. *How to Use Cooperative Learning in the Mathematics Class.* Reston, Va.: The Council, 1990b.

Artzt, Alice F., and Eleanor Armour-Thomas. "Development of a Cognitive-Metacognitive Framework for Protocol Analysis of Mathematical Problem Solving in Small Groups." *Cognition and Instruction* 9 (1992): 137–75.

Davison, David M., and Daniel L. Pearce. "Writing Activities in Junior High Mathematics Texts." *School Science and Mathematics* 88 (October 1988): 493–99.

Havens, Lynn. "Writing to Enhance Learning in General Mathematics." *Mathematics Teacher* 82 (October 1989): 551–54.

Johnson, Marvin L. "Writing in Mathematics Classes: A Valuable Tool for Learning." *Mathematics Teacher* 76 (February 1983): 117–19.

Johnson, David W., Roger T. Johnson, and Edythe Johnson Holubec. *Revised Circles of Learning: Cooperation in the Classroom.* Edina, Minn.: Interaction Book Co., 1986.

LeGere, Adele. "Collaboration and Writing in the Mathematics Classroom." *Mathematics Teacher* 84 (March 1991): 166–71.

McIntosh, Margaret E. "No Time for Writing in Your Class?" *Mathematics Teacher* 84 (September 1991): 423–33.

Meyers, Chet. *Teaching Students to Think Critically.* Jossey-Bass Higher Education Series. San Francisco: Jossey-Bass, 1986.

Miller, L. Diane. "Writing to Learn Mathematics." *Mathematics Teacher* 84 (October 1991): 516–21.

Nahrgang, Cynthia L., and Bruce T. Petersen. "Using Writing to Learn Mathematics." *Mathematics Teacher* 79 (September 1986): 461–65.

Slavin, Robert. "Student Team Learning in Mathematics." In *Cooperative Learning in Mathematics*, edited by N. Davidson, 69–102. Menlo Park, Calif.: Addison-Wesley Publishing Co., 1990.

Sutton, Gail O. "Cooperative Learning Works in Mathematics." *Mathematics Teacher* 85 (January 1992): 63–66.

PLANNING FOR CLASSROOM PORTFOLIO ASSESSMENT

Diana V. Lambdin and Vicki L. Walker

Three years ago, the mathematics teachers from grades 4–12 in our school met for two weeks during the summer for an in-service program related to assessment and decided to begin using portfolios with our students in the fall. I was enthusiastic, although I had no idea at that time how drastically my approach to assessment—and to teaching in general—would change as a result of the portfolio decision.

> *Portfolios are more than student folders.*

In the three years since that assessment meeting, I've struggled with learning how to use portfolios for classroom assessment and discovered many tips toward planning for their use. Among the most important things that I've learned are (*a*) the importance of having a clear idea of the reason for assigning students to compile portfolios; (*b*) the importance of establishing workable routines for managing the production, organization, and storage of the portfolios; and (*c*) the importance of giving students clear guidance about expectations for their portfolios.

Diana Lambdin teaches at Indiana University in Bloomington, IN 47405-1006. Her special interests include problem solving, curriculum development, assessment and evaluation, and writing to learn mathematics. Vicki Walker teaches middle school mathematics at Louisville Collegiate School, Louisville, KY 40207. She is interested in alternative methods of assessment, particularly portfolio assessment.

WHY USE PORTFOLIOS?

The mathematics teachers in my school established certain goals for our use of students' portfolios. First, we were looking for a better way to assess the whole child than just relying on test scores. Second, and perhaps most important, we wanted to help students develop better self-assessment skills and become less reliant on the grades we assign to their work. Third, we wanted to establish a better means of communication among students, parents, and teachers about the kinds of mathematical learning taking place in our classrooms.

These were lofty goals. Although it seemed that portfolios could help us attain them, early on it was not clear exactly how. In retrospect, I realize that I really had very little idea at first what good portfolios should look like, much less how I intended to manage or evaluate them. I discussed the portfolio project with my students during the first weeks of school and sent home a letter informing their parents, but for quite a while, I was actually just feeling my way along. As the year went on, the students and I all raised questions about portfolios, shared thoughts, and communicated about mathematics (and about what we thought demonstrated mathematical learning), and gradually a clearer picture developed. Table 1, taken from guidelines distributed in 1992 by the Kentucky Department of Education as part of an Educational Reform Act mandating the use of portfolios in mathematics assessment, furnishes an overview of the philosophy of portfolio assessment that I have gradually come to espouse. Although the process of searching for meaning has been important to my own growth as a professional, I might have been able to grow more quickly and efficiently had I realized certain things. In this article, I share some of the insights I've gained about portfolio assessment. (Resources I've found especially useful are listed in the Bibliography.)

TABLE 1
Mathematics-Portfolio Philosophy

A workable mathematics-portfolio philosophy—

- supports a method of evaluation that allows students to demonstrate their strengths rather than their weaknesses;
- values a variety of learning styles;
- values mathematics as a subject that requires careful and thoughtful investigation;
- promotes self-assessment and students' confidence in mathematics;
- encourages students to communicate their understandings of mathematics with a high level of proficiency;
- promotes a vision of mathematics that goes beyond correct answers; and
- emphasizes the role of the student as the active mathematician and the teacher as the guide.

(Adapted from Kentucky Department of Education [1992, pp. 1–4])

<table>
<tr><td colspan="1">

TABLE 2
Mathematics-Portfolio Entries

A complete portfolio will include—

- a completed table of contents;

- a letter to the reviewer written by the student that describes the portfolio;

- five best entries reflective of the topics studied and the activities completed in the course.

Each entry must include the original question, task, or problem posed; a title; the date; and the student's name. Entries must be in the same order as listed in the Table of Contents and must be numbered accordingly. If an entry is in the category of photographs, audiotapes, videotapes, or computer disks, then the entry must be accompanied by a brief paragraph describing the activity and its rationale.

(Adapted from Kentucky Department of Education [1992, pp. 1–4])

</td></tr>
</table>

lios meant that portfolio selection was just one more thing to fit into all the many instructional activities I must orchestrate. In that first year, whenever the end of a grading period approached, l scrambled to squeeze in class time for portfolio work and processing. As the portfolios were dug out, I proclaimed to my classes that we all needed to value this process of compiling portfolios.

Portfolios can improve communication with students and parents.

Students were instructed to choose papers that would demonstrate their competencies and their insights. After the first grading period, when many portfolios appeared to be random selections of papers, I required students to attach a comment to each piece telling why they had chosen it for their portfolio. I pleaded that they reflect thoughtfully about their mathematical endeavors and hoped they would turn in masterpieces of mathematical revelation. Then I was extremely disappointed when many portfolios consisted primarily of computa-

PORTFOLIOS ARE NOT THE SAME AS FOLDERS

In the beginning, I tended to equate portfolios with student folders in my mind. I'd often kept folders containing examples of students' work and conference comments, and I initially thought that was more or less what the portfolios would be like. I now realize that a very important element was missing in that conception of the portfolio process—the element of self-evaluation. In the portfolio process that has evolved in my classroom, students are much more in control when putting together their portfolios than they ever were with my old folders. Developing a portfolio involves reflection, writing, and self-critiquing in an effort to present a composite picture of oneself. This approach makes a portfolio much different from simply being a collection of sample pieces of a student's work.

Deciding what kind of envelopes or folders to use as portfolios and where to store them seemed at first to be relatively minor details, but I later realized that such routine decisions can have important implications. The department had decided that students would keep a *working portfolio* (a manila file folder) and a *permanent portfolio* (a dark blue, cardstock accordion-style folder). Throughout the grading period, students placed those papers they were considering as possible portfolio entries in their working portfolio, which served as a sort of holding tank for their selections. At the end of each grading period, students reevaluated their work and made the final selections to transfer to their permanent portfolio. During the first year, all the portfolios were kept in storage boxes that tended to

float around my classroom, depending on where space was available at any given moment. When it came time for a class period devoted to working on portfolios, the storage boxes were pulled out usually from underneath a mass of papers, books, and dust.

Looking back, I can see that something was fundamentally wrong with my whole approach toward the management of the portfolios. The idea of having a working portfolio and a permanent portfolio was, and remains, an essential part of my portfolio procedures. Yet my early method of managing the working portfo-

<table>
<tr><td>

TABLE 3
Mathematics-Portfolio Entry Types

Writing

This type of entry includes journal entries, mathematics autobiographies, explanations, reflections, justifications, and so on.

Investigations or Discovery

This type of entry can be described as an exploration that leads to understanding of mathematical ideas or to the formulation of mathematical generalizations. Examples include gathering data, examining models, constructing arguments, and performing simulations.

Application

This type of entry is to include the selection and use of concepts, principles, and procedures to solve problems in a well-grounded, real-world context.

Interdisciplinary

This type of entry demonstrates the use of mathematics within other disciplines.

Nonroutine Problems

This type of entry includes problems for which the solution or strategies are not immediately evident. This category may include mathematical recreations such as puzzles and logic problems.

Projects

This type of entry includes activities that extend over a period of days and requires a formal presentation of the material learned. This category may include research projects, designs, constructions, and original computer programs.

Note: A portfolio entry may fall into more than one of the foregoing types.

(Adapted from Kentucky Department of Education [1992, pp. 1–4])

</td></tr>
</table>

tional work with comments such as "I chose this because it is neat" or "I chose this because I got all the right answers." Because I had talked about demonstrating good problem solving and displaying mathematical thinking and because I had set aside what I felt to be very valuable instructional time for students to select portfolio pieces and to write comments about them, I had naively assumed that my students would share my expectations about what constituted thoughtful reflection. That first year I sat at my desk facing a huge mound of blue folders, upset not only because most of my students' choices seemed to be off target and their reflections rather shallow but also because I had no earthly idea what I should do to evaluate the portfolios.

> At first I did
> not know how to
> evaluate portfolios.

TIPS FOR GETTING STARTED WITH PORTFOLIO ASSESSMENT

What seems obvious to me now is that by keeping portfolios in storage boxes and only pulling them out occasionally, I was inadvertently conveying a message to my students about the value of the portfolios that was quite contrary to my preaching. By stressing portfolio work only at the end of each grading period, I was defeating my own goal of having my students invest themselves in a process of self-reflection that would culminate in a product called a portfolio. I never imagined that I was instilling anything but positive ideas about maintaining portfolios in my students. Yet, little by little, I began to realize some important adjustments that needed to be made.

Portfolios need to be accessible

First of all, I rearranged things in my room, purchased some inexpensive shelves, and made a permanent home for the portfolios. At present the shelves are located in the front of my room, the area

---

TABLE 4
Portfolio "Thinking Questions"

Please think through these questions carefully as you begin finalizing your portfolio selections and preparing your written summaries.

- What activity or mathematical topic was involved?
- How did the activity help you learn something new?
- What did you learn from this experience?
- Can you describe any connections between the activity and other subject areas or real-life situations?
- Would you do anything differently if you had more time?
- What strategies did you use? (What did you *think* as you worked through the task?)
- What mathematical skills were used in your solution process?
- How would you rate your overall performance related to the activity?
- What are your areas of strength in mathematics?
- What goals have you set for yourself in mathematics?

---

is clearly labeled "Portfolios," and student samples and selection guidelines are posted on the wall directly above the shelves. Since the portfolios are visible and accessible every day, they are tended to more consistently. They are now an integral part of my classroom and of its activities.

Students need guidance in labeling and choosing

Getting my students to label their portfolio selections clearly is a challenge. I expect not just names and page numbers but also dates, assignment titles, and descriptions that clarify what the work is all about. l did not ask for this information initially, and consequently, I did not get it. As I began to give students more specific guidelines about how to label their entries, I began to see marked improvements in their portfolio work. Moreover, I believe my students began to be much more aware of the range of activities in which we were involved and the reasons we were doing these different types of work.

Initially I gave students key phrases for the types of items I expected to go into their portfolios: for example, *favorite piece, best effort, most improved, awesome problem-solving work*. I supplied self-stick notes on which they were to indicate the reasons for their selections; the notes were to be attached to the corresponding pieces. Some students spent considerable time thinking about which pieces of their work might qualify for inclusion in their portfolio and why. Most

students, however, just raced through their notebooks and their working portfolios grabbing things they thought might fit the bill. Those who just wanted to get finished fast tended to focus primarily on superficial aspects like neatness and correctness and on computational tasks, rather than reflecting on the thinking they had done in solving nonroutine problems.

The many changes I have made in my guidelines for portfolio selections and portfolio writings have convinced me that I will probably continue to make adjustments with each passing year, but I can share some ideas about what I do currently. I give my students written guidelines about the different types of work to include in their portfolios (see tables 2 and 3). I also supply a handout of "thinking questions" for them to work through before preparing the written reflections that I now require to accompany each entry (see table 4). (These written reflections have replaced the self-stick notes, which I decided were too small and informal for my purposes.) In general, my goal is to guide students through a process of reflecting, and then writing, about why they've chosen specific pieces—in particular, what they've learned from the activities or work that they select and what kind of connections they can make between this work and other school topics or other aspects of their lives. (See fig. 1 for an example of one student's work on an assignment involving estimation and her rationale for including that work in her portfolio.)

FIGURE 1
Student Work with Portfolio Reflection

Portfolio paragraph

Anne
5-25-93

I chose my "books in the library" project for an entry because it shows my work and has a clear explanation of the process I used. I enjoyed this project because we got to work our own way and find the answer alone. This project taught me to collect data, organize it, and to understand what I did enough to put it in words. Even though my answer whasn't very exact I feel that for the beginning of the year it is pretty good.

Books in the Library

Anne
9/16/92

When I began the Library Books project I thought there might be 400 books. First of all I counted 3 shelves—1 full, 1 medium, and 1 with barely any. Next I avraged them. After that I counted the number of shelves upstairs and multiplied the average amount of books per shelf by the number of shelves. Then I went downstairs and counted the books on the spinners, counted the books in the Kiddie Library, and counted all the books on the downstairs shelves. The total amount of books in the library is ...

26,057

This is how I got my answer:

Upstairs:
51 per shele
x 198 shelves
10,098 on the shelves
+ 97 countertop
10,195

Downstairs:
961 Kiddie Room
14,770 all shelves
9 atlases
+ 122 spinners
15,862

Downstairs 10,195
Upstairs + 15,862
26,057 total

A table of contents is essential

I now require students to have a table of contents for their portfolios, and I have seen remarkable improvement in their portfolios since doing so. Offering students help in preparing a table of contents is fairly easy, yet extremely critical. I generally display a sample table of contents on the overhead projector (see fig. 2) so that students can take notes on the format. Since I've required a table of contents, I get far fewer portfolios that are just piles of papers with fragmented thoughts attached. Students seem to be more thorough regarding the layout of their work and the overall appearance of their portfolio, perhaps because they have more of a sense of a completed project. Each portfolio now has a definite beginning and end and a clearer vision-at-a-glance of what it contains and what message it is meant to convey. Furthermore, the table of contents allows for easier perusal on my part and has saved me a great deal of time during my evaluation process.

> *Whole-class discussions prompt reflection.*

STUDENTS NEED GUIDANCE IN BEING REFLECTIVE

I never realized before I began using portfolios the importance of giving students opportunities to categorize, edit, critique, and analyze their own work and the work of other students, so that they can develop an intuitive sense of what constitutes quality. Projecting transparencies of students' work for whole-class discussion about mathematical content and quality of work has now become a common instructional activity in my class. My students seem to benefit considerably from these whole-class discussions. Similarly, I have learned a lot about which areas of my instruction have made sense to them and on which topics they have remained confused. As we have begun to spend more time analyzing and processing material in class, my students and I have both become more engaged in reflecting on the value of various activi-

---

FIGURE 2

Sample Portfolio Table of Contents

NAME _____
GRADE _____
DATE _____

TABLE OF CONTENTS

Title of Entry	Date Completed	Page
1. Will All Quadrilaterals Tessellate?	15 Nov. 1991	1
2. Buckets of Trouble	27 Oct. 1991	3
3. M&M Probability	16–18 Mar. 1992	5
4. Statistical Project on Immigration	2–12 Feb. 1992	8
5. My Sixth-Grade Mathematics Experience	19 Apr. 1992	10

---

ties. Even though I had included problem-solving activities, writing tasks, group work, and special project work in my classes for years, I was surprised to discover that many of my students had never thought about the distinctions among these types of learning activities. A case in point is one student who chose only computational selections for his portfolio and justified his selections with the statement that he had spent a lot of time working the "problems." Time spent was what made them problem *solving* for him.

In addition to having the whole class share and discuss examples presented on the overhead projector, I frequently engage students in peer-evaluation activities. I pair students or have them work in small groups to make portfolio selections and record comments about their selections. This type of activity may involve having students respond to some important questions I've placed on the overhead projector or may occur at the end of a particular unit when I ask students to summarize the main ideas related to the unit. (See table 5 for some examples of students' writing from a peer-evaluation activity.)

I involve students in peer-evaluation activities a couple of times a month. During such activities, I am able to circulate around the room, take note of valuable comments I hear, make informal assessments of students, and exchange thoughts with small groups or individuals about the type or quality of work they've completed. In this manner, my instructional style and my assessment procedures have become more unified, and portfolio selection is no longer a one-day activity at the end of each marking period. The primary goal of my peer-evalua-

tion activities is that the students spend time thinking about, and sharing their ideas related to, mathematics. The additional benefits of such activities are that students become more aware of what they have studied and what they have learned, I gain valuable insights about my instruction, and the entire portfolio-assessment process becomes an integral part of all that we do.

PORTFOLIO EVALUATION

Evaluating students' portfolios is very time-consuming. I have found it easier to handle if I evaluate one class of portfolios at a time rather than try to grade all classes at once. The letter grade that I assign to each portfolio is included as part of the overall grade for the marking period and is based on three things: the diversity of selections, written reflections about selections, and the organization of the portfolio. Note that I do not grade portfolios on the quality of the selections included (homework, group work, writing assignments, tests, etc.) because many of these have already been graded. Thus, it is possible for a student who gets below-average grades on the mathematics work to receive a better portfolio grade than a student with very high grades on her or his work if the former portfolio is more thoughtfully chosen and carefully documented than the latter.

I use a two-step procedure for portfolio assessment. First I read through all the portfolios and sort them into three piles: *excellent*, *satisfactory*, and *needs improvement*. Then I go back through each pile and assign a score to each portfolio by using a five-point scale (1–5) for each of my three categories (selection, reflection, and organization). Assigning these points is a difficult,

---

TABLE 5

Selected Peer-Evaluation Portfolio Reflections

Activity: Students engaged in partner conferences to discuss their portfolio selections, give advice to one another, and comment on stand-out selections.

1. When I looked at the portfolio selections with Shawn, I noticed a lot of things I could have done better on. For instance, on my problem-solving section I did not do so good because it was the beginning of the year and I had not really gotten into school yet.

2. I worked with Jeff today. He helped me see many things about my papers but most of all he helped pick my best work. This is "How many books are in the library?" This work shows reasoning, estimation, observations, and many other things. This is why this work stands out so well. It shows what my work was. This was also challenging and exciting to me. Even though my estimation was 5600 and the actual was 19,000, I still think my reasoning and attitude towards this project was very good.

3. Today I worked with Andrew. He helped me see the things I was doing wrong. I had a codecracker which didn't show a lot but he helped me see how to make it work. He told me to add an explanation about it for it to fit. I think a standout piece is my million's project. It shows everything I need. It has the original problem plus it shows all my work. It has an explanation about the problem and what we did.

4. One piece of work I think I did super was the "Buckets of Trouble." Even though the explanation wasn't perfect, it showed what our group had done and had pictures to show strategies and the solution. This was a standout piece, and was a fun experiment too. Our group had to work with cups to visualize what we were doing and if it would work.

5. Today I conferenced with Jenny. She pointed out that some of my work needed explanation and helped me choose another piece of work that helps make my portfolio stand out. We chose the Library Book project. The piece was neat, colorful, and had a wonderful explanation!

---

fairly subjective, process. But I try to set general guidelines ahead of time.

When assigning points for the selection category, I consider the diversity of the entries, the time periods represented (work should be represented from throughout the school year thus far), and the overall appropriateness of the selections. Points assigned for reflection are based on the students' written reflections about their choices. I consider clarity of thought, analysis of the problem or the mathematical concepts being displayed, use of complete sentences, legibility, and overall quality of the reflections. The category for organization involves the more technical aspects of the portfolio, such as whether it contains a table of contents, has all its pieces correctly ordered and labeled, and includes the required parental signature. I generally assign five points per category for those portfolios that show excellent work, three points for those that are satisfactory, and one point for those needing improvement. (Four points and two points are assigned, as needed, for work that seems to fall in between.) For example, a student might receive four points for diversity of selection, three points for written reflections, and five points for organization, for a total of twelve points (of fifteen possible) for the portfolio.

The final step of the evaluation process involves writing personal comments to each student about the strengths and weaknesses of his or her portfolio. Although this writing takes a great deal of my time, it greatly enhances my communication with my students and reinforces the value I place on reflection and on written expression.

PORTFOLIOS FACILITATE COMMUNICATION

Using portfolios has changed my communication with students and their parents in ways I had never considered before. For example, portfolios now serve as a powerful tool in parent-teacher or student-teacher conferences. As we examine together examples of such things as group work, problem solving, or written reflections, I can clarify my goals for such assignments, we can compare this type of work with more traditional textbook assignments, and students can ask ques-

tions or try to clarify thoughts that they might not have expressed well on paper. Valuable student-teacher communication also takes place through portfolio writings in which students are assigned to share their reactions to class activities or assignments and to reflect on their personal goals for mathematics learning. (Fig. 3 presents an example of a student's reflection on his personal strengths and weaknesses in mathematics.)

Student-parent communication has also benefited from my use of portfolios, especially since I began requiring parental signatures on the portfolios and encouraging input from parents on students' selections. During my second year of using portfolios I began sending home a newsletter at the end of each grading period to summarize the major topics and ideas that had been covered in class. The newsletter not only has helped me review important ideas with my students as they prepare their portfolios but has facilitated student-parent communication about what has been stressed in class and why.

> *Portfolios have to be accessible all the time.*

SOME FINAL THOUGHTS

Portfolio assessment has helped me and my students make progress toward a number of the goals recommended by the NCTM's *Curriculum and Evaluation Standards for School Mathematics* (1989). My students are more thoughtful about what mathematics they are studying and why. They seem to be developing a better understanding of what is meant by problem solving and mathematical reasoning, less often resorting to the blind application of computational algorithms when confronted with problems. In making portfolio selections, my students are learning to look for connections among mathematics topics (and between mathematics and other aspects of their lives), and they are learning to take personal responsibility for self-assessment. In writing their portfolio reflections, they are improving their abilities to communicate about mathematical ideas and about their own personal strengths and weaknesses.

I must admit, quite honestly, that portfolio assessment is time-consuming and labor-intensive for teachers, especially those who have many students. But careful planning and establishment of routines can eliminate much wasted effort and will make the job easier to do. I have found the results well worth it. Since using portfolios with my classes, I have no doubt that my students are learning more mathematics, and that has always been my ultimate goal.

This article, although written in the first person singular, is actually a collaborative effort of the two authors, who shared equally in its conceptualization and writing. The authors became acquainted in 1990 when Louisville Collegiate School requested that mathematics educators at Indiana University give them some advice about bringing their mathematics teaching more in line with the NCTM's curriculum and evaluation standards. Frank Lester suggested the use of portfolio assessment as a catalyst for change. He and Diana Lambdin consulted with the Collegiate teachers for several years as they worked through the process of establishing the use of portfolio assessment in all their mathematics classes, grades 4–12. In 1992, the state of Kentucky began mandating the use of portfolios in mathematics assessment. For a related article see "Implementing the K–4 Mathematics standards in Kentucky" in the *Arithmetic Teacher,* November 1993.

BIBLIOGRAPHY

Kentucky Department of Education. *Kentucky Mathematics Portfolio: Teacher's Guide.* Frankfort, Ky.: The Department, 1992.

Mumme, Judith. *Portfolio Assessment in Mathematics.* Santa Barbara, Calif.: University of California, 1990. (A publication from the California Mathematics Project.)

National Council of Teachers of Mathematics. *Curriculum and Evaluation Standards for School Mathematics.* Reston, Va.: The Council, 1989.

Petit, Marge. *Getting Started: Vermont Mathematics Portfolio—Learning How to Show Your Best!* Cabot, Vt.: Cabot School, 1992.

Stenmark, Jean Kerr, ed. *Assessment Alternatives in Mathematics: An Overview of Assessment Techniques That Promote Learning.* Berkeley: University of California, 1989.

———. *Mathematics Assessment: Myths, Models, Good Questions, and Practical Suggestions.* Reston, Va.: National Council of Teachers of Mathematics, 1991.

Vermont Portfolio Committee. *The Vermont Mathematics Portfolio: What It Is, How to Use It.* Montpelier, Vt.: Vermont Department of Education, 1991.

FIGURE 3

Student Self-Reflection

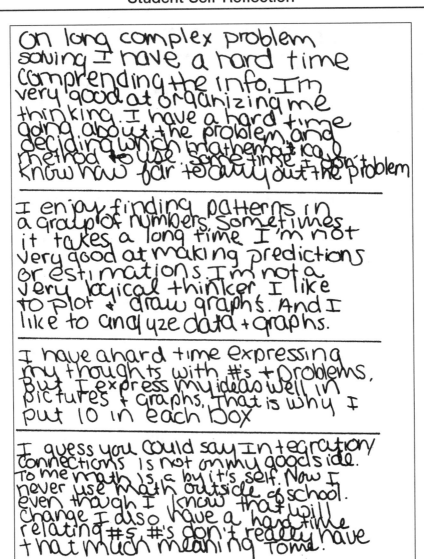

On long complex problem solving I have a hard time comprending the info. I'm very good at organizing me thinking. I have a hard time going about the problem and deciding which mathematical method to use. Some time I don't know how far to carry out the problem

I enjoy finding patterns in a gralpof numbers. Sometimes it takes a long time I'm not very good at making predictions or estimations. I'm not a very logical thinker I like to plot & draw graphs. And I like to analyze data + graphs.

I have a hard time expressing my thoughts with #'s + problems, But I express my ideas well in pictures + graphs. That is why I put 10 in each box

I guess you could say Integration connections is not on my good side. To me math is a by it's self. Now I never use math outside of school. even though I know that will change I also have a hard time relating #s #'s don't really have that much meaning to me. have

STUDENT MATHEMATICS PORTFOLIO: MORE THAN A DISPLAY CASE

Mary L. Crowley

Records of students' progress should be more than a set of numerical grades or checklists—they can include brief notes or samples of students' work. (NCTM 1989, p. 197)

Teachers have traditionally relied heavily on tests and homework to gather information on students' performance. They are finding, however, that as the goals of mathematics education expand to include (1) valuing mathematics, (2) developing mathematical confidence, (3) becoming problem solvers, (4) communicating mathematically, and (5) reasoning mathematically (NCTM 1989), these tools do not always yield sufficient or suitable information. New and revised assessment techniques are needed.

The student mathematics portfolio has been identified as a potentially valuable, and currently underused, assessment resource (NCTM 1989; Stenmark 1989; Clarke, Clarke, and Lovitt 1990). What is a portfolio? Why should a teacher use a portfolio? How can a teacher collect, organize, and evaluate a portfolio? This article will address these questions and present specific examples for portfolio use. Although the examples come from a junior high school class, many of the ideas should be of interest to teachers at other levels.

WHAT IS A MATHEMATICS PORTFOLIO?

The mathematics portfolio is a collection of selected student work. It can dis-

Mary Crowley teaches at Dalhousie University, Halifax, NS B3H 3J5. She is interested in advancing pedagogical reform at the college level, particularly in the mathematics classroom.

play a student's best or most significant efforts across a range of mathematical activities or couple early work with later and stronger work to illustrate a student's mathematical progress. In each of these examples, the portfolio serves as a place to store previously evaluated materials. These concrete examples can show the teacher or parent the student's performance in more detail than would an abstract number or letter grade.

> *The portfolio can reinforce what is valued in the program.*

In addition to being a display case for completed work, the portfolio can contain items, or itself be an item, for evaluation. With younger students, merely assembling the portfolio might become an evaluation tool. Presentation, neatness, artistic quality, and so on, might be appraised. However, if the portfolio collection is to be graded on the basis of the mathematical activities included, some new work will undoubtedly need to be incorporated. This work could be an assignment designed specifically for the portfolio or an extension of some previously completed work (see "Debugging" in fig. 3). A word of caution, however: The portfolio loses its "selected" feeling when a lot of new work is included for evaluation.

The previous points indicate that the portfolio can house selected samples of students' work, which, in turn, can be used to document students' accomplishments as well as to assess their work. The

portfolio can also serve a more subtle and equally important function of reinforcing what is valued in the mathematics program. If the portfolio contains only examples of activities that primarily reward correct answers (e.g., traditional tests), the message to students and others who view the portfolio is that this sort of activity is what matters in mathematics. If, however, the portfolio contains items that represent a broad range of goals and activities, that demonstrate the student's ability to apply problem-solving knowledge, to use mathematical language to communicate ideas, to reason and analyze, or that show a positive attitude toward mathematics, students will learn that these mathematical outcomes are desirable.

WHAT GOES INTO A PORTFOLIO?

The portfolio's contents will vary according to its purpose, the way in which it will be used, the age of the students, and the types of assessment activities used in the class. It might, of course, include examples of traditional student output, such as tests, quizzes, and homework.

A richer student profile, however, is derived when the portfolio contains a wide range of assessment artifacts. A brief list of items that might be considered includes the following:

- Samples of journal writings
- A mathematics autobiography
- Mathematical research completed either individually or with a group

- Several solutions to a challenging problem
- An elegant proof that can be either intuitive or formal, depending on the student's abilities
- Student-formulated problems
- Student-made concrete representations
- A book review
- Group projects
- Photographs of student dramatizations
- Audiotapes of student and teacher interviews

A more elaborate list of suggestions can be found in the two publications by Stenmark cited in the References. The choice of materials depends on what the portfolio is meant to reflect. Figure 1 contains excerpts from three student portfolios.

HOW DO YOU ORGANIZE A PORTFOLIO?

A portfolio can be collected over a term or even over the entire school year. It is important, therefore, to introduce the concept early on. At that time, the types of activities from which the student can select portfolio items, the grading scheme, the presentation format, the due dates, and the purpose of the portfolio should be discussed. Students should also be reminded over the course of the term to be thinking about items to submit to their portfolio.

Figure 2 contains instructions for a portfolio that can be collected over a four-month period from September to December. The directions are presented in a letter that is distributed to students and parents. The instructions are also discussed with the students in class.

A portfolio containing both new and completed work is presented in figure 3. To give the portfolio a focus, categories for submissions are identified. A few of these categories require that all students submit the same assignment, for example, an autobiography. For most categories, however, the student selects the included item from several possible candidates. Two categories are totally unrestricted: The student can submit a mathematical product of his or her choice, and, similarly, the teacher can also contribute an item. Using these selection options gives both the student and the teacher a voice in creating the profile of the student's performance and attitudes. This portrait is further illuminated by the various activities represented in the submission categories: group work, individual work, a presentation to the class, writing, standard testing, attitudes toward mathematics, problem solving, and mathematical reflection.

Several criteria can be used to evaluate them.

HOW DO YOU EVALUATE A PORTFOLIO?

Not all portfolios need to be assessed. For example, if the primary function of the portfolio is to display a student's accomplishments, the teacher has no reason to assess the individual's work again. Nonetheless, some comments from the teacher about the collection would be appropriate.

If, however, the merits of the portfolio are to be assessed, identify evaluation guidelines. Stenmark, in *Mathematics Assessment: Myths, Models, Good Questions, and Practical Suggestions* (1991), presents an excellent starter set of such criteria. These include such evaluating characteristics as the student's—

a) *problem-solving skills:* "[F]ormulates and understands the problem or task ..." and "[C]hooses a variety of strategies" (p. 43);

b) *ability to make mathematical connections:* "[R]elates mathematics to other subject areas and to the real world" (p. 43);

FIGURE 1
Samples of Students' Writing

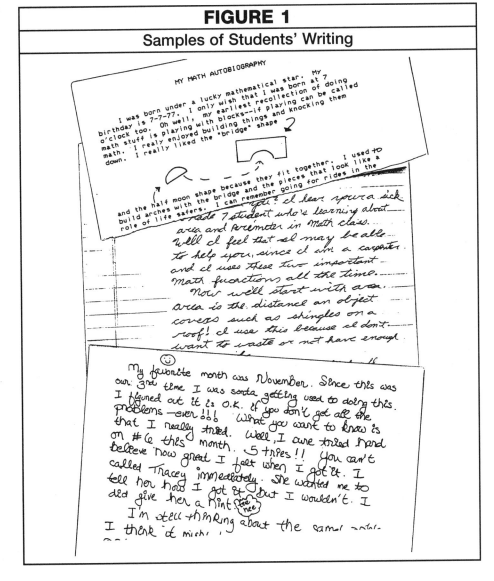

FIGURE 2

An Informational Letter for Students and Parents

```
Dear Mathematician,

    This term, I am asking you to keep a mathematics portfolio.
This is a collection of various types of mathematics activities
that you will be doing in class. Several different types of
things should be included. I've described them on the attached
sheet. Read carefully; sometimes you can choose what to
include.

    Depending on what you submit, your portfolio could become
quite cumbersome. If possible, I would like you to use an
expandable folder to house all the documents. Please use
dividers or labels to indicate each category and subcategory.
If you find that you cannot fit everything into this type of
container, please discuss this situation with me.

    I would like to keep your portfolios in the classroom. This
arrangement will help me when I am filling out report cards and
when I meet with your parents on parent-teacher night. To help
you get started, I would like you to hand in a portfolio of
"work in progress" on 5 October. The final portfolio is due 15
December.

    I will be assigning a grade to the portfolio. The marking
scheme is attached.

    Happy collecting.

                                        Sincerely,

                                        Your Mathematics Teacher
```

c) *ability to communicate mathematically:* "[U]ses appropriate mathematical language and notation" (p. 43); and

d) *attitudes toward mathematics and self:* "[S]hows development of positive attitudes—confidence, flexibility, willingness to persevere, appreciation of the value and beauty of mathematics" (p. 43).

Stenmark also includes implementation tips for evaluation, such as recommending that only two or three of the criteria be evaluated at any one time and that students be informed in advance of which criteria will be evaluated (Stenmark 1991, p. 43).

Portfolios focus on strengths.

CONCLUSION

Assessment is an integral component of any mathematics program. Well-designed and appropriately selected evaluation procedures can be used to (*a*) identify areas of students' strengths and weaknesses, (*b*) give feedback on instruction, (*c*) assign grades, and (*d*) supply information on students' achievement of program goals. A range of assessment tools should be used when gathering information in any of these areas. The techniques selected should be consistent with the purposes of the evaluation.

Many mathematics teachers are finding the portfolio to be a valuable addition to their assessment repertoire. It can be used by students, teachers, parents, and administrators as a record of students' accomplishments. It can reflect what is valued in the mathematics program. It can appeal to students with differing learning styles through a range of highlighted activities. Its focus on strengths rather than weaknesses can help to promote a positive self-image in the student. And, best of all, with a little preplanning it can be easy and fun to do. Why not try it?

REFERENCES

Clarke, David J., Doug M. Clarke, and Charles J. Lovitt. "Changes in Mathematics Teaching Call for Assessment Alternatives." In *Teaching and Learning Mathematics in the 1990s,* 1990 Yearbook of the National Council of Teachers of Mathematics, edited by Thomas J. Cooney, pp. 118–29. Reston, Va.: The Council, 1990.

National Council of Teachers of Mathematics. *Curriculum and Evaluation Standards for School Mathematics.* Reston, Va.: The Council, 1989.

Stenmark, Jean K. *Assessment Alternatives in Mathematics: An Overview of Assessment Techniques That Promote Learning.* Berkeley, Calif.: EQUALS, Lawrence Hall of Science and California Mathematics Council, 1989.

———. *Mathematics Assessment: Myths, Models, Good Questions, and Practical Suggestions.* Reston, Va.: National Council of Teachers of Mathematics, 1991.

FIGURE 3
Portfolio Materials

Six categories of portfolio inclusions are listed. Category 2 lists five items; all other categories list only one item. Your portfolio will have ten different items once complete.

1. *Getting to know you*

Please write a mathematical autobiography. Explain how you feel about mathematics, what you like about the subject, and what you dislike about it. Include any other information that you believe reflects your attitudes toward mathematics. These thoughts should be completed early in the term and turned in as part of the 5 October submission.

2. *I'm proud of several items.* You should have one entry for each of the Eve sections.

   a) *Letter to a sick friend.*
   Several times over the term you will be asked to write a letter to friend who was not in school when we studied a specific topic (fractions, negative numbers, and so on). In the letter, explain the concept to the student. Include here the letter that you think is your best effort.

   b) *Problem without words.*
   From time to time during the term, you will be given a "problem without words" and asked to write a word problem to correspond with the information. Include in the portfolio the problem that you like best and explain why you like it.

   c) *Calendar conversations.*
   Each month I will hand out a calendar of activities for you to solve. Keep a journal of how you have attempted to solve these problems. I will collect these journals each month, read them, and return them. Include the month of your choice and explain why you chose that particular month.

   d) *Testing time.*
   Include the test that you think shows your best work of the term.

   e) *One special item.*
   Include something mathematical that you have done this term of which you are particularly proud. It does not have to be work that we did as part of class. Explain why you chose this item.

3. *Mathequarade*

During the week of Halloween, present, in dramatic form, a mathematical concept of your choice. I will photograph you during the presentation or use a video camera, if possible. Please include the still picture. Also, include a journal of your idea development. Comment on why you chose to present the topic, what sort of research and preparation you did, and what you learned.

4. *Debugging*

Include a problem from one of the tests or homework assignments that you did not complete or did not answer correctly but realized later how it should have been done. Include a correct solution and an explanation of why it works and what made you think of it. Also, include your false or incomplete start.

5. *Critics corner*

Your group will be asked to help me present a section from the textbook to the class. You will be graded on that presentation. I will also ask your group to write a letter to the publishing company discussing your reaction to the section. I would like you to discuss the writing style, including vocabulary used, and to comment on the diagrams or pictures, layout,

6. *Teacher's pet*

I will give you something to and effectiveness of the examples. Include that letter in the portfolio. include in your portfolio. For example, I might include a test that in my view was good, so don't throw away those tests when I return them. It might be a description of work I saw you doing in class. I will explain why I included this item.

(Calendar conversations and Mathequarade are based on activities that were suggested by two junior high school teachers, Marie Thomson and Susan Wilkie.)

INFORMING LEARNING THROUGH THE CLINICAL INTERVIEW

Madeleine J. Long and Meir Ben-Hur

The National Council of Teachers of Mathematics's *Curriculum and Evaluation Standards for School Mathematics* (1989) and *Professional Standards for Teaching Mathematics* (1991) endorse the view that assessment should be made an integral part of teaching. Although many of the student outcomes described in the *Standards* cannot properly be assessed using paper-and-pencil tests, such tests remain the primary assessment tools in today's classroom.

During the course of a National Science Foundation teacher-enhancement project, Fellows for the Advancement of Mathematics Education (FAME), a method was developed that permits classroom teachers to assess students' performance in mathematics in an alternative fashion through a series of clinical interviews. A clinical interview is an exchange between two or more people in which the interviewer (teacher) seeks to elicit information from the interviewee (student) about how the latter thinks and learns. Although the interview was originally designed to study children's thinking in a clinical setting, the authors have adapted it for use by teachers in classroom settings.

Madeleine Long and Meir Ben-Hur serve as director and assistant director, respectively, of the Institute for the Advancement of Mathematics and Science at Long Island University—Brooklyn campus, Brooklyn, NY 11201. Long has directed a number of National Science Foundation–funded projects in mathematics and science. Ben-Hur's interests include learning difficulties in mathematics and effective teaching strategies.

The clinical interview yields information not easily available from other sources. It gives insights into students' experiences by permitting the teacher to understand the meanings that students find in mathematical problems and to appreciate their feelings and confidence about learning mathematics. It furnishes the teacher with information about students' backgrounds and learning styles, their strengths and weaknesses, and

> *Interview time was well spent.*

about cultural differences that may affect their views of, or success in, mathematics. It also allows teachers to stress process over product, encourages talking about mathematics, and gives teachers and students instant feedback. Through the clinical interview it is possible to ascertain prior to formal exposure to a topic whether students can construct their own strategies. Unlike paper-and-pencil tests, it makes possible the discovery of whether students restrict themselves to, and place more trust in, a single method of solving a problem or are able to use alternative methods. It also makes possible a determination of their understanding that answers obtained through the use of different methods can actually coincide.

Consider, for example, the fourth-grade student who was able successfully to perform the following computations:

$$1/3 + 1/6 = \underline{\hspace{1cm}}$$

$$1/2 + 1/4 = \underline{\hspace{1cm}}$$

$$1/8 + 1/4 = \underline{\hspace{1cm}}$$

The same student was asked to identify fractional parts of a pie during an interview in which the following scenario occurred:

> The Teacher Interviewer (TI) shows the student a fraction circle with one-half, one-third, and one-sixth portions shaded (see fig. 1). She points to the one-half part.
>
> TI: What portion of the pie does this represent?
> Student: One-half (writes "1/3").
> TI: And this? (points to the one-third portion).
> Student: A third (writes "1/3").
> TI: And this? (points to the ones-sixth portion).
> Student: A small third (writes "1/3").

A series of similar questions revealed the same pattern, which, in this instance, implied that the same student who was able to add fractions had little idea of what the fractional parts meant.

THE INTERVIEW PROCESS

The clinical interview has three components: the initiation, the formulation of hypotheses about the student and the student's understanding, and the testing of these hypotheses through questioning. The formulation of hypotheses can occur at any time during the interview, and questions can be altered to test the hypotheses. Many interviews involve a fourth step, characterized by the interviewer's attempt to modify the student's knowledge and ascertain which materials and methods are best suited to bring about the modification.

Initiating the interview

During this very important initial stage TIs should ask students nonthreatening, personal questions, as well as questions about favorite classroom activities. They should orient the students, explain that the purpose of the interview is to help them learn, and justify recording or videotaping the interview. TIs should also ask questions that help to ascertain whether the students are familiar with the materials to be used. The questioning stage should begin when the interviewees' behavior shows that they are comfortable with the process and willing to proceed.

Although TIs know their own students best and make their own determinations, classic indicators of interview comfort and readiness on the part of the student include these:

- The emergence of student-initiated questions
- The volunteering of information beyond that requested by the TI
- Involvement in the organization of materials to be used in the interview

The questioning stage

Although this stage can begin with a standard question or the presentation of a task to be completed, the questions must be rephrased in the student's language and tasks must be continually modified for each student. Throughout, students should be encouraged to rephrase, elaborate on their responses, and support responses with explanations and arguments. Because they often appear to know more than they actually do, additional questions should be asked to check their degree of understanding. For example, the TI asks a sixth-grade student the following question: "What is the first day of the month if the last Friday of the month is the twenty-fifth?" The question is presented orally and in writing, and the student demonstrates an understanding of the question. He or she then attacks the problem in a trial-and-error fashion and fails to find an appropriate approach. At that point, the TI suggests a modification of the problem that causes the child to think visually: "Draw a calendar." The child draws a seven-by-

FIGURE 1

four grid, numbers the days consecutively from the first box, and finds that Friday falls on the twenty-seventh.

The TI then asks two slightly different questions: "Suppose a Friday falls on the twenty-fifth. On what date was the previous Friday?" and "Can we find out what the date of the first Friday of the month is?" Note that the TI helps eliminate an obstacle but does not solve the problem. At this stage the student discusses the principle of counting in reverse in increments of seven days but still does not complete the solution. The TI then asks, "If the first Friday is on the fourth, on what day of the week was the first day of the month?"

> *Creative teachers found time for interviews.*

TIs should pause sufficiently between questions and should encourage students to elaborate further on each response. It is critical that they remain nonjudgmental in their acceptance of responses and at the same time show respect for the student's thinking and curiosity. Experienced interviewers have found the following phrases to be helpful in this regard:

- I am interested in your thinking.
- Please help me understand. Suppose you are the teacher and I am your pupil.
- I don't think that this problem is easy. Sometimes I get confused with dates and days of the week. Don't you?
- Sometimes when I have difficulties

with a problem, I break it down into small steps. Let's do that here and find out.... (The problem is modified.)

- I like it when you take the time to think.
- I understand now, but....

Formulating and testing hypotheses

The purpose of the interview is to identify, in an increasingly analytical way, the difficulties students confront while they solve problems. Thus, as the TI encourages students to respond to carefully formulated questions and elicits responses in a nonthreatening manner, a series of hypotheses about the student's learning should be formulated and tested. Examples of hypotheses that were formulated during the interviews described earlier include these:

- The student is familiar with the calendar.
- The student is able to gather relevant information before attempting to solve the problem.
- The student approaches the problem systematically rather than by trial and error.
- The student can use arithmetic efficiently.

Teachers, of course, are interested in helping students understand mathematics, a goal much easier to reach if they understand and can analyze the difficulties students confront while attempting to learn.

Intervention

Interventions can occur during or after the interview. When satisfied with her or his identification of the difficulties, the TI should attempt different kinds of interventions to determine the effectiveness of each in ameliorating the difficulties. The intervention serves as an excellent means of ascertaining the effectiveness of various instructional approaches. The intervention can be undertaken with individuals or groups of students who share a common difficulty. After an intervention, the TI should return to testing hypotheses.

The clinical interview can quickly become a diagnostic tool that enables sensitive teachers to gain a better understanding of, and insight into, all students' learning through the careful analysis of the problems confronted by one or two of them. Conducting the interview leads teachers to listen to their students, to see problems through the eyes of the students, to respond to each student's particular needs, and to focus on stages of learning rather than answers.

When the clinical interview was initially introduced to FAME's middle school teachers in New York City, the teachers feared that it would be overly time-consuming and would not help them in their central role as teachers of mathematics. As the interviews were conducted and analyzed, the teachers came to see them as "cost effective," since information they gained from a dialogue with one or two students was often generalizable to the entire class. From just a single interview, one teacher learned of her failure to consider the importance of reading comprehension when teaching problem solving. She also learned that every problem, regardless of how simple or seemingly straightforward, assumes knowledge that some students might not possess. (One student was not familiar with the calendar.) Lastly, she discovered that her own instruction had

been mainly verbal, making little use of diagrams, graphs, and manipulatives.

Teachers also found that the time put into developing and refining individual interview questions made them better able to frame meaningful interview questions for the entire class and to sustain a whole-group dialogue. The question of where to find time in a crowded day to

Interviews uncover learning difficulties.

conduct interviews was solved creatively and differently by different teachers. Some teachers conducted five-to-twenty-minute interviews while the rest of the class was engaged in independent learning or cooperative-group work. Others borrowed a brief part of lunch or recess for interviews; others conducted interviews before class or after school. As the teachers' emphasis passed from the "pain" of how to manage the interviews to the joy of discovery, more and more possibilities opened up. In fact, two teachers have trained high school volunteers to conduct interviews with their elementary school students. One teacher reflected that "reteaching a topic that students had difficulty understanding always left a small group still baffled. The clinical interview has replaced some of the reteaching."

The clinical interview should be considered by classroom teachers as an important teaching-and-assessing tool because it permits the teacher to encourage individual students to learn mathematics, to uncover typical learning difficulties among groups of students, to plan strategies for dealing with the difficulties, to get students to "talk mathematics," and to reinforce concepts. The only requirements for the successful use of the interview are an understanding of mathematics, sensitivity to students, willingness to work in a new arena, and practice.

BIBLIOGRAPHY

Peck, Donald M., Stanley M. Jencks, and Michael L. Connell. "Improving Instruction through Brief Interviews." *Arithmetic Teacher* 37 (November 1989): 15–17.

National Council of Teachers of Mathematics. *Curriculum and Evaluation Standards for School Mathematics.* Reston, Va.: The Council, 1989.

———. *Professional Standards for Teaching Mathematics.* Reston, Va.: The Council, 1991.

Thompson, Alba G., and Diane J. Briars. "Implementing the *Standards*: Assessing Students' Learning to Inform Teaching: The Message in NCTM's Evaluation Standards." *Arithmetic Teacher* 37 (December 1989): 22–26.

ASSESSING STUDENTS' BELIEFS ABOUT MATHEMATICS

Denise A. Spangler

The beliefs that students and teachers hold about mathematics have been well documented in the research literature in recent years (e.g., Cooney 1985; Frank 1988, 1990; Garofalo 1989a, 1989b; Schoenfeld 1987; Thompson 1984, 1985, 1988). The research has shown that some beliefs are quite salient across various populations. These commonly held beliefs include the following (Frank 1988):

- Mathematics is computation.
- Mathematics problems should be solved in less than five minutes or else something is wrong with either the problem or the student.
- The goal of doing a mathematics problem is to obtain *the* correct answer.
- In the teaching-learning process, the student is passive and the teacher is active.

Educators generally agree that these beliefs are not conducive to the type of mathematics teaching and learning envisioned in the *Curriculum and Evaluation Standards for School Mathematics* (NCTM 1989).

A cyclic relationship appears to exist between beliefs and learning. Students' learning experiences are likely to contribute to their beliefs about what it means to learn mathematics. In turn, their beliefs about mathematics are likely

Denise Spangler is a doctoral student at the University of Georgia, Athens, GA 30602. Her research interests include students' and teachers' beliefs about mathematics and children's constructions of arithmetic.

to influence how they approach new mathematical experiences. According to the *Standards* document, "[Students'] beliefs exert a powerful influence on students' evaluation of their own ability, on their willingness to engage in mathematical tasks, and on their ultimate mathematical disposition" (NCTM 1989, p. 233).

This apparent relationship between beliefs and learning raises the issue of how the cycle of influence can be used to reinforce positive attitudes. A rich collection of mathematical experiences in the spirit of the curriculum standards may help enrich students' beliefs. Another approach is to help students become

> *Discussing open-ended questions helps illuminate students' beliefs.*

aware of the beliefs that they hold about mathematics. The *Standards* document suggests that assessing students' beliefs about mathematics is an important component of the overall assessment of students' mathematical knowledge. Beliefs are addressed in the tenth standard of the evaluation section, which deals with assessing mathematical disposition. Mathematical disposition is defined to include students' beliefs about mathematics. The document recommends that teachers use informal discussions and observations to assess students' mathematical beliefs (NCTM 1989). Although teachers' awareness of students' mathematical beliefs is important, of equal importance may be students'

awareness of their own beliefs toward mathematics.

One medium for bringing students' beliefs to a conscious level is open-ended questions. As students ponder their responses to such questions, some of their beliefs about mathematics will be revealed. As groups of students discuss their responses to these questions, some students' beliefs will likely be challenged, leading to an examination of these beliefs and their origins and, possibly, to the modification of these beliefs.

This article presents some open-ended questions that have been used by the author with elementary, junior high, and senior high school students; preservice and in-service elementary, junior high, and senior high school teachers; and graduate students in mathematics education. The questions have been culled from a variety of sources and do not necessarily represent the author's original ideas. Each question is followed by a summary of typical responses. The responses from the various populations were quite similar, which is not surprising, since the research shows a striking similarity between the beliefs held by these groups. For some questions possible origins of the belief or possible avenues for further discussion are included.

These questions can be presented to students in various formats. Students can be given a question or series of questions to ponder for homework, or they can be assigned to gather responses to questions from an adult, an older student, and a younger student. Some questions can be posed as journal-writing entries, whereas others can be presented for class discussion with no prior preparation on the part of the students. Regardless of the manner of presentation of the questions, however, students should receive some response to their thinking. This important feedback may come in the form of a class or small-group discussion, or it may be in the form of questions or comments from the teacher in students' journals.

• If you and a friend got different answers to the same problem, what would you do?

The most common answer to this question is that the students would both rework the problem. When asked what reworking accomplishes, the students reply that one person might find an error in his or her work. Another popular answer is that it depends on who the other student is. If the other student is perceived to be "smarter," then the tendency is to accept that person's answer. If the student feels mathematically superior to the other person, though, he or she will stick with the original answer. Only on rare occasions do students suggest that both students could have a correct answer. When this option is presented to students, they tend to think of examples in which both students have represented the same numerical value in a different form (e.g., 1/2 and 3/6 or 0.5 or 1:2). Students rarely consider possibilities in which the two answers are completely different but equally correct, as often occurs in problem solving. These responses lend support for Frank's findings (1988) that students perceive mathematics as a search for *the* one right answer.

• If you were playing "Password" and you wanted a friend to guess the word *mathematics*, what clues would you give? ("Password" clues must be one word and may not contain any part of the word being guessed.)

The four most common answers are, predictably, "add," "subtract," "multiply," and "divide." Other clues include "numbers," "problems," "operations," "calculate," "hard," and "subject." These responses suggest that students tend to view mathematics as synonymous with arithmetic. This revelation can lead nicely into a discussion of other branches of mathematics, the types of problems that

are posed in the branch, and the types of tools used, such as ruler, compass, graphing calculator, and so on. This discussion, along with some classroom activities in such other branches of mathematics as geometry, probability, and data analysis, can help dispel students' belief that mathematics is merely computation.

Students generate counterexamples to popular beliefs.

• If given a choice, when solving a problem would you prefer to have (*a*) one method that works all the time or (*b*) many methods that work all the time?

Most students indicate that they would prefer to have one method for solving a problem because they would not have to remember as much as if they had multiple methods. This response suggests that students perceive memorization as a major component of mathematics learning. Some students, however, indicate that they would prefer to have several methods from which to choose when solving a problem because they could check their answers using a different method. Other students point out that sometimes one method is more efficient for solving a particular problem than other methods. For example, many methods can be used to determine the center of a circle, including (*a*) folding paper or using a Mira to find the point of intersection of two diameters of the circle and (*b*) finding the point of intersection of the perpendicular bisectors of two chords of the circle. Sometimes the use of paper folding is impractical, so one of the other methods would be better. At other times, the perpendicular-bisector method may be cumbersome and time-consuming, so one of the other methods would be preferred. Also, some students will likely understand one method better than others, and all students are not likely to understand the same method. Students can debate this question among themselves, offering examples of mathematical situations that support their opinions.

• Is it possible to get the right answer to a mathematics problem and still not understand the problem? Explain.

Unfortunately, students are all too often able to obtain correct answers without understanding what they are doing. How many elementary school students can perform the invert-and-multiply algorithm for dividing fractions but cannot tell a story to go along with the number sentence? How often do students solve word problems by extracting the numbers and selecting an operation on the basis of relative sizes of the numbers without understanding how the mathematical operation relates to the action in the problem? After pondering the initial question for a while, many students admit that they often get an answer without understanding the problem. Students can generate examples of mathematical tasks that they perform by rote without understanding the reasons for the steps they perform. This reflection can present opportunities for meaningful reteaching of concepts by the teacher or for interesting research projects for individual students. This type of reteaching is often the focus of the first course in mathematics content taken by preservice elementary school teachers. This course typically consists of the conceptual underpinnings of the four basic operations on subsets of the real numbers. Class discussions are often punctuated by such comments as "So that is why the decimal point goes there!" Discussions of this nature can help students see that studying mathematics involves more than merely obtaining correct answers.

• How do you know when you have correctly solved a mathematics problem?

Reworking the problem, checking with the teacher or a classmate, looking in the back of the book, working backward (for arithmetic problems), or plugging in values (for algebra problems) are common answers to this question. Seldom do students suggest that they check to see if the answer makes sense in the context of the initial problem. This discussion offers an opportunity to introduce such a problem as the one given in the Third National Assessment of Educational Progress:

An army bus holds 36 soldiers. If 1128 soldiers are being bused to their training site, how many buses are needed?

This problem was given to 45 000 high school students, and one-third of them

Emphasis on Assessment

responded that the answer was 31 remainder 12 without checking to see if such an answer made sense in the context of the problem (Schoenfeld 1987). All too often the check-back stage of the problem-solving process is neglected, either because students are in a hurry to finish the problem or because they do not perceive checking back as an essential component of problem solving. Many students equate checking back with checking numerical computations. They do not perceive looking for generalizable results, examining the efficiency of the method used, looking for additional answers, or identifying the underlying mathematical concepts as part of the problem-solving process. This limited view is likely due to their prevailing belief that the objective of working a mathematics problem is to obtain an answer.

• What subject or subjects is mathematics most like? Least like? Why?

The most popular answer to this question is that mathematics is most like science because it involves memorizing formulas and working with numbers. Virtually all other subject areas are nominated in the category of being least like mathematics. Nevertheless, during a class discussion, something interesting usually occurs. Someone may say that mathematics and music are not alike, but a student who has some musical background may reply, "Oh, yes they are!" The student will go on to explain that music involves patterns, counting beats, using fractions to determine how long to hold a note, time signatures, and a variety of other mathematical concepts. A similar discussion usually ensues about art. This discussion furnishes a nice opportunity to talk about the golden ratio and its uses in art and architecture (see Billstein and Lott [1986]) or about visualization of abstract concepts of point, line, and plane (see Millman and Speranza [1991]). Some students will claim that mathematics is not similar to studying a foreign language, whereas other students will contend that mathematics *is* a foreign language! In both French and mathematics, it is necessary to adopt the conventions of the language, learn new vocabulary, and determine how isolated words or ideas connect to form meaningful sentences or concepts. And in both

instances, practical experiences in the real world help to refine newly acquired skills and concepts.

For other subject areas, students are less likely to formulate an explanation of how the subject is similar to mathematics. This explanation usually has to be

Mathematics is more than computation.

initiated by the teacher, and then students contribute their own ideas. For example, history and mathematics are alike because just as we cannot change history, we cannot alter certain mathematics facts (at least not without changing a great deal of mathematics). The Boston Tea Party occurred in Boston, not Orlando, and we cannot change that fact. Similarly, the probability of the occurrence of any given event must be between 0 and 1, inclusive, and we cannot change that fact. (The best tactic is to use an example that relates directly to the topic being studied when this discussion takes place.)

Although a great deal of history is past and cannot be changed, history is being made right this very moment, just as new mathematical knowledge is constantly evolving (see Peitgen, Jürgens, and Saupe [1992] for a discussion of fractals and chaos). Students tend to perceive mathematics as a static discipline in which everything has already been created or discovered; however, the frontiers of mathematical knowledge are being pushed farther every day. Also, the knowledge we have about past historical events affects the way we live our lives today, just as the mathematics that has been known for several hundred years shapes the mathematics with which we work today. For example, the bombing of Pearl Harbor in 1941 affects the current location of the United States naval fleet, namely, that a majority of the fleet is not kept in the same harbor. Likewise, the fact that infinitely many prime numbers exist affects the modern-day work of cryptographers, who develop coding schemes using prime numbers.

Many similarities occur between mathematics and language arts, but they require some thoughtful consideration to uncover. Spelling, grammar, and mathe-

matics are alike in that they have certain rules that must be memorized and followed. A key difference, however, is that rules in spelling and grammar are frequently broken, whereas rules in mathematics are generally universally applicable. Literature and mathematics are alike because two people may read the same story or poem and come away with entirely different messages. In mathematics, two people may interpret a problem differently and thus may get different answers or may take different approaches to the problem.

• Describe someone in your class or school who you think is mathematically talented.

This discussion needs to be handled with some tact so as not to hurt anyone's feelings. Encourage students not to use the name of an individual but rather to describe characteristics of that person that show evidence of mathematical talent. Many students, particularly elementary school students, will say that mathematically talented people can do mathematics quickly—those who raise their hand first to answer a question, finish a test first, or advance the farthest in the "around the world" flashcard game. This response likely stems from students' belief that mathematics problems should be done quickly. Older students often indicate that mathematically talented people are more logical and analytical and can do things in their heads. This view may explain some students' reluctance to draw diagrams or write down information to solve a problem. In addition to the aforementioned characteristics of mathematically talented people, students invariably mention stereotypical physical or personality characteristics of such people. The next question presents an opportunity to examine these stereotypes.

• Can you think of any television characters who are mathematically talented?

The first answers from students are usually characters who fit the archetypal "nerd" image. Such characters as Steve Urkel from "Family Matters" and Arvid from "Head of the Class" come readily to mind. These characters are equipped with pocket protectors, eyeglasses, briefcases, and white socks, and they are the intellectual giants of the situation comedies on which they appear. With a little bit of prompting, however, students can usually think of another popular, prime-time television character who is mathematically talented but who does not fit the "nerd" stereotype. Dwayne Wayne of "A Different World" is a college student majoring in mathematics who is good-looking, popular, fashionably dressed, and well respected by both his peers and his teachers. Several episodes of the show have dealt directly with mathematics, including episodes where Dwayne tutored students who were struggling with their mathematics classes. Another episode of the show found Dwayne enrolled in a poetry class in which he felt his intellectual talents were being wasted and could be better spent on coursework in his field. Once students begin thinking along these lines, they can think of other characters and nonfictional people who are mathematically talented but who do not fit the negative stereotype.

• Close your eyes and try to picture a mathematician at work. Where is the mathematician? What is the mathematician doing? What objects or instruments is the mathematician using? Open your eyes and draw a picture of what you imagined.

Ask students a variety of questions about the mathematician they imagined. Was their mathematician male or female? How old was their mathematician? What was their mathematician wearing? What did their mathematician look like? In what types of activities was the mathematician engaged? Were other people around?

This activity is used in science education to help students overcome stereotypes about scientists. The results of the activity are quite similar regardless of whether it is done using a scientist or a mathematician. In the instance of the mathematician, students generally picture an older male having gray Einstein-like hair, wearing glasses, and sitting at a desk. He is usually using pencil and paper, books, a calculator or computer, and sometimes a ruler. The mathematician is often in a nondescript room, and no other people are around. These obser-

vations suggest that students view mathematics as a solitary endeavor that is carried out in a place very different from their everyday surroundings. They also apparently view mathematics as a male-dominated discipline.

> *Some problems have more than one answer.*

• Do you suppose McDonald's has a mathematician on its corporate staff? What might that person do for McDonald's?

The initial reaction of most students is that a mathematician is employed to help with inventory and accounting tasks. A common response from elementary school students is that a mathematician is needed to keep track of how many hamburgers have been sold so that the signs on the golden arches that proclaim "*x* billion hamburgers sold" will be accurate! These responses again suggest that students are considering only the computational aspect of mathematics. To stimulate additional thought, the teacher can pose such questions as "How does McDonald's decide where to build a new restaurant?" "How does McDonald's decide on new food products to offer?" and "How are the promotional games created?" These questions open the doors for discussions about data collection, probability, and decisions based on data.

• What businesses in our town might employ a mathematician? What would the mathematician do?

Responses to this question vary depending on the businesses in the town, but students generally have a limited view of the career opportunities for mathematicians. These questions can be used to initiate a discussion of careers in mathematics and careers that use mathematics. Students can interview townspeople who are mathematicians or who use mathematics in their jobs to gather information about various careers. Students can share their findings with the class or the entire school through oral reports, written reports compiled into a class book, pictures, murals, and videotapes or audiotapes. Carpenters, archi-

tects, nurses, engineers, scientists, actuaries, pharmacists, statisticians, and operations researchers are among the people who use a great deal of mathematics in their careers.

CONCLUSION

The preceding questions, individually or collectively, cannot supply teachers with definitive information about each student's beliefs about mathematics. However, such questions and discussions, coupled with observations of students' interactions in mathematical settings, can give teachers valuable information about the beliefs that influence their students' study of mathematics. Students' beliefs about mathematics are manifested in the classroom in whether and how they ask and answer questions, work on problems, and approach new mathematical tasks. The assessment of students' beliefs about mathematics can help teachers plan instruction and structure the classroom environment so as to help students develop more enlightened beliefs about mathematics and mathematics learning (NCTM 1989).

This article is based on one by the same title that appeared in the winter 1992 issue of *Mathematics Educator,* the publication of the Mathematics Educator Student Association at the University of Georgia, an affiliate of NCTM.

REFERENCES

Billstein, Rick, and Johnny W. Lott. "Golden Rectangles and Ratios." *Student Math Notes* (September 1986): 1–4.

Cooney, Thomas J. "A Beginning Teacher's View of Problem Solving." *Journal for Research in Mathematics Education* 16 (November 1985): 324–36.

Frank, Martha L. "Problem Solving and Mathematical Beliefs." *Arithmetic Teacher* 35 (January 1988): 32–34.

———. "What Myths about Mathematics Are Held and Conveyed by Teachers?" *Arithmetic Teacher* 37 (January 1990): 10–12.

Garofalo, Joe. "Beliefs and Their Influence on Mathematical Performance." *Mathematics Teacher* 82 (October 1989a): 502–5.

———. "Beliefs, Responses, and Mathematics Education: Observations from the Back of the Classroom." *School Science and Mathematics* 89 (October 1989b): 451–55.

Millman, Richard S., and Ramona R. Speranza. "The Artist's View of Points and Lines." *Mathematics Teacher* 84 (February 1991): 133–38.

National Council of Teachers of Mathematics. *Curriculum and Evaluation Standards for School Mathematics*. Reston, Va.: The Council, 1989.

Peitgen, Heinz-Otto, Hartmut Jürgens, and Dietmar Saupe. *Fractals for the Classroom, Part One: Introduction to Fractals and Chaos*. New York: Springer-Verlag New York and National Council of Teachers of Mathematics, 1992.

Schoenfeld, Alan H. "What's All the Fuss about Metacognition?" In *Cognitive Science and Mathematics Education*, edit- ed by Alan H. Schoenfeld, pp. 89–215. Hillsdale, N.J.: Lawrence Erlbaum Associates, 1987.

Thompson, Alba Gonzalez. "The Relationship of Teachers' Conceptions of Mathematics and Mathematics Teaching to Instructional Practice." *Educational Studies in Mathematics* 15 (1984): 105–27.

Thompson, Alba G. "Teachers' Conceptions of Mathematics and the Teaching of Problem Solving." In *Teaching and Learning Mathematical Problem Solving: Multiple Research Perspectives*, edited by Edward A. Silver, pp. 281–94. Hillsdale, N.J.: Lawrence Erlbaum Associates, 1985.

———. "Learning to Teach Mathematical Problem Solving: Changes in Teachers' Conceptions and Beliefs." In *The Teaching and Assessing of Mathematical Problem Solving*, edited by Randall I. Charles and Edward A. Silver, pp. 232–43. Hillsdale, N.J.: Lawrence Erlbaum Associates, 1988.

VALUING WHAT WE SEE

Doug Clarke and Linda Wilson

As teachers explore alternative forms of assessment for the classroom, interest increases in all aspects of observational assessment—what to look for, how to look for it, how to document it, and how to use it. This article offers some guidance in each of these areas and some hints from the experiences of teachers who have experimented with observational assessment.

In leading workshops on assessment alternatives for mathematics teachers, we often pose a brief interview activity, which we invite the reader to try, preferably with a second teacher so you can interview each other:

Picture the roster of one of your classes, in alphabetical order. Picture the third student on your list. Now talk about that student, using the following three questions as a structure (adapted from Graue and Smith [1993]):

- Tell me about the mathematical *content* the student knows.
- Tell me about the student's mathematical *processes,* such as reasoning, communicating, problem solving, and making connections.
- Tell me about the student's mathematical *disposition,* such as attitudes, persistence, confidence, and cooperative skills.

As teachers take turns being interviewed about their own student, we find that they have little difficulty in speaking for at least five minutes. Depending on

Doug Clarke teaches at the Australian Catholic University, Oakleigh, Victoria, Australia. His interests include making mathematics enjoyable and relevant and the professional growth of teachers. Linda Wilson teaches at the University of Delaware. She is interested in assessment issues in the mathematics classroom and is assistant project director of the NCTM Assessment Standards.

the choice of student, teachers may have some difficulty discussing the student's knowledge of either content or processes, but few teachers have difficulty with disposition—one aspect that students make very obvious to us.

> When starting the process of documenting classroom observations, "start small."

When we ask teachers to describe how they came to know so much about the student, that is, what sources of data they relied on, the responses tend to fall into three main groups:

1. Written products—tests, quizzes, journals, class work, homework, drawings, posters, assignments, or project work
2. Things that they hear students say—comments during individual, group, or whole-class discussion
3. Things that they see students do

As we discuss the ways in which the "products" of these various forms of assessment are typically used, it becomes clear to teachers that although all three approaches furnish rich assessment information, their mathematics grading and reporting practices draw almost exclusively on the first category, written products. If, as David Clarke (1988) and others claim, "we show students what we value by the ways in which we assess them," then our actions tend to give the message to students that only their written products—particularly tests and assignment work—are of genuine value. Although grading is only one small part of assessment, a recent research study found that "what gets graded is what gets valued" (see Wilson [1994]).

Teachers agree that during class time they observe and hear a great deal that has the potential to inform their teaching. However, insights gained during these times can be quickly lost in the hurly-burly of the classroom if some form of documentation does not occur during the course of instruction. A particular insight may be observed, but within thirty seconds another significant event may occur, and the original insight is lost.

In the remainder of this article we shall discuss several ways in which teachers can use observational assessment to inform students, parents, and themselves. Our hope is that teachers will consider observational assessment a useful alternative that can enhance the arsenal of tools available for assessing what students know about, and can do in, mathematics. As with other alternative forms of assessment, this strategy should not be simply an "add on" to the usual written assessments but should occasionally take the place of these tasks.

WHEN TO DOCUMENT OBSERVATIONS

Though teachers are continually observing students in the classroom, certain activities are more conducive to opportunities for documentation. For example, when students are engaged in small-group work, the teacher has more freedom to circulate about the room. As classrooms become more student-centered and less teacher-centered, teachers will have more freedom to observe.

WHAT TO LOOK FOR

Although the focus of a teacher's observations quite reasonably is influenced by the nature of the mathematical activity in which students are engaged, the three interview questions at the beginning of this article constitute an overall structure.

Mathematical content

The nature of the task or tasks for the day will determine the content, although a balance of concepts, skills, and applications seems appropriate. A periodic check against the NCTM's *Curriculum and Evaluation Standards* (1989) will ensure that important content is being addressed.

Mathematical processes

The first four curriculum and evaluation standards (NCTM 1989) furnish a structure here:

- *Problem solving*—Does the student choose wisely among a variety of strategies? Can the student monitor her own problem-solving process? Can the student pose good problems?

- *Communication*—Can the student communicate mathematics at a high level of quality in written and oral form to the teacher and other students? Does the student reflect on and clarify his thinking about mathematical ideas? Does the student use multiple representations appropriately in a given situation?

- *Reasoning*—Can the student make and test conjectures? Does the student understand the nature and purpose of counterexamples? Can the student construct simple arguments and carefully evaluate the arguments and conjectures of others?

- *Connections*—Does the student see the links among these and similar problems? Does the student demonstrate an understanding of the links among mathematical topics, such as the various forms of rational number? Does the student see the link between a mathematical activity and its real-world application? Does the student see appropriate connections between mathematics and other disciplines?

Mathematical disposition

Disposition has many aspects. What do students think mathematics is? How do they believe mathematics is best learned? What, in fact, does it mean to learn or to understand mathematics? In what circumstances do they particularly appear to enjoy the subject? Do they demonstrate confidence? What kinds of classroom environments do they appear to prefer? How much perseverance do students demonstrate in working on difficult problems?

> *Teachers have been able to identify "invisible students."*

HOW TO OBSERVE AND DOCUMENT

When starting out on the process of documenting classroom observations, "start small." Even three or four brief notes on the first few days is a good start. Remember that the goal is not to record an observation on every student every day. Rather, focus on a small number of students on any given day. Over time, sufficient information should accumulate about all students.

One approach for recording observations is to create a grid with the students' names down one side and the focus aspects across the top. These focus aspects could be mathematical concepts, processes, dispositional factors, or a mix-ture. Teachers can then put a checkmark beside a student's name as a particular insight or behavior is observed (see fig. 1).

Software to assist this approach is currently being developed. Using either a bar-code reader or a personal digital assistant (PDA), teachers can scan a student's name and an observation that they have chosen to look for, along with qualifiers that describe the level of achievement (see fig. 2). The information is stored and can be downloaded to a computer for future retrieval and analysis.

Although it is possible to watch for a predetermined list of things, which are then checked off as they are observed, many teachers have found it at least as useful to view such checklists only as sources of ideas for observations. These teachers have simply written next to students' names comments about any feature of the students' work that they see as noteworthy (see fig. 3, taken from Clarke, Clarke, and Lovitt [1990, p. 121]). The types of comments that are recorded are both general and very specific and both positive and negative: "prefers visual ways of looking at problems"; "confused x- and y-axes"; "listens well to the ideas of others"; "has difficulty transferring ideas from two to three dimensions"; "uses simple cases well in problem solving"; and "shows leadership in group situations."

To save transferring these comments from the class lists to a more permanent record under a given student's name, some teachers have used sticky labels.

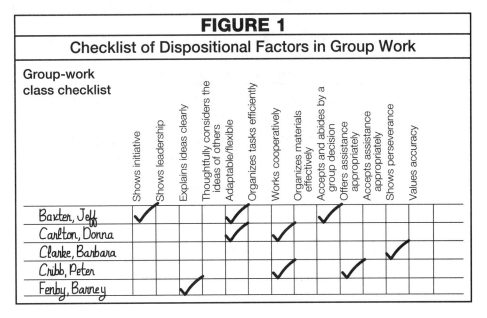

FIGURE 1

Checklist of Dispositional Factors in Group Work

Group-work class checklist	Shows initiative	Shows leadership	Explains ideas clearly	Thoughtfully considers the ideas of others	Adaptable/flexible	Organizes tasks efficiently	Works cooperatively	Organizes materials effectively	Accepts and abides by a group decision	Offers assistance appropriately	Accepts assistance appropriately	Shows perseverance	Values accuracy
Baxter, Jeff	✓				✓				✓				
Carlton, Donna					✓		✓						
Clarke, Barbara												✓	
Cribb, Peter							✓		✓				
Fenby, Barney				✓									

These labels can immediately be attached inside a student's folder.

Teachers' initial reactions are often, "This is all too much for me!" Certainly, some days the classroom is so hectic that the teacher may be spending all the time just ensuring that the purpose and the steps of an activity are clear and may have time for nothing else. However, if writing even a small number of written comments each week is emphasized, then most days some comments on at least one or two students can be recorded. As teachers who have tried this approach successfully have commented, "Even if we only get down five or six comments a week, that's five or six more than we used to do."

HOW TO USE THE INFORMATION

Having gathered all this assessment information—and it does accumulate surprisingly quickly—what should teachers do with it?

Informing teaching

One approach is to look at the comments for a given week or a given topic and consider what further teaching action, with individuals or the whole class, is necessary. Perhaps a misconception is widespread and requires attention. For example, several tenth-grade students have indicated by their comments that they think that two figures with the same perimeter must have the same area. A teacher may wish to note this error and plan further confrontation with this notion through some appropriate exploratory activities. Perhaps a given

> *Notes from observations can add life and substance to descriptive comments written about students.*

student has shown a preference for applying mathematics to sports and can be assigned an extension project. Another student may have shown considerable preference for spatial approaches during problem solving. A teacher can note this preference, with a view to acknowledging and encouraging it in subsequent instruction.

Another consequence of this approach is that teachers have been able to identify "invisible students." After sev-eral weeks of such documentation, teachers might notice that some students have no comments beside their names. The teachers then realize that they have little idea about the progress of these students. This realization might lead to giving greater attention to these students during subsequent observations.

Monitoring students' progress

A further benefit of such documentation is that trends over time emerge for a given student or across a particular content area. A glance back over the notes on one student may clarify the path of that student's progress during the school year. Sharing this information with students can help them become more aware of their own progress. The power of documenting observations lies in the specific details that can be noted and referred to in the future rather than trusted to memory. Memory may say, "A couple of weeks ago Sydney really spoke out in our class discussion," but a quick note might bring back the details: "Sydney pointed out today that the two data sets had nearly the same mean but that the important difference was in the standard deviation. She showed some good insights into the implications of that difference in interpreting the data."

Writing reports and conferring with parents

Teachers who have used documented observations have reported that they find themselves possessing a far wider amount of useful information than in the past, which can inform both their written reports and their conferences with parents. Rather than only draw on test results as a basis for discussing mathematical growth, teachers who observe have a "bigger picture" of a child's mathematical progress, and parents appreciate this more complete view.

Decisions about how to include observational documentation in the grading scheme for a course will depend on the particular policy of a given school or grade level. Such information cannot easily be quantified and "averaged in," but it certainly constitutes evidence on which grading decisions can be based. Teachers who use portfolio assessment may find that these observations offer another dimension of students' growth. Other

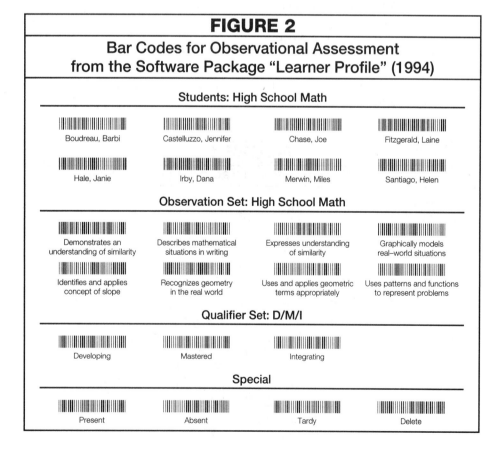

FIGURE 2

Bar Codes for Observational Assessment from the Software Package "Learner Profile" (1994)

Students: High School Math

Boudreau, Barbi Castelluzzo, Jennifer Chase, Joe Fitzgerald, Laine

Hale, Janie Irby, Dana Merwin, Miles Santiago, Helen

Observation Set: High School Math

Demonstrates an understanding of similarity Describes mathematical situations in writing Expresses understanding of similarity Graphically models real–world situations

Identifies and applies concept of slope Recognizes geometry in the real world Uses and applies geometric terms appropriately Uses patterns and functions to represent problems

Qualifier Set: D/M/I

Developing Mastered Integrating

Special

Present Absent Tardy Delete

FIGURE 3
An Example of an Annotated Checklist

Week beginning August 3	Annotated classlist	ACTION	
	COMMENTS (Aberrations and insights)	REQUIRED	TAKEN
Bastow, Barry	No concept of odd and even	✳	
Carlton, Donna	Showed leadership in the group		
Carss, Marjorie			
Clements, Ken			
Caughey, Wendy			
Del Campo, Gina	Thought 63 and 36 the same	✳	✓
Ganderton, Paul	Really tried		
Grace, Neville	Sequencing problems	✳	
Howe, Peter			
Lee, Beth	Spatial thinker		
McDonough, Andrea	Recognised significance of a counter example		
McIntosh, Alistair			
Moule, Jim			
Mulligan, Joanne			
...ner, Kevin			
...er, Fay	M.A.B. needed ...e tens		

From Clarke, Clarke, and Lovitt (1990)

teachers may find this information most useful when writing end-of-term progress reports and when communicating with students and parents. The notes from observations can add life and substance to the descriptive comments that often accompany grades in students' reports.

CONCLUSION

This article has discussed some ways in which observational assessment can enrich teachers' *documented* knowledge of students and subsequently inform their practice. The authors advocate devoting to mathematics assessment not more time but more *quality* time. If fewer tests and quizzes are given and "what comes naturally"—listening to and observing students—is documented, the overall assessment mix is richer and far more informative for students, teachers, parents, and other interested parties.

All teachers spend a large portion of their teaching time observing students as they do mathematics in the classroom. By documenting this evidence of students' learning, teachers place more value on that information and can make more use of it. Students will quickly learn that what they do in class as they discuss, argue, explain, conjecture, and reason aloud about mathematics is valued just as much as what they show through paper and pencil. Capturing such moments and then using such evidence in addition to the traditional means of assessment can lead teachers to make more valid inferences about what students know and can do.

REFERENCES

Clarke, David J. *Assessment Alternatives in Mathematics*. Melbourne, Victoria, Australia: Curriculum Corp., 1988.

Clarke, David J., Doug M. Clarke, and Charles J. Lovitt. "Changes in Mathematics Teaching Call for Assessment Alternatives." In *Teaching and Learning Mathematics in the 1990s*, 1990 Yearbook of the National Council of Teachers of Mathematics, edited by Thomas J. Cooney, pp. 118–29. Reston, Va.: The Council, 1990.

Graue, M. Elizabeth, and Stephanie Z. Smith. "Conceptualizing Assessment from an Instructional Perspective." Paper presented at the annual meeting of the American Educational Research Association, Atlanta, Ga., 1993.

Learner Profile. Pleasantville, N.Y.: Sunburst/Wings for Learning, 1994. Software.

National Council of Teachers of Mathematics. *Curriculum and Evaluation Standards for School Mathematics*. Reston, Va.: The Council, 1989.

Wilson, Linda D. "What Gets Graded Is What Gets Valued." *Mathematics Teacher* 88 (September 1994): 412–14.

SECTION IV

Looking Within—
Evaluating Our
Own Effectiveness

Classroom teachers are being asked to try many new and different forms of teaching and assessment. How can we judge the effectiveness of these efforts? The articles in this final section suggest some first steps for teachers interested in answering this question through self-assessment.

James Schwartz's "How Can We Evaluate Ourselves?" begins by pointing up the important distinction between teacher assessment for evaluative or accountability purposes and teacher assessment undertaken to improve instruction. He then proceeds to focus attention on the latter. Schwartz proposes four components that teachers might consider as they self-assess their efforts to teach according to the vision of the *Standards*: (1) attention to how students behave, (2) consideration of the extent to which the teacher emphasizes procedural understanding compared with conceptual understanding, (3) identification of the teaching model with which the teacher identifies most closely, and (4) indications of the teacher's depth of content knowledge. Schwartz stops short of furnishing definitive answers about teacher self-assessment, but his article raises important questions for consideration.

Miriam Leiva argues that teachers need to "take charge and become central to the evaluation process" by engaging in planning, instruction, reflection, documentation, and professional development as described in the *Professional Standards for Teaching Mathematics*. Her article, "Empowering Teachers through the Evaluation Process," provides guidance for putting together a teaching portfolio to document professional growth. It includes suggestions for documenting teaching outcomes through careful selection of student work, teacher commentary, teacher-written reflection, and video clips. Leiva also suggests indicators of good practice that classroom observers can look for and discuss during preobservation and postobservation dialogues with the teacher being observed. The entire evaluation process is seen as a collaborative effort among professionals who desire to "reflect, analyze, evolve, mature, and learn."

"The Teacher and Evaluation," by Roberta Koss and Rick Marks, similarly describes a vision of teacher evaluation where teachers work collaboratively to support each other in improving their practice. In this vision, "changes in the evaluation of teaching should mirror those in the assessment of student learning," and "authentic assessment is just as valid for teachers as for students."

Another way that teachers can become involved in self-assessment is by taking on the very powerful role of teacher-as-researcher. Building on experiences gained through work in several projects designed to help teachers reconsider how they teach and assess, Jean Moon discusses in her article entitled "Connecting Learning and Teaching through Assessment" the benefits that accrue when teachers become researchers of their own practice. The teachers involved in Moon's projects explored the teacher-as-researcher role through guided observations of their own teaching, critiques of videotaped classroom lessons from other school settings, and extensive collaborative and reflective discussions.

Finally, Vicky Kouba describes three methods she has found useful in helping novice teachers evaluate their own practice. She describes how constructing a concept map of the mathematical knowledge and connections a teacher has in mind for a lesson helps both to increase the teacher's understanding of the content and to draw attention to misconceptions or gaps in understanding. Another method for helping teachers become better self-evaluators is the analysis of videotapes and case studies. Self-analysis and reflection become much easier when one has first prepared for them by analyzing and reflecting on the teaching of others. Finally, Kouba suggests the use of a cooperative team approach to postobservation analyses, where the teacher who was observed is encouraged to take the lead in identifying strengths and weaknesses in the lesson.

HOW CAN WE EVALUATE OURSELVES?

James E. Schwartz

Teachers in Rochester, New York, recently rejected a proposed contract under which they could have received a generous bonus in any year in which they received an exemplary evaluation. Why did they turn down this proposal? Although probably many different personal reasons could be cited for negative votes, the issue that received the most attention in the press was the issue of the evaluation process. Teachers were concerned that the process was too vague and undefined. They wanted to know the criteria by which they would be evaluated. They wanted to know who would be involved in the evaluation process.

In 1989 the NCTM published the *Curriculum and Evaluation Standards for School Mathematics* in its most recent effort to effect reform of the teaching of school mathematics. To what extent are teachers adopting these standards? Is the teaching of school mathematics being changed and improved because of this document?

The dual mandates of teachers' accountability and improvement of instruction are the two most important reasons for concern about the evaluation of teachers. Any discussion of the topic of teacher evaluation should keep the distinction clear. Any teacher-evaluation instrument should be designed with one or the other of these perspectives as its priority. An instrument designed to improve instruction may or may not prove to be helpful in teacher accountability. A teacher-accountability instrument may or

James Schwartz teaches at the State University of New York at Buffalo, Buffalo, NY 14260. He is currently completing his doctoral research on the relation between teachers' mathematical understanding and their ability to teach mathematics constructively.

may not help to improve instruction. This article is devoted to teacher evaluation designed to improve instruction.

THE QUESTION OF WHAT MAKES GOOD TEACHING

Virtually all attempts at teacher evaluation must begin with the question of what constitutes good teaching. Joyce and Weil (1980) paint a picture of a pluralistic educational world in which many different models of teaching are good. Ball and McDiarmid (1988) have developed a study that recognizes that people subscribe to various models of teaching. Ball and McDiarmid's evaluation instruments are unusual in that they attempt to minimize a bias toward one particular model. Most evaluation instruments are not so ambitious. Typical instruments reflect the view of their designers about the things that constitute good teaching.

> How do you rate an unexpected mathematical discussion?

An example may illustrate the importance of this point. A teacher attempting to implement the *Curriculum and Evaluation Standards* (NCTM 1989) may choose to engage the class in a lively debate about some mathematical conjecture made by a student. The teacher's role would be to draw out the students' thinking, keep discussion more or less confined to the topic at hand, pose important questions, and generally moderate the debate. This entire debate may arise quite unexpectedly as the students are engaged in a mathematical game or activity. The *Standards* document would encourage this sort of spontaneous exploration.

However, if this lesson were being rated by an observer using one of a number of direct-instruction-observation scales, the evaluation might be unfavorable. Possibly no review or anticipatory set would have been used for the topic under debate. No seatwork or homework may have been assigned for the topic under debate. No purpose for the activity may have been stated at the beginning of the lesson. In fact, the entire debate might be judged to be off the topic of the planned lesson. This illustration demonstrates the fact that the criteria by which we judge teaching are extremely important.

DIFFICULTIES OF EDUCATIVE TEACHER EVALUATION

Carver (1974) envisioned a difference between psychometric and edumetric testing. His view was that standardized tests tended to serve the purposes of statisticians better than they served the purposes of educators. He proposed using tests in a manner that would be instructive rather than merely evaluative. In a similar spirit, Gitlin and Smyth (1990) have recently called for educative teacher evaluation. The concept of educative teacher evaluation is consistent with NCTM's *Professional Standards for Teaching Mathematics* (NCTM 1991) . These professional standards emphasize the roles of self-evaluation and peer evaluation as necessary components in the improvement of mathematics teaching. Among the problems associated with traditional teacher evaluation is the problem of authority-imposed, or hierarchy-imposed, evaluation. Such evaluation tends to be ineffective because of such elements as fear and resentment experienced by the teacher in the evaluation process.

Other problems with traditional forms of evaluation, as identified by Gitlin and Smyth, are that they separate knowing from doing, they disregard the history and context of the teaching act, they consist of a monologue instead of a dialogue, and they foster individualism and competition. If teacher evaluation is to be made truly educative, ways will need to be found to overcome at least some of these problems.

TIME TO DREAM

What would educative teacher evaluation look like? How would it address the problems of traditional forms of teacher evaluation?

First, a way of overcoming the threatening nature of evaluation must be devised. Self-evaluation may be the answer here. As each of us looks in the mirror each morning, we observe things about ourselves about which we would certainly be offended if they were noted by someone else. Although self-evaluation is a relatively new and unproved method, it should be taken seriously as a possible avenue for teacher evaluation. Let us visualize all the following ideas in the context of self-evaluation.

A self-evaluation instrument could overcome the problem of an authoritative, or hierarchical, evaluation. No hierarchy is involved when a teacher privately evaluates her or his own teaching. The nature of the instrument would need to be collegial and supportive rather than authoritarian, but these qualities could easily be embodied. Because of the elimination of threat, an environment would more likely develop in which dialogue would occur.

The logical follow-up for an individual's self-evaluation would be peer dialogue leading to peer evaluation. As with students, true intellectual growth of teachers occurs as a result of perplexity, cognitive dissonance, and cognitive conflict. Meaningful discussion with teaching colleagues can be an ideal source of the sorts of challenges that lead to growth. Since for many teachers the change from a transmission philosophy of teaching to a constructivist view of learning will be profound, peer dialogue and peer evaluation will be necessary parts of the assessment and growth processes.

In the initial stages of this change in teaching philosophy, teachers will need their peers to supply ideas and arguments that seem to run completely counter to previously held attitudes and beliefs. One constructivist teacher can have an almost subversive effect among transmission and behaviorist teachers. Through the sharing of these different beliefs and the justification of beliefs that accompanies the sharing, teachers are led to change their beliefs.

In later stages of change, when like-minded teaching peers discuss and reflect on their teaching, the nature of the peer evaluations can be expected to change. In place of debate and justification of positions, the dialogue at this stage would more closely resemble a brainstorming session. Here one person's ideas would be expected to stimulate and provoke a series of ideas from the other participants. In the light of these new perspectives, each of the participants would be likely to perceive and acknowledge the points at which their former ideas, methods, and attitudes fell short of the goals. Through peer evaluation, informed by prior self-evaluation, the monologue of traditional means of evaluation can be replaced by dialogue.

The problem of a separation of knowing and doing is more difficult to resolve. Certainly a teacher's knowledge must be evaluated. Evidence can be cited that teachers' understanding of mathematics needs more depth (Bamberger and Duckworth 1982, Ball 1990, Tirosh and Graeber 1990). Shulman (1986) has emphasized the role of knowledge in developing excellence in teaching. Unfortunately, even in self-evaluation a need for better understanding of content and pedagogy may be too painful for teachers to face. This problem will probably be with us for some time to come.

For the most part, however, self-evaluation combined with peer evaluation offers more promise of being educative than do traditional methods. If teachers engage regularly in structured self-evaluation and peer evaluation, if they work together to develop a dialogue about their results, and if they can demonstrate that their teaching is improving as a result of this approach, then perhaps this form of evaluation can be used to replace the tra-

ditional methods. At the very least, this form should be able to supplement the traditional forms.

WHAT AND HOW DO WE SELF-EVALUATE?

I envision a mathematics-teaching evaluation instrument that includes four components: a classroom student-behavior checklist, a procedural-conceptual-discrimination component, a projective-teaching-model-identification component, and an assessment of content understanding.

Scoring and interpreting this instrument would involve examination of correlations between the various components of the instrument. Because of the complexity involved in scoring, it would probably be desirable to use an interactive computer program to present this instrument.

Debate and research into teacher evaluation have focused on the question of whether to evaluate teaching behaviors or students' performance as measured on achievement tests. Difficulties arise in both approaches. I suggest that we can learn much about a teacher by examining the classroom behaviors of the students. Students who regularly engage in pencil-and-paper seatwork are under the influence of a certain kind of teacher; conversely, students who regularly participate in mathematics games, mathematics writing, and mathematics discussion are under the influence of a very different kind of teacher. The differences in students' behavioral patterns result from different teaching philosophies and methods.

Immediately following a lesson, the teacher could identify from a checklist those behaviors the students engaged in most frequently during the lesson. The behaviors on the checklist would be representative of behaviors that could be expected in a variety of different teaching models. The scoring of this component would involve looking for consistency in the selection of students' behaviors. If a clear pattern of behaviors was selected, the instrument would give the teacher information about the teaching model indicated by the students' behaviors. If no consistent pattern occurred, the teacher would be informed that the results were inconclusive, indicating either an inconsistent teacher or an eclectic teacher. The teacher would have to decide which condition was true.

The procedural-conceptual-discrimination component of the evaluation instrument is needed because teachers differ in the emphasis they place on these aspects of mathematics. Most teachers would find illuminating the ability to identify which of these aspects they tend to emphasize. The format of this component could be patterned after one of Ball's (1988) interview questions. She asked teachers to respond to the following student's error in multiplication by telling how they would go about correcting it.

Student's work:
$$
\begin{array}{r}
123 \\
\times 456 \\
\hline
615 \\
492 \\
738 \\
\hline
1845
\end{array}
$$

Ball's work indicated that such an approach can yield important information about whether a teacher is concept driven or procedure driven.

The third component of the self-evaluation instrument would employ a projective technique to help a teacher assess self-regard, that is, what sort of teacher is she or he? This component would present the teacher with carefully designed descriptions of typical classroom situations that demand a teacher's decision. By indicating a response to the situation, the teacher would be furnishing information about her or his thinking and philosophy. Scoring and interpreting this component would be similar to scoring and interpreting the student-behavior checklist. In addition, the composite picture obtained by this component would be correlated with the picture obtained in the first component, and a report about the teacher's consistency would be obtained.

The final section of this instrument would be designed to inform the teacher about her or his depth of understanding of content. Because of vast differences in the content to be taught, this component would need to be different for elementary school teachers and secondary school teachers. An example of the importance of deep content understanding will high-

light the need for this section of the instrument.

One of the goals emphasized by the NCTM's *Curriculum and Evaluation Standards* (1989) is the development of better estimation and mental mathematics. Most teachers today received their education before these areas were strongly emphasized. As a result, we tend to place less confidence in our mental estimates than we do in our pencil-and-paper work. As we exercise our mental-mathematics and estimation skills, we gain a deeper understanding of mathematics.

Questions in this section could be of the type in figure 1. Only one of the answer choices is above 9. Estimation (6 + 3) would indicate that the answer must be above 9, but most teachers use scrap paper and the addition-of-unlike-fractions algorithm to answer the question. Questions such as this one, along with a response about which items required scrap paper to solve, will yield information about the teacher's mathematical sophistication.

FIGURE 1
An Item Assessing Use of Mental Mathematics

$$6\frac{1}{3}$$
$$+2\frac{5}{6}$$

a) $8\frac{1}{6}$ b) $8\frac{1}{2}$
c) $8\frac{6}{9}$ d) $9\frac{1}{6}$

Another type of question for this part of the instrument is again proposed by Ball (1990). Teachers were asked to generate representations of problems involving such topics as division of fractions, division by zero, and basic algebraic expressions. These seemingly simple tasks have a great deal of power to discriminate between a shallow and a deep understanding of elementary mathematics in the mind of the teacher.

Scoring and interpreting this component of the instrument would not need to be personalized. The answer key would supply correct answers, as well as suggestions for how to deepen a shallow understanding of mathematics.

Overall scoring and interpretation of the instrument could be in the form of a

personalized report. This format would be realistically possible only if the instrument was presented by computer. The report would include such information as the teaching model indicated by the responses, degree of consistency, depth of content knowledge, and research-based recommendations for self-improvement based on the results.

> ## Student's activities reflect teachers' values.

PIE IN THE SKY?

The vision presented here is admittedly a dream at this point. Could such an instrument be devised? Would it work? Would it aid in bringing about needed reform? These questions should be debated and researched.

REFERENCES

Ball, Deborah. "Knowledge and Reasoning in Mathematical Pedagogy: Examining What Prospective Teachers Bring to Teacher Education. Vols. 1 and 2." *Dissertation Abstracts International* 50 (1988): 416A. University Microfilms no. 8900008.

———. "Prospective Elementary and Secondary Teachers' Understanding of Division." *Journal for Research in Mathematics Education* 21 (March 1990): 132–44.

Ball, Deborah, and Bill McDiarmid. "Research on Teacher Learning: Studying How Teachers' Knowledge Changes." *Action in Teacher Education* 10 (Summer 1988): 17–23.

Bamberger, Jeanne, and Eleanor Duckworth. *Analysis of Data from an Experiment in Teacher Development.* Washington, D.C.: National Institute of Education, 1982. Grant no. G-81-0042.

Carver, Ronald. "Two Dimensions of Tests." *American Psychologist* 29 (July 1974): 512–18.

Gitlin, A., and J. Smyth. "Toward Educative Forms of Teacher Evaluation." *Educational Theory* 40 (Winter 1990): 83–94.

Joyce, B., and M. Weil. *Models of Teaching.* 2d ed. Englewood Cliffs, N.J.: Prentice Hall, 1980.

National Council of Teachers of Mathematics. *Curriculum and Evaluation Standards for School Mathematics.* Reston, Va.: The Council, 1989.

———. *Professional Standards for Teaching Mathematics.* Reston, Va.: The Council, 1991.

Shulman, Lee. "Those Who Understand: Knowledge Growth in Teaching." *Educational Researcher* 15 (1986): 4–14.

Tirosh, Dina, and Anna O. Graeber. "Evoking Cognitive Conflict to Explore Preservice Teachers' Thinking about Division." *Journal for Research in Mathematics Education* 21 (March 1990): 98–108.

EMPOWERING TEACHERS THROUGH THE EVALUATION PROCESS

Miriam A. Leiva

Mr. Hille had been student teaching for three weeks when I made an announced observation in his second-year-algebra class. His lesson on ellipses had been carefully planned, and he was ready with models, string, calculators, overhead transparencies, and a lesson plan. Somewhere at the beginning of his enthusiastic presentation, he slipped from equations of ellipses to hyperbolas, while naming and graphing them as ellipses! Suddenly he realized what he was doing and looked at me in horror, but he went on for a few more minutes, "keeping his cool" as he would explain later. He asked questions and assigned a few problems from a previous section. The period ended. To an observer with little or no mathematics background, Mr. Hille's lesson appeared to be excellent.

Most teachers—novice and veteran—are uncomfortable with evaluations based on classroom observations, in particular those observations mandated for accountability purposes. *Teacher evaluation* conjures up images of limited classroom observations using a check sheet of items related to technicalities rather than substance. Although technicalities are very important for effective teaching and classroom management, they are only a small part of what must be evaluated to

Miriam Leiva is the Bonnie Cone Distinguished Professor for Teaching and a mathematics professor at the University of North Carolina at Charlotte, Charlotte, NC 28223, where she teaches mathematics and mathematics education. Her areas of interest include mathematics teacher education and improving university mathematics instruction.

paint a portrait of a mathematics teacher as an instructor and a professional. Mr. Hille may have exhibited some appropriate teacher behaviors, but the mathematics and the lesson were flawed. Classroom observations in isolation may give insight into some aspects of teaching but may be deceiving if based on out-of-context episodes or glitzy activities planned for the observer. Teachers also have "bad" days that can occur when observers visit!

> *Teachers must assume ownership of the evaluation process.*

Thus, it is imperative that teachers take charge and become central to the evaluation process. Just as our practices are changing with respect to the evaluation of students, the practices and uses of the evaluation of teaching mathematics must also change.

THE *PROFESSIONAL TEACHING STANDARDS* AND TEACHER EVALUATION

NCTM's vision for the evaluation of mathematics teaching is developed through eight standards in the *Professional Standards for Teaching Mathematics* (NCTM 1991). Key to these guidelines is the assumption that the primary purposes of teacher evaluation are to improve teaching and to guide individual professional development. Teacher self-evaluation and the analysis of teaching are central to improving mathematics teaching

within the framework of the *Standards* document.

The evaluation of teaching envisioned by NCTM is a multidimensional, ongoing process that engages teachers in planning, instruction, and reflection and in collecting evidence to document all the elements of their teaching. It supports involving colleagues and promotes professional discussions based on the episodes and artifacts that document teaching. Supervisors and administrators participate in the process to inform, suggest, support, and guide. Their interpretation of classroom observations and their assessment of the documentation—teacher portfolios—furnished by teachers is guided by the *Curriculum and Evaluation Standards for School Mathematics* (1989) and the *Professional Standards for Teaching Mathematics* (1991). The involvement of colleagues, supervisors, and administrators establishes the process as a catalyst for individual reflection, collegial dialogues, and collaborative efforts to enhance the teacher and the teaching. Through a comprehensive, mutually developed evaluation plan, teachers are empowered to take charge of their own assessment and, in concert with their evaluators, make decisions about instruction and professional development.

DOCUMENTATION

The selection of items in a portfolio documents the teacher's philosophies and beliefs, gives a glimpse into her or his mathematical knowledge, and indicates what she or he values and considers acceptable practice. The portfolio, together with classroom observations, should offer evidence of the teacher's—

- actions that promote student confidence and participation;
- sensitivity to students' needs; and
- love for students, teaching, and mathematics.

Because teachers grow continuously as professionals, evidence of their competence should be thought of as *evolving*— a draft in the formative stage, with many opportunities for revisions. Such documentation could be organized into the three professional components of teaching (Shulman 1994):

- Plan and design—what, why, and how
- Enactment of teaching—doing it
- Outcomes of planning and teaching—what happened

Planning for teaching includes designing and developing individual lessons and all supporting course and program elements in the context of the mathematics curriculum and pedagogy. It demonstrates the teachers' knowledge of content and pedagogy, their sense of what mathematics is important for students to learn, and their proposed teaching method. Planning is documented through many sources:

- Course lesson plans or outlines that reflect the mathematics to be taught, both concepts and procedures
- Course goals and the teacher's expectations in terms of students' goals
- Selected, annotated lesson plans that indicate the use of technology and other teaching resources in the context of a course
- Key students' assignments including projects, papers, investigations, and problem sets that are indicative of what the teacher expects and values

In all such plans and assignments, the mathematics teacher must consider from where the students are coming and where they are going. Previous knowledge, learning modes, cultural backgrounds, and confidence all play a significant role as teachers prepare to teach mathematics and open doors to all students.

The enactment of teaching is usually evaluated through classroom observations or videotapes. As with the other elements of evaluation, information from many sources enters into the evaluation of classroom teaching. Observations by a mathematics colleague or supervisor should focus more on the teaching of mathematics than on the technicalities that can be evaluated by a generalist observer.

In the case of Mr. Hille, the planning and technical aspects of the lesson were appropriate, but the teaching observed showed a novice teacher not secure in his teaching or in the mathematical content and connections within the topic. He concluded, on his own, that his reaction to his mix-up was inappropriate, and postobservation discussion focused on how he could handle such a situation in the future. His decision to return to a previous section for discussion and assignments was cautiously supported on the basis of his limited experience and teaching repertoire.

Dialogues between observer and teacher must take place.

It is often difficult to judge a teacher's knowledge of mathematics through classroom observation. However, certain indicators give insights into the mathematical depth of a teacher. Are connections within mathematics being made? Is the mathematics presented from multiple perspectives? Are the activities suitable for developing the concepts or skills? Are the tools of instruction appropriate? Do the questions get at an understanding of the concept or the why of a procedure? Do they guide understanding, student participation, and learning? Does the development of the lesson pave the way for future work? Is it based on the previous work and curriculum? Is the treatment of a topic reasonable given the areas of emphasis in mathematics?

Dialogues between observer and teacher must take place before and after observations. If the teacher places the lesson in the context of the mathematics course and supplies an outline to guide the observation, the observer will have a more informed view of the class.

Reactions, suggestions, and perceptions about the teacher and the teaching are shared and analyzed. A written evaluation of the classroom observation should be developed jointly or include remarks from both teacher and observer. All documents pertaining to the observation become part of the portfolio.

Videotapes also offer windows into classrooms and should be reviewed and evaluated jointly. This medium furnishes a powerful tool for self-evaluation. Videotapes may also become part of the teacher's portfolio. Teachers should select clips and episodes that not only show elements of effective teaching but also demonstrate mathematical content and pedagogical knowledge. As with all the components in the portfolio, teachers must select and organize the evidence to give the most comprehensive and accurate picture of themselves and their teaching.

Teaching outcomes are documented through many sources:

- Graded students' work, including tests, that demonstrates the level of mathematical depth, an understanding of concepts, and proficiency with procedures
- Students' journals and other writings that reveal students' confidence in, and beliefs about, mathematics
- Teacher's comments on students' papers, tests, and journals
- Teacher's written reflection on what was accomplished in a given course or unit and what changes would be made when the same unit is taught again

Figure 1 shows a student's response to an assignment in an algebra class. The students were asked to create patterns and to describe them algebraically, geometrically, and verbally. Amy's paper is indicative of mathematics teaching that makes connections within the discipline; revisits mathematics learned in a previous level and justifies it using newly acquired knowledge; and expects students to communicate mathematics symbolically, pictorially, and verbally. The richness of the activity and the response suggests that important mathematical content, procedures, and connections are taught and learned in this class. Any

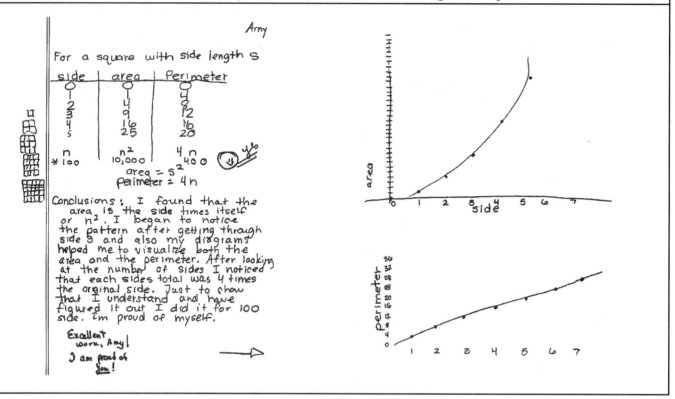

FIGURE 1
Amy's answer to the following problem from a first-year algebra class:
Create a pattern; describe it numerically and algebraically.
Connect the algebraic representation with geometry.

mathematics teacher would be proud of Amy's mathematical knowledge and the confidence that she demonstrated as she wrote "I am proud of myself."

PROFESSIONAL DEVELOPMENT AND EVALUATION

When teachers participate in the evaluation process together with administrators and mathematics colleagues, the end results must be specific recommendations for improvement, plans for ongoing teacher support, and realistic goals for continued growth. Professional support could take many forms: staff development, course work, attendance at professional meetings, and resource materials for the teacher and classroom. Even the most experienced and excellent teachers benefit from documenting the changes in their practices and professional growth. This visionary model assumes that teachers and administrators share equal responsibility for the evaluation process, the professional-development plan, and the resulting improvement in instruction.

SUMMARY

As teachers, we must assume ownership of the process of evaluating teaching and recognize its value in our professional growth. Enlisting the support of other mathematics teachers to collaborate in the evaluation process ensures that special attention will be paid to the mathematics content and the mathematics pedagogical knowledge exhibit-

> *Even excellent teachers benefit from documenting change.*

ed in the teaching and in the teaching artifacts in the portfolio. As we continue our efforts to improve our teaching and make changes in mathematics teaching and the assessment of students, we must recognize teacher evaluation as our professional domain and our tool to help us reflect, analyze, evolve, mature, and learn.

BIBLIOGRAPHY

Borko, Hilda, Margaret Eisenhart, Catherine A. Brown, Robert G. Underhill, Doug Jones, and Patricia C. Agard. "Learning to Teach Hard Mathematics: Do Novice Teachers and Their Instructors Give Up Too Easily?" *Journal for Research in Mathematics Education* 23 (May 1992): 194–222.

National Council of Teachers of Mathematics. *Curriculum and Evaluation Standards for School Mathematics.* Reston, Va.: The Council, 1989.

———. *Professional Standards for Teaching Mathematics.* Reston, Va.: The Council, 1991.

———. *Assessment Standards for School Mathematics.* Reston, Va.: The Council, 1995.

Noddings, Nel. "Professionalization and Mathematics Teaching." In *Handbook of Research on Mathematics Teaching and Learning,* edited by Douglas A. Grouws, pp. 197–208. New York: Macmillan, and Reston, Va.: National Council of Teachers of Mathematics, 1992.

Shulman, Lee. "On the Evaluation of Teaching." Keynote address at the American Association of Higher Education, Peer Review of Teaching Conference, June 1994.

THE TEACHER AND EVALUATION

Roberta Koss and Rick Marks

Evaluation of teaching is usually something done *to* a teacher. In contrast, the *Professional Standards for Teaching Mathematics* (NCTM 1991) supports evaluation of teaching done *by* and *for* a teacher. That is, the teacher participates actively in designing and carrying out any evaluation, and the process contributes substantially to the teacher's professional growth. This vision dramatically changes the roles and responsibilities of the teacher as well as others involved in evaluating teaching. To begin moving effectively in this direction, both teachers and supervisors need to understand the rationale for change and to see how this change could occur.

A recent evaluation incident illustrates the need for change. Ms. Jay received a reminder to set several instructional goals that could be observed and evaluated by the new assistant principal at her school. The assistant principal later visited one of Ms. Jay's geometry classes. The written evaluation report included a recommendation that she begin classes with a warm-up problem because students were observed to be talking in their groups for the first few minutes of the class. Ms. Jay met with the administrator to explain that she *expected* students to talk in groups, discussing questions from the previous night's assignment. For further clarifica-

tion, she gave the administrator a copy of the sections on students' and teachers' roles in discourse from the professional teaching standards.

RATIONALE FOR CHANGE

Before we can make sense of *how* to evaluate teaching, we should understand *why* it is needed. The professional teaching standards give a clear and simple reason: the purpose of evaluating teaching is to improve instruction. Evaluation should function primarily as a stimulus and a guide for the teacher to continue learning and growing in ways that will enhance students' learning of mathematics. This purpose contrasts sharply with evaluation that emphasizes judgments about a teacher's competence based on compliance with detailed, preset criteria at a single point in time.

> *Evaluation should stimulate and guide teachers' continued learning and growth.*

If the intent of evaluation is to improve teaching, then the process must generate enough data—including time exposures, not just snapshots—to compose an accurate picture of some significant aspects of teaching. These data need to be interpreted in light of goals, options, and constraints in a given situation. The results should commend desirable teaching practices, yield substantive and mutually agreeable plans for improvement, and support any follow-up action. This process ought to be ongoing, though the focus on what to evaluate will change over time.

Changes in the evaluation of teaching should mirror those in the assessment of

students' learning. Many mathematics teachers are expanding their assessment of students' work to include writing, miscellaneous projects, oral presentations, small-group work, portfolios, and other nontraditional forms of assessment. They are gathering performance data over time to increase validity and acknowledge growth. They are using these data more to enhance students' learning—that is, as a pump—than to label and filter students. The parallel is clear: authentic assessment is just as valid for teachers as for students.

Focusing on evaluation to further professional growth and improve instruction may help teachers work with change more easily. This form of evaluation corresponds to the teacher's own personal goals and those of students. The teacher is a more active participant and has a greater measure of control over the process. If the evaluation pinpoints not the *teacher* but the *teaching*, it is less threatening and promotes possibilities for change. As evaluation becomes better aligned with other aspects of teachers' professional work, it should become more natural, useful, and even empowering.

CURRENT PRACTICE

The evaluation of teaching varies somewhat from one school to another, but the process in one California district seems to be more or less typical. California schools operate under collective bargaining, and the agreement specifies that the teachers control the conditions of the evaluation. When collective bargaining first began over ten years ago, the elected bargaining agent in one district insisted that only administrators conduct evaluations so as not to place teachers in the position of formally eval-

Roberta Koss teaches at Redwood High School, Larkspur, CA 94939. She is a member of the NCTM Board of Directors and was a member of the Working Group of the Commission on the Professional Standards for Teaching Mathematics. Rick Marks is an associate professor at Sonoma State University, Rohnert Park, CA 94928. He teaches in both the mathematics and education departments and supervises both elementary and secondary preservice teachers.

uating their colleagues. Every two years each teacher must define several goals relating to curriculum, learning environment, pedagogy, student progress, and participation in school and professional activities. The teacher discusses these goals with an administrator, who then makes an appointment to visit one class. Sometime after the visit, the administrator interviews the class without the teacher. Finally, the administrator records the visit and supplies written commendations and recommendations.

This clause in the district's contract has not changed, but the elected post of bargaining agent does change. In more than thirty years of teaching, one veteran teacher's evaluation reports have ranged from the ridiculous—"Ms. Kay dresses in a professional manner"—to the sublime—"Ms. Kay needs to make certain that every student is engaged for every minute during the class." These evaluation sessions generally fail to improve her teaching; they result only in interrupted instruction and additional paperwork.

The evaluation process described earlier does not meet the spirit of the professional teaching standards. The teachers in this district agree that this matter needs attention. In a recent survey, the faculty cited the evaluation of teaching as its top priority for districtwide reform.

IMPLEMENTING THE PROFESSIONAL TEACHING STANDARDS

Fortunately, changing evaluation in this particular district has begun. Several teachers learned years ago that working with colleagues was a better way to improve their own teaching. Two "next-door neighbors" at one school developed a special, collegial relationship. They both attended National Science Foundation–sponsored summer institutes in transformation geometry, then jointly created a curriculum for tenth graders. That fall they each taught one section of the new course in a shared classroom, since one of the pair was on a part-time teaching schedule. They often prepared for class by observing and analyzing the other's teaching, and they found time each day to discuss their experiences and to modify future lessons accordingly.

Both teachers believed that this daily interaction helped them to improve the curriculum and their work with students not only in that course but in subsequent teaching.

> *Authentic assessment is just as valid for teachers as for students.*

Although these two teachers no longer share a room, their collaboration continues. Lately they have integrated technology and authentic assessment into their courses and have found time to discuss concerns and successes. Their discussions are honest and explicit because over time they have built a relationship of mutual respect, affection, and confidence in each other's ability and skill. Currently they are grappling with using technology in the curriculum, discussing such issues as to whether they should eliminate the in-depth study of rational expressions in favor of recursive relations. Both teachers gain valuable insights from their collaboration, and their students benefit from improved teaching.

Opportunities for collaborative evaluation and growth can arise in varied settings. For instance, the California Mathematics Council—Northern Section recently held a leadership conference focusing on the *Professional Standards for Teaching Mathematics* (NCTM 1991). One of the authors had been invited to lead the participants in a sample lesson, and she chose a lesson from her geometry class on exploring line reflections and symmetries using Miras. Just before the lesson, both authors decided to work together to model some of the evaluation and professional development standards through a postinstructional interview. A real evaluation setting, of course, would include a prelesson conference as well. While one led the activity, the other wrote the following set of questions:

- What were your goals for this lesson?
- What mathematics was in this set of tasks?
- Why did you choose these particular tasks? How were they related to these "students"? To your goals?

Did you consider other tasks? If so, what?

- How did you structure this activity? How did you think about the balance between your input and the students' construction of their own ideas?
- What kinds of things did you hear the students saying in their discussions? What difficulties did they encounter? How did you respond? Why?
- What other materials might have worked to teach this topic? What are the relative advantages and disadvantages of the various materials?
- What surprised you in this lesson? What do you think about this situation now?
- How did you get the students to consolidate their learning? How successful was this lesson? How do you know? What ideas *didn't* come out?
- Did the students enjoy this activity? How do you know?
- How might you follow up or extend this lesson with these students? Why?
- If you were to reteach this same lesson to a similar group of students, how might you modify it? Why? How might you teach it differently to high school students? Why?

After the lesson, the evaluator interviewed the teacher for forty-five minutes as conference participants listened. The interview served several purposes. In writing the questions, the evaluator was forced to think about the most important aspects of the lesson being observed and of the teacher's thinking that lay behind them. In responding to the questions, the teacher was forced to elaborate on the many planning decisions that had helped shape the lesson and to reveal and clarify the spur-of-the-moment changes made during the lesson. The observers benefited in two ways. First, they heard the teacher reflect on the many ideas and considerations that were implicitly part of this particular lesson and they were encouraged to think more deeply about mathematics and mathematical pedagogy. Second, they saw a model of evaluation that acknowledged and even capitalized on the rich complexity inherent in teaching, that recognized the importance of the teacher's thinking and decision making, and that encouraged reflection as a way to grow individually and improve instruction.

Many teachers regularly engage in peer evaluation, discussion, and reflection on their teaching, and many more might do so if such practices were part of the culture of teaching. One of the missing pieces is an assessment system that values these activities and supports teachers in this kind of professional growth and instructional improvement. Several models for structuring collaborative evaluation are described in the October 1993 issue of *Educational Leadership*. Two articles describe how such models can be implemented despite constraining contracts between teachers and district officials — either by renegotiating evaluation procedures (Black 1993) or by working carefully within the established system "to bend without breaking" it (Rooney 1993, p. 43).

A CONSTRUCTIVIST VIEW

Reforming evaluation needs to be part of a larger reform effort in mathematics education. This effort, grounded in a constructivist view of learning, fosters growth in each student's mathematical thinking through active exploration, communication of ideas, and reflection over an extended period. To achieve this goal, a teacher may acknowledge various learning styles, present worthwhile tasks and time to explore mathematical ideas, emphasize making sense of the mathe-

matics, encourage each student to express his or her own thinking and share it with peers, and use the teacher's knowledge of students to design instruction that will lead them toward greater understanding. The teacher accepts that mathematics is complex and often difficult and that students' learning is a continuous process that takes time as well as effort to develop. Teaching mathematics is complex and difficult.

> *The evaluation model capitalized on the rich complexity inherent in teaching.*

If constructivist principles apply to students' learning, then they surely apply to teachers' professional development. A teacher will likely grow in an atmosphere that encourages a personal setting of goals and commitment to action; that focuses on a few important areas rather than many scattered details; that stimulates both personal reflection and collegial sharing; and that aims for continuous, coherent development toward improved teaching practice. We must all recognize that professional growth occurs only with effort and over time, and we need to infuse these ideas into our procedures for evaluating teaching.

CONCLUSION

The increasing role of the teacher in evaluation is a natural consequence of other aspects of mathematics-education reform. By the same token, this shift cannot occur independent of other changes.

The recommendations in the "Standard for the Evaluation of the Teaching of Mathematics" section of the *Professional Teaching Standards* are intertwined with those in the "Standard for the Development of Teachers of Mathematics" section, and neither can be implemented without substantial support by schools and school systems, educational policymakers, colleges and universities, and professional organizations, as outlined in the chapter on support and development. This interdependence reminds us that assessing students' learning *and* evaluating teaching is part and parcel of the larger process of promoting quality mathematics education for all learners.

BIBLIOGRAPHY

Black, Susan. "How Teachers Are Reshaping Evaluation Procedures." *Educational Leadership* 51 (October 1993): 38–42.

Costa, Arthur L., and Bena Kallick. "Through the Lens of a Critical Friend." *Educational Leadership* 51 (October 1993): 49–51.

National Council of Teachers of Mathematics. *Professional Standards for Teaching Mathematics*. Reston, Va.: The Council, 1991.

Nolan, Jim, Brent Hawkes, and Pam Francis. "Case Studies: Windows onto Clinical Supervision." *Educational Leadership* 51 (October 1993): 52–56.

Rooney, Joanne. "Teacher Evaluation: No More 'Super'vision." *Educational Leadership* 51 (October 1993): 43–44.

Stobbe, Colleen. "Professional Partnerships." *Educational Leadership* 51 (October 1993): 40–41.

Walen, Elizabeth, and Mimi DeRose. "The Power of Peer Appraisals." *Educational Leadership* 51 (October 1993): 45–48.

CONNECTING LEARNING AND TEACHING THROUGH ASSESSMENT

C. Jean Moon

We are beginning to understand that the teacher-as-researcher role encourages a teacher to reflect on teaching practices and students' learning, which is a promising strategy for changing the way mathematics is taught, learned, and assessed (Tobin 1989). When teachers actively participate in evaluating classroom lessons, they can begin to create new, more effective frameworks in which to help their students make mathematical connections.

Using assessment to make connections between learning and teaching requires both conceptual and reflective involvement by classroom teachers, such as thinking about the big ideas that evolve into designing a lesson. The success of the project described in this article reflects some of the benefits of the teacher-as-researcher role in making assessment a true part of mathematics teaching.

PROJECT DESCRIPTION

In 1988 and 1990, the Exxon Education Foundation awarded several grants to the Center for Math/Science Education Research at the University of Wisconsin—Milwaukee (UWM), in cooperation with the Milwaukee Public School (MPS) system. These grants supported a partnership between UWM and

Jean Moon is the director of the Center for Mathematics, Science and Technology in Education at Lesley College in Cambridge, MA 02138-2790. From 1988 through 1992 she was project director of the Exxon-sponsored K–3 Mathematics Specialist and assessment projects, which served as the basis for this article.

Garfield Elementary School, an inner-city MPS mathematics and science specialty school, so that a K–3 mathematics-specialist position might be created. An assessment project to align teaching, learning, and assessment in grades K–3 with the NCTM's *Curriculum and Evaluation Standards* (1989) followed the creation of the specialist's position. One of the goals of the project was to develop assessment models that focused on communications, problem solving, and number sense as outlined in the standards for grades K–4.

> ## Guided observations of your own teaching can be helpful.

The project also sought to help teachers understand the link between assessment and teaching in a manner quite different from traditional after-school or Saturday in-service sessions. The project offered guided opportunities for twelve Garfield Elementary School teachers to participate in assessment by acting as researchers in their classrooms as they identified, piloted, and refined assessment criteria related to communications, problem solving, and number sense in mathematics. Throughout the assessment project, each of the twelve teachers was given one release day a month; substitute-teacher costs were supported by Exxon grant funds. Further, teachers participating in the monthly meetings were awarded district in-service credit as part of a program contained within the districtwide Staff Development Academy.

During each of these release days, the teachers and I met for guided discussions and reflection, focusing on specific questions at the heart of identifying assessment criteria. These questions are addressed subsequently. In addition to monthly release days, the Garfield teachers agreed to meet one day a week, before the start of the school day, for support and discussion. Later in the project, videotaped class lessons were reviewed.

The Garfield mathematics specialist became part of a larger network of K–3 teachers who met once a month on Saturday mornings. This network was composed of teachers from eight Milwaukee Public Schools who were interested in assessment. Funds from the Exxon grant enabled these teachers to earn a college credit from the University of Wisconsin—Milwaukee for actively participating in this network.

The project supported critical areas as defined by the Garfield teachers. The support permitted the following:

- Time for teachers to meet in a group
- A partnership structure with a university
- A meaningful reward by allowing district in-service credit
- A link to a larger national network through the Exxon K-3 Mathematics Project
- The backing of the group by school and district administrators

In addition, funds from the grant allowed the purchase of limited teaching materials helpful to implementing certain mathematics lessons.

THE ROLE OF TEACHERS IN DEFINING ASSESSMENT

The critical bridges among teaching, learning, and assessment at Garfield were constructed as each of the K–3 teachers began to explore a teacher-as-researcher role. They engaged in this exploration through guided observations of their own teaching and through watching videotaped classroom lessons from various school settings. They observed lessons taught by the Garfield mathematics specialist, as well. The assumptions contained within the NCTM's curriculum and evaluation standards suggests that this new role is helpful for all mathematics teachers. When teachers are given an opportunity to observe and reflect on the classroom process, two of the exciting outcomes of the standards are achieved: (1) greater involvement in making instructional and assessment decisions on the part of teachers, and (2) development of a sense of expert judgment in instruction and assessment.

BEGINNING QUESTIONS

The K–3 staff at Garfield, which included teachers, the mathematics specialist, and the science-resource person, began exploring assessment by observing classroom lessons while examining several questions:

- What is assessment?
- How do the NCTM's evaluation standards describe assessment?
- In what ways is performance-based assessment different from traditional evaluation practices?
- How does the role of the teacher change in the context of performance-based assessment?
- What is the role of the student in the assessment process?
- How can assessment and instruction be integrated?

These questions were not difficult for the Garfield staff, since most had previously studied both the standards and the concept of performance-based assessment. More problematic to the group was defining, in a clear and explicit manner, what assessment might look like in a mathematics class. For example, if we were to assess problem solving in a sec-ond-grade mathematics lesson, what exactly would we do? What would problem-solving activities look like? How would we know if a student is successful?

These questions reveal a significant truth about the relationship between teaching and assessment because the behaviors being assessed affect the way in which teaching takes place: Teachers need to create and evaluate assessment

> *Determining student criteria is necessary in linking assessment and instruction.*

activities. The connection between learning and assessment cannot occur unless teachers themselves know the abilities they are asking their students to develop. This new view of assessment is asking us what we want students to know and be able to do, which is very different from a mathematics classroom that focuses on correct answers or content, readily scored from an answer sheet, as evidence of learning. The combination of new questions and new answers, or student outcomes, forces a broader view of evaluation and assessment. While the Garfield staff became more cognizant of this broader view, they continued to struggle with discerning the format of specific assessment models.

As the Garfield staff grappled with the question "What could assessment in problem solving look like?" it was helpful for them to work through the following questions in rich detail:

- What is problem solving in mathematics?
- How could we describe the behavior of a child who has a well-developed sense of problem solving? What are those behaviors?
- How could we describe the behaviors of a child who does not have a well-developed sense of problem solving? What are those behaviors?

Our experience in the Exxon project showed us that these questions directed us toward the heart and soul of the assessment and the teaching process: the *criteria* on which to evaluate students' performance. Identified criteria represent a slice of the range of behaviors that make up a broader outcome, such as

problem solving or number sense. Responses to these questions, and others like them, present a solid picture of what counts in the classroom as acceptable performance in a given mathematics ability or outcome.

THE ROLE OF CRITERIA IN LINKING TEACHING AND ASSESSMENT

Determining criteria may be the most difficult aspect of the process of assessment; it certainly was for the staff participating in this project. We were tempted to leave the discussion and dialogue too early, before we had articulated the criteria we believed to be most appropriate. Our discussions tended to look for quick descriptions without first completing the necessary reflective work. At some point within the process, however, it became clear to us that determined, often collaborative, work is needed to examine what is at the heart of any competent performance within a specific ability, whether that ability is mathematical reasoning, problem solving, or connection-making. This work should not be done in isolation, apart from colleagues. The moment of clarity differed among the staff, but gradually the work became more openly collaborative and, as a result, more productive in meeting project goals.

After six months of dialogue, reflection, revision, practice, and feedback, the Garfield staff identified a set of behavioral criteria for grades K–3 within the context of problem solving, communications, and number sense in mathematics. They had come to a professional agreement that these criteria reflected the behaviors they expected their students to demonstrate, the behaviors they valued as part of the problem-solving, number-sense, and communications outcomes. A sample of the problem-solving criteria developed for grades K–3 is presented in table 1. Teachers created criteria in which development could be observed over time. It is assumed that these criteria will not necessarily be achieved by students at the earlier grades. However, it was agreed that all students should demonstrate these stated abilities by the end of the third grade.

In defining the K–3 problem-solving criteria, the staff had simultaneously set up a direct connection to instruction. For example, when they identified assessment criteria related to the construction of problems from everyday life, they were making a statement about how they would be constructing their daily lessons. Lessons had to furnish consistent opportunities for students to practice constructing mathematics problems in their own language and symbols. Lessons also had to teach students that being able to talk and write using mathematical symbols and words was an important skill on which they would be evaluated. As a result, the connection between criteria in problem solving and communications became quite clear.

Throughout our work we viewed criteria as guides for learning and not as ends in and of themselves. Criteria became guides for assisting teachers and students in making connections between daily mathematics lessons and understanding the whole of mathematics.

A NEW SET OF QUESTIONS AND CONNECTIONS

On the basis of their new understanding of criteria, the Garfield staff is now addressing a new set of questions:

- What learning experiences are necessary to offer practice for students in the identified criteria or students' behaviors?
- How can we share these criteria with our students in a meaningful way? How can we model these criteria in the teaching process?
- How can we sample students' per-

formance during ongoing learning experiences in a way that is informative yet manageable?

- What kind of learning experiences or lessons provide a context in which the students can most effectively demonstrate their learning?
- How can we best give feedback to students on their performance?
- How can we encourage students to assess their own work using the identified criteria and not just their subjective interpretations?

Students need to know assessment criteria.

To facilitate answering these questions, we are now videotaping many of the K–3 mathematics classes at Garfield. By viewing these tapes as a professional community and applying the assessment criteria to students' performances, we are beginning to find concrete suggestions, connections, and solutions. In retrospect, the Garfield staff has taken several important steps: (1) they have begun to develop a clearer sense of what assessment means and how to implement it within the mathematics classroom; (2) they have found a clear role in working together with university personnel to identify a base of professional knowledge within assessment; and (3) they have received feedback from parents and students stressing the important link among teaching, learning, and assessment. According to a second-grade teacher at

Garfield, "I feel the assessment criteria we developed have helped me become more aware of the 'how and why' of my math lessons. They have also provided me with the 'language' necessary to talk with parents during conferences." The idea of a "language" for talking with parents refers to the ability of the teachers to use problem-solving criteria or number-sense criteria to inform parents about the goals of their mathematics instructions. The assessment criteria fortified for teachers, students, and parents the often abstract goals critical to mathematics instruction.

Teachers need to be an integral part of defining and building assessment criteria. Until teachers can address the "how and why" of their mathematics lessons, they will be unable to model the connections essential to helping students understand. Students and teachers are best informed when they have explicit assessment criteria to help guide and make connections in teaching and learning mathematics.

BIBLIOGRAPHY

Diez, Mary, and Jean Moon. "What Do We Want Students to Know?...and Other Important Questions." *Educational Leadership* 49 (May 1992): 38–41.

Meek, Anne. "On Thinking about Teaching: A Conversation with Eleanor Duckworth." *Educational Leadership* 48 (March 1991): 30–34.

National Council of Teachers of Mathematics. *Curriculum and Evaluation Standards for School Mathematics*. Reston, Va.: The Council, 1989.

Schon, Donald. *Educating the Reflective Practitioner*. San Francisco: Jossey-Bass, 1987.

Tobin, Kenneth. "Teachers as Researchers: Expanding the Knowledge Base of Teaching and Learning." In *Looking into Windows: Qualitative Research in Science Education*, edited by Marsha Lakes Matyas, Kenneth Tobin, and Barry Fraser, pp. 1–7. Washington, D.C.: American Association for the Advancement of Science, 1989.

The author wishes to express her appreciation to the Exxon Education Foundation and foundation personnel for their consistent support.

TABLE 1
Examples from K–3 Problem-Solving Criteria for Mathematics

Illustrate, describe, and model various problems by—
- using objects, illustrating with graphs, and drawing pictures; and
- repeating a problem in one's own words.

Verify, interpret, and justify solution strategies by—
- explaining the problem-solving process in her or his own words;
- seeing relationships between problem types and solution strategies; and
- checking and testing the reasonableness of a solution in appropriate units.

Construct problems from everyday life with various mathematics concepts by—
- forming a mathematics problem and thinking about it;
- telling in one's own words through embedding a mathematics problem in a story or illustrating to others through pictures, graphs, charts, or written composition; and
- demonstrating an understanding of how a problem can be solved.

SELF-EVALUATION AS AN ACT OF TEACHING

Vicky L. Kouba

A common call heard today is that we want "reflective teachers" who have the skills and experiences necessary to engage in a high-level examination of teaching. Indeed, the authors of the NCTM's *Professional Standards for Teaching Mathematics* (hereafter *Professional Teaching Standards*), published in 1991, recommend that teachers assume more of the responsibility for both self-evaluation and peer evaluation.

To become a reflective teacher, one must "reflect" in situations that place value on the quality and outcome of that reflection. Because reflection needs to be more than just *thinking about* the teaching, the teacher doing the reflecting must

> ## Concept maps can help us see connections of related topics.

also have the power and support to act on those reflections. In addition, that teacher must have sound knowledge about mathematics—content knowledge—and about the act of teaching—pedagogical knowledge. When Brown and Borko (1992, p. 218) examined patterns in studies of preservice teachers learning to teach mathematics, they found that limitations in these two areas of knowledge were associated with difficulties in making the transition to higher-order thinking and reasoning about

Vicky Kouba teaches at the State University of New York at Albany—SUNY, Albany, NY 12222. She works with preservice and in-service teachers.

teaching itself, "an inability to connect topics during classroom discussion, and a focus on procedural rather than conceptual understanding." This kind of higher-order reasoning is at the very heart of being a reflective teacher and of being able to carry out effective self-evaluation and peer evaluation as the *Professional Teaching Standards* describes them.

HELPING PRESERVICE AND BEGINNING TEACHERS EVALUATE THEMSELVES

What, then, are some approaches that may help the preservice or beginning teacher, both novice teachers, become a good evaluator of his or her level of content knowledge and level of pedagogical knowledge, regardless of the style of teaching used? The following are methods that the author and her colleagues have found successful in their mathematics teacher education program. These methods also seem to promote the development of a teacher-as-facilitator style of teaching.

Concept maps and critical listening

When helping preservice teachers design their first teaching unit, we require that they create a concept map of the mathematical knowledge and connections they want the students to know by the end of the unit. This use of concept maps in mathematics education was suggested by Farrell and Farmer (1988, pp. 193–94) as one way to approach long-range planning. We use Novak and Gowan's (1984, p. 15) description of con-

cept mapping, "a schematic device for representing a set of concept meanings embedded in a framework of propositions." A sample map constructed by a preservice teacher in a methods course is shown in figure 1.

As part of their methods course and before working on their individual concept maps, the preservice teachers learn how to construct concept maps. They study and discuss sample concept maps, work in groups to construct maps when given a list of concepts, and then work in groups both to generate a list of concepts and to create a corresponding propositional concept map. In addition, cooperating teachers and other school-based personnel attend a seminar in which they learn how to construct and use concept maps.

The act of constructing the map helps both to increase that teacher's understanding of the content in the unit and to draw his or her attention to any gaps or misunderstandings in the mathematical content and connections of the unit. The concept map itself serves as a graphic representation of the nature of the preservice teacher's understanding of a topic. If, on the one hand, the map has parallel, disconnected strands (i.e., it resembles a hand with a small palm and overly long fingers), the preservice teacher has a linear, fragmented view of the topic. We have found that preservice teachers who produce such linear, disconnected concept maps often need help with making transitions. They also need help in thinking through and making connections between concepts and procedures and among various representa-

FIGURE 1

A Preservice Teacher's Concept Map of a Unit on Ratio and Proportion

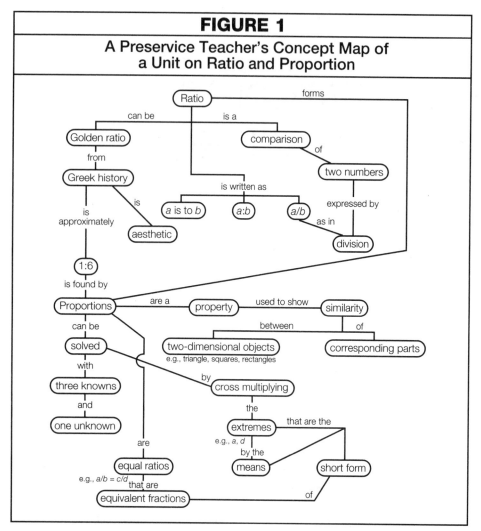

rent map connects to the preceding or the next instructional unit, and the modes of instruction. Such a discussion seems to increase the preservice teacher's awareness of his or her own philosophy of teaching. In addition, the preservice teacher learns to identify and value the bases for making decisions about instruction.

The preservice teacher–cooperating teacher interaction is also an individual interview. Cooperating teachers ask the same types of questions as those asked by the methods professor. However, the cooperating teachers often probe more deeply into the content. For example, in the informational seminar on concept mapping, cooperating teachers said they would ask the following questions of the

> **Single words in a veteran teacher's map are rich with connections.**

preservice teacher who constructed the map in figure 1:

- What do you mean in the portion of the map where you say that "proportions are a property"?

- How will you help students understand the relationship between cross-multiplication and equivalent fractions? You might want to consider adding a little more detail to your map to show that this relationship involves a procedure for finding a common denominator for two equivalent fractions.

- Your map seems to be missing some applications for using proportions. What other ones will you explore in this unit besides those related to the golden ratio and similarity in geometric figures? Where might these fit in your map?

- When you say that a ratio is a comparison of two numbers, do you mean *any* two numbers, or are restrictions placed on the nature of the numbers? Can a ratio be a comparison of two irrational numbers?

Both the preservice teachers and the

tions of mathematical ideas. If, on the other hand, the concept map produced by a preservice teacher somewhat resembles a web with connections or cross-links (as in fig. 1), that teacher has a more integrated understanding of the mathematical content of the unit than the person who produces a linear map.

The concept map also serves as a stimulus for communication between (*a*) the preservice teacher and other preservice teachers, (*b*) the preservice teacher and the methods instructor, and (*c*) the preservice teacher and the cooperating teacher.

The preservice teacher–preservice teacher interaction takes place in the methods classroom as an exercise in peer evaluation. The exercise employs a "critical listener" approach, in which preservice teachers work in pairs taking turns being the "reader" and the "critical listener." A set of guidelines and explanations of the roles and the exercise are given to the preservice teachers (see table 1).

These guidelines foster an environment for focused discussion of the concepts, subconcepts, cross-links, hierarchical levels, and connections that may be present in the map. The guidelines also help the preservice teachers reflect on appropriate and varied modes of instruction.

Preservice teachers who have participated in this activity report that it helps them identify gaps in their mathematical understanding and be more aware of what to look for in the content as they design a unit plan.

The preservice teacher–methods instructor interaction based on the concept map is done on an individual-interview basis. The concept map serves as the means for the methods instructor to probe the preservice teacher's beliefs about the nature of mathematics and instruction. As the map is discussed, the methods instructor asks questions about the placement of concepts in the map, the choice of words used to form the propositions, the ways in which the cur-

cooperating teachers report that using the map as a focal point helps to identify and correct misconceptions or incomplete conceptions about the mathematical content that the preservice teacher may have. Cooperating teachers also report that the discussion of the concept map has paid an unexpected dividend. Often veteran teachers write instructional plans composed of key words that cue them to entire teaching protocols or scenarios based on their years of experience. The key words do not convey the same rich meaning to preservice teachers who look at the plans. During the discussion of a preservice teacher's concept map, a veteran teacher's questions and follow-up explanations typically make more visible to the preservice teacher the richness of the veteran teacher's planning for, and understanding of, a unit. The preservice teacher gains a greater awareness of, and appreciation for, the kinds of mathematical connections that the veteran teacher consciously makes during instruction.

Often during the discussion of a concept map, the cooperating teacher and the preservice teacher discuss how best to approach specific concepts. In particular, they frequently discuss how the classroom learning environment can be structured to help mathematics students construct their own concepts and connections.

Novice teachers vary in the extent to which they use concept maps during their practice-teaching experience and first year of teaching. When, of their own volition, novice teachers construct a concept map, it is typically because they "feel shaky" about the content of the selected unit. The concept-mapping and critical-listening experiences seem to help preservice teachers develop one tool not only for evaluating the extent of their mathematical knowledge but also for extending the depth and breadth of that knowledge. These novice teachers are also more willing and able to use concept maps or other types of mapping tasks,

Small groups of 4–7 work best when analyzing videos.

such as "mind mapping" (Entrekin 1992) or thematic webbing (Piazza, Scott, and Carver 1994) with their students.

Analysis of videotapes and case studies

In the teacher education program at the State University of New York at Albany—SUNY, videotapes and written case studies of teachers are used as a means to help preservice and beginning teachers evaluate and develop their teaching strategies. At first, the novice teacher is uncertain as to just what to look for in tapes or how to use such tapes without the "knowing eyes" and analyses of a cooperating teacher or supervisor. However, experience in case-study analysis has been shown to help develop skills for looking at oneself.

Preservice teachers have been found to make progress in learning sound analytical skills when they begin with videotapes of cooperating teachers or with written scenarios as case studies. In methods classes, the instructor takes the lead and models how to analyze the teaching depicted in a videotape or written case study. During the same session, the preservice teachers are gradually given more of the responsibility for analyses of additional cases. By the end of the two-hour session, individual or pairs of preservice teachers are leading all aspects of the analysis. The methods instructor acts as a coach.

After these initial experiences, the preservice teachers analyze videotapes of the actual classroom teaching or microteaching of their peers. Experience with peer and self-analysis of videotapes of teaching has resulted in the following guidelines:

1. The person who was videotaped must be the first person to offer criticism of the episode. More important, that first criticism must be positive. Teachers must be as adept at analyzing what went right with a lesson as they are with what went awry. Teachers who know their own strengths, successes, and the underlying reasons for those strengths and successes have a pool of information that serves as a resource when planning for improvements in less successful areas of teaching. This statement leads to the second guideline.

2. Positive and negative comments must be followed by an analysis of the probable cause for the positive or negative aspect of the teaching episode. Negative comments also must be followed by suggestions and plans for improvement that make as much use as possible of the person's strengths.

3. An environment of respect is necessary when analyzing videotapes. The methods instructors help their students achieve this climate by modeling tact and compassion in their comments about others' teaching.

4. Groups of from four to seven people seem to work best when analyzing videotapes. However, preservice teachers should not engage in analyses without the presence of the methods instructor,

---

TABLE 1
Critical Listening Guidelines for Concept Map Review

Work in pairs taking turns being the reader and the critical listener. The reader (the person who prepared the materials) presents the materials. The critical listener (a) listens well, (b) asks questions to increase accuracy and clarity of the reader's materials, (c) checks for clarity of writing for the match between what the reader has written, and (d) checks for errors in the content.

1. The reader and listener talk through the concept map. The reader identifies the major levels for the concepts and subconcepts and the important cross-links, identifies the hierarchical levels and explains how each level differs from the level preceding it and the level following it, and explains what active tasks or projects the students could do to develop an understanding of the cross-links.
2. The reader explains in what ways the map moves from the general to the specific and in what ways the map has balance in terms of symmetry and location of closely related concept clusters.
3. The reader explains and clarifies any of the relationships that connect concepts. Both the reader and the listener check the map to ensure that all relationships (line segments between concepts) are labeled.
4. The reader and listener determine if the map matches the goals and objectives for the unit, if any gaps exist in concepts or relationships, and if the map has adequate examples written near appropriate concept labels.

supervisor, or cooperating teacher until the preservice teachers have had sufficient practice in the techniques and have demonstrated tact and a sense of professional integrity during the exercises.

Cooperative teams and postobservation analyses

In teaching situations, novice teachers may be helped to take a greater role in their own evaluation through the use of a cooperative-team approach. Feldt (1993) describes the advantages of a coaching environment in which colleagues can benefit from multiple perspectives on almost any aspect of teaching. The State University of New York at Albany—SUNY program combines the team approach with a structured postobservation analysis of the actual classroom teaching of a preservice teacher. The program uses a team consisting of the cooperating teacher, the supervisor, and the preservice teacher. Occasionally, the team includes the methods instructor as well.

As with the analyses of videotapes, novice teachers gain insight into how to examine their own teaching if they see the techniques modeled and then participate as a team member with experienced teachers. The scenarios in the *Professional Teaching Standards* can serve as models for the analysis of a teaching episode.

Following introductory experiences, the novice teachers examine their own teaching. After the novice teacher conducts a class observed by the rest of the team members, a postobservation conference is held. During this conference, the novice teacher takes an active part in identifying strengths and weaknesses in the lesson rather than primarily listens to the cooperating teacher's or supervisor's analysis. The novice teacher takes an equally active role in suggesting changes in the lesson and in constructing plans for bettering the teaching overall. The cooperating teacher and supervisor function as questioners whose questions help to focus the discussion on the structure of the lesson, the content, the students' understanding of the content, and the preservice teacher's notion of how to improve. The questions might include the following:

Novice teachers construct plans for bettering their teaching.

- What went as planned?
- What would you do differently and why?
- When were you feeling the most pressure and why?
- When were you feeling most comfortable with the lesson? Why?
- How did you control the pace of the lesson?
- Which examples and teaching modes were the most effective and why? Which were the least effective and why?
- What were the main content points for your lesson and how well do you think you structured the lesson to allow students to reach those points? Were the students aware of those points?
- What do you think the students learned and how can you tell?
- What can you use from today's lesson in the refinement of tomorrow's lesson?
- What aspects of your teaching do you want to work to improve? How will you go about doing so?

After the novice teacher has answered the questions, the cooperating teacher or supervisor may offer further suggestions and ideas.

Additional techniques

Preservice and beginning teachers also can learn to evaluate themselves effectively through the use of shared journals, role-playing, and cross-observation of other novice teachers. If an opportunity exists for the novice teachers to participate as members of a team designing a teacher-evaluation program for a school or a teacher education program, such participation has been shown to help novice teachers construct a framework for examining their own teaching.

The overall goal for all the approaches described is to help novice teachers become the same kind of effective problem solvers regarding their own teaching as they hope to help their students become regarding mathematical problem solving.

REFERENCES

Brown, Catherine A., and Hilda Borko. "Becoming a Mathematics Teacher." In *Handbook of Research on Mathematics Teaching and Learning*, edited by Douglas A. Grouws, pp. 209–39. New York: Macmillan Publishing, 1992.

Entrekin, Virginia S. "Mathematical Mind Mapping." *Mathematics Teacher* 85 (September 1992): 444–45.

Farrell, Margaret A., and Walter A. Farmer. *Secondary Mathematics Instruction: An Integrated Approach.* Providence, R.I.: Janson Publications, 1988.

Feldt, Constance Curley. "Becoming a Teacher of Mathematics: A Constructive, Interactive Process." *Mathematics Teacher* 86 (May 1993): 400–403.

National Council of Teachers of Mathematics. *Professional Standards for Teaching Mathematics.* Reston, Va.: The Council, 1991.

Novak, Joseph D., and Bob Gowan. *Learning How to Learn.* New York: Cambridge University Press, 1984.

Piazza, Jenny A., Margaret M. Scott, and Elizabeth C. Carver. "Thematic Webbing and the Curriculum Standards in the Primary Grades." *Arithmetic Teacher* 41 (February 1994): 294–98.

BIBLIOGRAPHIES
AND MATRICES

This section contains three bibliographies with brief annotations on each of the 96 articles on assessment published in the school-based NCTM journals from January 1990 to May 1995 as well as the 11 articles dealing with assessment that appeared in the *Journal for Research in Mathematics Education* (*JRME*) during that same time period. (Boldfaced titles indicate that the articles are reproduced in this book.)

Each of these 107 articles is also cross-listed here in an article-by-topic matrix. One matrix is for articles from the *Arithmetic Teacher* or *Teaching Children Mathematics* and from *Mathematics Teaching in the Middle School*; a second matrix lists articles from the *Mathematics Teacher*; and a third matrix lists the *JRME* artcles. Topics are listed down the left side of each matrix, and articles are listed along the top of the matrix by number (according to their number in the corresponding annotated bibliography).

For example, the *Mathematics Teacher* matrix identifies three articles associated with portfolio assessment (numbers 3, 14, and 27); an asterisk in the matrix indicates that number 27 is reprinted in this book. Refer to the *Mathematics Teacher* annotated bibliography (where the articles are numbered alphabetically by author) for an annotation of each of the three articles about portfolios. In the bibliography, the title of article number 27 is boldfaced, since that article is reprinted in this book.

In compiling these annotated bibliographies, we used the *Current Index to Journals in Education* (produced by the ERIC Clearinghouse for Science, Mathematics, and Environmental Education—ERIC/CSMEE) to search for appropriate articles. With permission from the clearinghouse, we have adapted ERIC's article abstracts for use in our bibliographies. Many thanks to ERIC for permitting this use of their abstracts.

ANNOTATED BIBLIOGRAPHY

Arithmetic Teacher/Teaching Children Mathematics
and Mathematics Teaching in the Middle School

1. **Badger, Elizabeth. "More than Testing." *Arithmetic Teacher* 39 (May 1992): 7–11.**

   Explains (through a measurement task requiring students to estimate the number of popcorn kernels in a container) a set of processes that teachers might use to evaluate students' learning and understanding. Illustrates the processes of setting goals, deciding what to assess, gathering information, and using the results.

2. Ball, Deborah Loewenberg. "Implementing the *Professional Standards for Teaching Mathematics*: What's All This Talk about Discourse?" *Arithmetic Teacher* 39 (November 1991): 44–48.

   Explores possible outcomes of using the *Professional Teaching Standards* as a set of tools to construct productive conversations about teaching. Presents a discussion taking place in the author's third-grade classroom illustrating discourse in the classroom, accompanied by the author's commentary on the lesson.

3. Berkman, Robert M. "Teacher as 'Kimp.'" *Arithmetic Teacher* 41 (February 1994): 326–28.

   Demonstrates a technique where, by taking on the disguise of one who is completely ignorant of a mathematical topic or by using incorrect examples, students can be challenged to reflect on their thinking and to be very precise about their language.

4. Biggerstaff, Margaret, Barb Halloran, and Carolyn Serrano. "Teacher to Teacher: Use Color to Assess Mathematics Problem Solving." *Arithmetic Teacher* 41 (February 1994): 307–8.

   Describes a technique using a color-coded holistic scoring system to achieve greater understanding of the assessment process on the part of students by having them score classmates' solutions to a problem.

5. Burns, Marilyn. "Timed Tests." *Teaching Children Mathematics* 1 (March 1995): 408–9.

   Describes some of the disadvantages of timed tests: children who work slowly are at a disadvantage, negative feelings toward mathematics are fostered, and timed tests do not necessarily measure children's understanding. Suggests that tests should send a message that it is important to apply numerical reasoning, not simply recall facts.

6. Bush, William S. "Implementing the K–4 Mathematics Standards in Kentucky." *Arithmetic Teacher* 41 (November 1993): 166–69.

   Describes efforts to reform K–4 mathematics instruction in Kentucky. Discusses the establishment of collaborative groups within Kentucky's mathematics education community, the Kentucky Education Reform Act of 1990, and reform efforts in the areas of assessment, curriculum, professional development for teachers, preservice teacher education, and public beliefs and attitudes.

7. Chambers, Donald L. "Improving Instruction by Listening to Children." *Teaching Children Mathematics* 1 (February 1995): 378–80.

   Gives examples of a teacher providing strategies for students to solve problems and later listening to the students' strategies. Provides action research ideas for assessing teaching and student progress in problem solving.

8. Clark, H. Clifford, and Marvin N. Nelson. "Evaluation: Be More than a Scorekeeper." *Arithmetic Teacher* 38 (May 1991): 15–17.

   Presents the elementary-level formative evaluation method of functional diagnosis that gives students immediate feedback on completed assignments. Gives three examples of the method as observed in the classrooms of master teachers: putting red dots next to problems needing attention, paired learning, and student answer keys.

9. Clark, John L. "The Toronto Board of Education's Benchmarks in Mathematics." *Arithmetic Teacher* 39 (February 1992): 51–55.

   In 1987, the Toronto Board of Education mandated the development of standards, called "benchmarks," for students' achievement in mathematics and language at the end of grades 3, 6, 8, and 10. The development and testing of benchmarks stressing higher-order thinking, problem solving, and the use of experiential approaches and manipulative materials are described. Specific examples and overall strengths are presented.

10. **Clarke, David J. "Activating Assessment Alternatives in Mathematics." *Arithmetic Teacher* 39 (February 1992): 24–29.**

    Presents practical methods that exemplify principles of assessment that involve minimal disruption of the instructional process and do not impose additional work on the teacher. Informal assessment methods include annotated class lists and student portfolios. Formal assessment methods include practical tests, student-constructed tests, and students' self-evaluation.

11. Collison, Judith. "Using Performance Assessment to Determine Mathematical Dispositions." *Arithmetic Teacher* 39 (February 1992): 40–47.

    Performance assessment, a method that makes possible the assessment of multiple dimensions of students' progress, including dispositions, is described. Criteria for good performance tasks are given, and their structure is illustrated through an example. A list of ten dispositions toward

Boldfaced titles in this bibliography indicate that the articles are reprinted in this book.

mathematics and a self-evaluation group-performance rating form to assess disposition are provided.

12. Cross, Lee, and Michael C. Hynes. "Assessing Mathematics Learning for Students with Learning Differences." *Arithmetic Teacher* 41 (March 1994): 371–77.

Discusses the use and adaptation of alternative assessment procedures, such as observation, interviewing, holistic scoring, checklists, and the reading of student journals, to accurately determine the progress of students with learning difficulties. Includes scoring rubrics and many samples of student evaluation.

13. Elliott, Portia C. "By Way of Introduction." *Arithmetic Teacher* 39 (February 1992): 4–7.

Two perspectives that frame the aspects of the debate on assessment issues are analyzed. The "count everybody" perspective calls for national standards over which all students would be tested. The "everybody counts" perspective favors assessments that are developed from multiple perspectives.

14. Folkson, Susan. "Who's behind the Fence? Creating a Rich Learning Environment with a Nontraditional Problem." *Teaching Children Mathematics* 1 (February 1995): 382–85.

Discusses a nonroutine problem used with small groups of students in kindergarten. Examples of students' solutions are provided along with an assessment of each student's work.

15. Garnett, Cynthia M. "Testing—Do Not Disturb? A Concerned Parent's View of Testing." *Arithmetic Teacher* 39 (February 1992): 8–10.

Presents a parent's viewpoint that criticizes assessment methods that diminish appreciation for diverse ways of understanding, discourage discovery and project-based learning, diminish the natural problem-solving aspects of play, and perpetuate the single-right-answer form of assessment. Assessment that values the child, includes all interested parties, and informs parents and teachers what children know is recommended.

16. Garofalo, Joe, and Jerry Bryant. "Assessing Reasonableness: Some Observations and Suggestions." *Arithmetic Teacher* 40 (December 1992): 210–12.

Offers five suggestions to help students assess the reasonableness of their answers: (1) giving students a variety of problems; (2) facilitating students' discussions and interpretations of the problems' conditions; (3) encouraging students to estimate answers before carrying out calculations; (4) encouraging students to ask whether their answers make sense; and (5) becoming aware of students' faulty assessment criteria.

17. Goldenberg, E. Paul. "A Mathematical Conversation with Fourth Graders." *Arithmetic Teacher* 38 (April 1991): 38–43.

Presents a conversation with students that gives an insight into the ways students think about decimals. Students were introduced, with the use of a calculator, to decimal notation and systematic experimentation. Discusses what students learned throughout this conversation.

18. Goldstein, Sue, and Frances A. Campbell. "Parents: A Ready Resource." *Arithmetic Teacher* 38 (February 1991): 24–27.

Presents highlights of a study of educational intervention in the elementary grades that contained a parent-participation component. Included are eight tenets of parental involvement, sample activities, and an evaluation form for home activities.

19. Graeber, Anna O. "Research into Practice: Misconceptions about Multiplication and Division." *Arithmetic Teacher* 40 (March 1993): 408–11.

Discusses the two overgeneralizations "multiplication makes bigger" and "division makes smaller" in the context of solving word problems involving rational numbers less than 1. Presents activities to help students make sense of multiplication and division in these situations.

20. Greenwood, Jonathan Jay. "On the Nature of Teaching and Assessing 'Mathematical Power' and 'Mathematical Thinking.'" *Arithmetic Teacher* 41 (November 1993): 144–52.

Offers seven criteria for developing mathematical thinking, plus suggestions for teaching and assessing students' progress that are compatible with each learning criterion. Provides evaluation sheets that help the teacher assess and grade students on the criteria.

21. Hart, Lynn C., Karen Schultz, Deborah Najee-Ullah, and Linda Nash. "Implementing the *Professional Standards for Teaching Mathematics*: The Role of Reflection in Teaching." *Arithmetic Teacher* 40 (September 1992): 40–42.

Discusses the role of teacher reflection in changes envisioned by the NCTM *Professional Teaching Standards*. Presents reasons why teachers should reflect on their teaching, what teachers should examine, when reflection should be done, and five methods on how reflection can take place.

22. Harvey, John G. "Teaching Mathematics with Technology." *Arithmetic Teacher* 38 (March 1991): 52–54.

Discusses the idea that if students are allowed to use calculators when doing classwork, they should be allowed to use calculators on tests. Presents examples of calculator-active items that are designed to assess accurately students' learning.

23. Helton, Sonia M. "I Thik the Citanre Will Holder Lase: Journal Keeping in Mathematics Class." *Teaching Children Mathematics* 1 (February 1995): 336–40.

Discusses the use of journal writing, including hints for getting started, with primary-aged students. Displays examples of student entries involving comparing quantities,

Boldfaced titles in this bibliography indicate that the articles are reprinted in this book.

practicing skills, and problem posing. Provides sample problems that students can investigate and write about in journals.

24. Jaberg, Patricia. "Assessment and Geraldine's Blanket." *Teaching Children Mathematics* 1 (April 1995): 514–17.

    Introduces problem situations from the context of children's literature. Discusses problem-solving strategies that first-grade students developed. Contains examples of problems involving place value, estimation, and fractions and assesses several student strategies.

25. Joyner, Jeanne M., and Nancy Nesbitt Vacc. "Implementing the *Professional Standards for Teaching Mathematics*: Linking Teaching, Learning, and Assessment." *Arithmetic Teacher* 41 (May 1994): 550–52.

    Discusses North Carolina's alternative assessment program for first and second grades, the process of implementation, knowledge gained from the program, and implications for implementing Standard 6 (focusing on analyzing and interconnecting teaching and learning) of the *Professional Teaching Standards*.

26. Kamii, Constance, and Barbara Ann Lewis. "Achievement Tests in Primary Mathematics: Perpetuating Lower-Order Thinking." *Arithmetic Teacher* 38 (May 1991): 4–9.

    Presents a study of eighty-seven second graders to demonstrate that achievement tests in primary school mathematics emphasize pupils' lower-order thinking by comparing answers to interview questions from constructivist and traditionally instructed groups. Results indicated that constructivist-instructed students demonstrated superior higher-order thinking on tasks involving place value, double-digit addition, story problems, and estimation.

27. Kroll, Diana Lambdin, Joanna O. Masingila, and Sue Tinsley Mau. "Cooperative Problem Solving: But What about Grading?" *Arithmetic Teacher* 39 (February 1992): 17–23.

    Many teachers use cooperative learning methods during instruction but face the problem of aligning assessment techniques with that instruction. Described are methods to include cooperative problem solving in assessment, including strategies to identify possible grading schemes, to make appropriate problem choices, and to evaluate individual versus group grading.

28. Krulik, Stephen, and Jesse A. Rudnick. "Reflect … for Better Problem Solving and Reasoning." *Arithmetic Teacher* 41 (February 1994): 334–38.

    Elaborates the final step of Polya's heuristic model, reflecting, to improve students' problem-solving performance. After checking answers for accuracy, the following steps are suggested: (1) test reasonableness and practicality, (2) write a summary paragraph, (3) find other solutions, (4) change the conditions, and (5) extend the problem.

29. **Lambdin, Diana V., and Vicki L. Walker. "Planning for Classroom Portfolio Assessment." *Arithmetic Teacher* 41 (February 1994): 318–24.**

    Discusses what a portfolio is and presents reasons for using portfolios to assess students' mathematical progress, along with tips for introducing, using, and assessing portfolios. Includes examples of students' work and guidelines for portfolio entries.

30. Lankford, Francis G., Jr. "What Can a Teacher Learn about a Pupil's Thinking through Oral Interviews?" *Arithmetic Teacher* 40 (October 1992): 106–11.

    Discusses students' computational strategies as discovered from audiotaped interviews. Based on interviews with 176 seventh-grade students. Contrasts strategies of good and poor computers and provides guides for interviewing. Uses examples to illustrate what teachers may learn about the thinking of their pupils.

31. Lappan, Glenda. "What Do We Have and Where Do We Go from Here?" *Arithmetic Teacher* 40 (May 1993): 524–26.

    Discusses four aspects of mathematics instruction envisioned by the *Professional Teaching Standards*: choosing worthwhile mathematical tasks, orchestrating classroom discourse, creating a constructive environment for learning, and analyzing students' understanding and the contribution of teacher practice to student learning. Presents principles to guide reform and examples of successful reform efforts.

32. Lindquist, Mary M. "Tides of Change: Teachers at the Helm." *Arithmetic Teacher* 41 (September 1993): 64–68.

    Adaptation from the Presidential Address at the 71st Annual Meeting of NCTM in April 1993. Topics include the growth and makeup of NCTM membership, publications and their changing mission, efforts toward professional development, and the expanded assessment standards. Calls for teachers to play leadership roles in bringing about change.

33. Long, Madeleine J., and Meir Ben-Hur. "Informing Learning through the Clinical Interview." *Arithmetic Teacher* 38 (February 1991): 44–46.

    Describes an alternative way for classroom teachers to assess students' performance in mathematics. The interview process is presented in stages: initiating the interview, questioning, formulating and testing hypotheses, and intervening.

34. Maher, Carolyn A., and Amy M. Martino. "Implementing the *Professional Standards for Teaching Mathematics*: Teachers Building on Students' Thinking." *Arithmetic Teacher* 39 (March 1992): 32–37.

    Provides excerpts from videotaped dialogue between two third-grade students and their interactions with their teacher while solving a counting problem to describe student thinking and communication during the task. Discusses the teacher's role in the dialogue and implications for classroom practice.

Boldfaced titles in this bibliography indicate that the articles are reprinted in this book.

35. Maher, Carolyn A., Robert B. Davis, and Alice Alston. "Teachers Paying Attention to Students' Thinking." *Arithmetic Teacher* 39 (May 1992): 34–37.

Reports an example of one lesson from a sequence of lessons on fractions from a sixth-grade class in which the teacher revises her plans after observing students' small-group work and interactions. The lesson illustrates the teacher's knowledge of mathematics, how students think, and how to observe that thinking.

36. **Moon, C. Jean. "Connecting Learning and Teaching through Assessment." *Arithmetic Teacher* 41 (September 1993): 13–15.**

K–3 teachers participated in a project to align teaching, learning, and assessment with the NCTM *Standards*. Goals included developing assessment models and helping clarify the link between assessment and teaching. Assessment criteria were based on student performance rather than on correct answers. Cooperative learning and support structures were used.

37. Mumme, Judith, and Nancy Shepherd. "Implementing the *Standards*: Communication in Mathematics." *Arithmetic Teacher* 38 (September 1990): 18–22.

Discusses the importance of teaching students to communicate mathematically and examines ways to develop this skill. Activities and open-ended questions are included. Stresses the use of physical materials, cooperative groups, listening skills, and writing.

38. **Norwood, Karen S., and Glenda Carter. "Journal Writing: An Insight into Students' Understanding." *Teaching Children Mathematics* 1 (November 1994): 146–48.**

Describes how journal writing is used to assess students' understanding of topics in progress. Contains examples of students' writing on multiplication and feelings about mathematics. Gives ten suggestions for using journal writing and seventeen sample journal prompts.

39. Owen, Lisa B. "Listening to Reflections: A Classroom Study." *Teaching Children Mathematics* 1 (February 1995): 366–69.

Encourages teachers to ask students to explain their thinking as a means of gaining understanding into their sense-making. Discusses reflection in the context of second-grade students' decisions to use mental mathematics, paper and pencil, or a calculator to solve problems.

40. Paull, Sandra. "Not Just an Average Unit." *Arithmetic Teacher* 38 (December 1990): 54–58.

Outlines an interdisciplinary unit on statistics. Discusses goals, organization, preinstruction survey, math lessons, results, and evaluation. The survey and examples of the students' work are provided.

41. Piazza, Jenny A., Margaret M. Scott, and Elizabeth C. Carver. "Thematic Webbing and the Curriculum Standards in the Primary Grades." *Arithmetic Teacher* 41 (February 1994): 294–98.

Presents thematic webbing in which students choose a theme and create major branches by brainstorming and the teacher compiles activities that connect the major branches while covering mathematics topics. Discusses implementation and assessment within the thematic-webbing approach. Uses bears as an example.

42. Romberg, Thomas A., and Linda D. Wilson. "Alignment of Tests with the Standards." *Arithmetic Teacher* 40 (September 1992): 18–22.

Examines six widely used grade 8 standardized tests for content, required processes, and level to determine their alignment with the grades 5–8 NCTM Curriculum and Evaluation Standards. Concludes that these tests inadequately covered the 5–8 standards. A follow-up study examined items from newly developed and foreign tests to demonstrate the existence of items that reflect the standards.

43. Ross, Rita, and Ray Kurtz. "Making Manipulatives Work: A Strategy for Success." *Arithmetic Teacher* 40 (January 1993): 254–57.

Describes a lesson in which a game involving base-ten blocks is used to teach place value. Discusses four steps to promote successful lessons involving manipulative materials: (1) manipulative choice, (2) lesson preparation, (3) active student participation, and (4) process evaluation.

44. Sammons, Kay, Beth Kobett, Joan Heiss, and Francis (Skip) Fennell. "Linking Instruction and Assessment in the Mathematics Classroom." *Arithmetic Teacher* 39 (February 1992): 11–16.

Presents assessment techniques to help improve instruction. Included are the formative-assessment techniques of observation and questioning, diagnostic interviews, and problem-solving investigations and the summative-assessment technique of performance-based tasks. Examples of these methods are provided together with at-home activities that encourage parental partnership.

45. Scheibelhut, Carolyn. "I Do and I Understand, I Reflect and I Improve." *Teaching Children Mathematics* 1 (December 1994): 242–46.

Encourages teachers to reflect on their teaching through writing activities and to learn more about their students' understanding of mathematics through having them write. Suggests using writing (1) at the beginning of a unit as a diagnostic tool, (2) as a follow-up to a lesson to see what students have learned, (3) to see if students can connect mathematics to real-life situations, and (4) to elicit information about students' beliefs concerning mathematics.

Boldfaced titles in this bibliography indicate that the articles are reprinted in this book.

46. **Schwartz, James E. "How Can We Evaluate Ourselves?"** *Arithmetic Teacher* 39 (February 1992): 58–61.

Teacher self-evaluation is proposed as a method to improve instruction. Envisioned is a mathematics-teaching evaluation instrument that includes a classroom student-behavior checklist, a procedural-conceptual-discrimination component, a projective-teaching-model-identification component, and an assessment of content understanding.

47. Sgroi, Laura A., Nancy Gropper, Mary Tom Kilker, Nancy M. Rambusch, and Barbara Semonite. "Assessing Young Children's Mathematical Understandings." *Teaching Children Mathematics* 1 (January 1995): 275–77.

Describes assessment integrated into instruction that probes the mathematical understanding of kindergarten and first-grade students. Uses a graphical example to gain insight into students' counting strategies. Provides analyses of student strategies gained from classroom discourse.

48. Slovin, Hannah. "Number of the Day." *Arithmetic Teacher* 39 (March 1992): 29–31.

Presents an activity for representing a given number in as many ways as possible using short periods of time to develop students' number sense and to give the teacher opportunities to make informal student assessments and diagnoses. Provides specific dialogue of the activity being used in a third-grade class.

49. **Spangler, Denise A. "Assessing Students' Beliefs about Mathematics."** *Arithmetic Teacher* 40 (November 1992): 148–52.

Presents eleven open-ended questions that can be posed to students and teachers at all educational levels in various formats to assess mathematical beliefs. The questions investigate beliefs toward mathematics, the problem-solving process, mathematicians, and mathematical applications.

50. Stenmark, Jean Kerr, Pam Beck, and Harold Asturias. "A Room with More than One View." *Mathematics Teaching in the Middle School* 1 (April 1994): 44–49.

A play is presented in which teachers, students, administrators, and parents discuss alternative forms of assessment and their impact on mathematics education. Samples of student work are provided and discussed.

51. **Stix, Andi. "Pic-Jour Math: Pictorial Journal Writing in Mathematics."** *Arithmetic Teacher* 41 (January 1994): 264–69.

Describes journal writing as an element of multimodal teaching. Discusses how students use journal writing that includes pictures, numbers, symbols, and manipulatives to help understand mathematical concepts. Provides a form to evaluate students' portfolio writing and examples of students' evaluated work.

52. Sullivan, Peter, and David Clarke. "Catering to All Abilities through 'Good' Questions." *Arithmetic Teacher* 39 (October 1991): 14–18.

Presents three features of "good" questions: they require students to do more than simply remember a strategy to answer; they promote student learning while answering the question; and they have several acceptable answers. Considers how questions can be used to cater to the range of student abilities.

53. Vacc, Nancy Nesbitt. "Implementing the *Professional Standards for Teaching Mathematics*: Teaching and Learning Mathematics through Classroom Discussion." *Arithmetic Teacher* 41 (December 1993): 225–27.

Proposes the technique of group discussions in the learning of mathematics. Examines the teacher's role in creating an environment that encourages student participation; presents four techniques to initiate discussions in elementary school classes; and offers five attributes teachers need to develop in students for effective discussions.

54. Vacc, Nancy Nesbitt. "Implementing the *Professional Standards for Teaching Mathematics*: Questioning in the Mathematics Classroom." *Arithmetic Teacher* 41 (October 1993): 88–91.

Encourages teachers to allow students to engage in conversation and discuss what they do and do not understand. Discusses different types of questions found in classroom instruction: factual questions, reasoning questions, and open questions. To promote communication, teachers must change their beliefs about instruction.

55. Walen, Sharon B., and James Hirstein. "Classroom Vignette: An Alternative Assessment Tool." *Teaching Children Mathematics* 1 (February 1995): 362–65.

Encourages teachers to use vignettes as a means of facilitating student discussion about mathematics and mathematics attitudes. Provides two vignettes, subsequent student discussion, and an assessment of the students' thinking.

56. Wilde, Sandra. "Learning to Write about Mathematics." *Arithmetic Teacher* 38 (February 1991): 38–43.

Discusses the value of making writing a regular part of the mathematics curriculum. Writing skills can be used in creating word problems, process problems, and mathematics journals. These writing samples can be used as diagnostic tools in the classroom, including bilingual classrooms. Includes examples of students' math work and written explanations.

Boldfaced titles in this bibliography indicate that the articles are reprinted in this book.

ANNOTATED BIBLIOGRAPHY

Mathematics Teacher

1. Arnold, Connie B., Sallee H. Reynolds, Cathy D. Stellern, Diane Bohannon, Katherine Harmon, Leanne Hill, Cathy Mamantov, and Suzanne H. Reed. "Grading." *Mathematics Teacher* 85 (September 1992): 442–43.

Shares a grading system based on a percentage of the total number of points attainable. The system requires students to maintain a personal notebook of their work and informs students how their grades will be calculated.

2. **Artzt, Alice F. "Integrating Writing and Cooperative Learning in the Mathematics Class." *Mathematics Teacher* 87 (February 1994): 80–85.**

Describes the use of writing to increase the effectiveness of student groups and the use of cooperative learning to enhance students' mathematical writing. Also discusses how to use cooperative learning and writing to help students learn from assessment instruments. Includes excerpts from student journals and sixteen references.

3. Asturias, Harold. "Using Students' Portfolios to Assess Mathematical Understanding." *Mathematics Teacher* 87 (December 1994): 698–701.

Examines reasons for using portfolios to assess students' understanding of mathematics. Offers general advice about what to include in portfolios and about how to generate student ownership of the portfolio idea.

4. Bagley, Theresa, and Catarina Gallenberger. "Assessing Students' Disposition: Using Journals to Improve Students' Performance." *Mathematics Teacher* 85 (November 1992): 660–63.

Clarifies the benefits of having students write about their understanding and dispositions toward mathematics. Discusses ways to manage journal writing and incorporate it into existing classes. Suggests nineteen assignments students can respond to in their journals.

5. Baker, Harold. "Soundoff: The SAT Should Be Revised." *Mathematics Teacher* 85 (January 1992): 14–15.

Suggests ways to improve the SAT and its face validity. Suggestions include greater emphasis on realistic problems, inclusion of realistic percent problems, modification of the multiple-choice format, and the use of the NCTM's *Curriculum and Evaluation Standards* as a guide to construct the test.

6. Baxter, Stephen, and Teresa Lasley. "Assessing Groups." *Mathematics Teacher* 85 (November 1992): 636–37.

Provides a strategy for assessing cooperative work. Includes ideas for forms that may help in recording information.

7. Braswell, James S. "Changes in the SAT in 1994." *Mathematics Teacher* 85 (January 1992): 16–21.

Describes important changes introduced in the mathematics sections of the new Scholastic Aptitude Test (SAT). The three main changes are (1) permission to use calculators, (2) inclusion of open-ended questions, and (3) content revisions consistent with the NCTM's *Curriculum and Evaluation Standards*.

8. Cain, Ralph W., and Patricia Kenney. "A Joint Vision for Classroom Assessment." *Mathematics Teacher* 85 (November 1992): 612–15.

Discusses teachers' roles and responsibilities in classroom mathematics assessment in the context of the "Standards for Teacher Competence in Educational Assessment of Students" (a document drafted in 1987 by representatives from the American Federation of Teachers, the National Council on Measurement in Education, and the National Education Association). Considers the issues of choosing and developing appropriate assessment methods, obtaining and using assessment results, and communicating assessment information.

9. Calahan, Rebecca. "From the Beginning." *Mathematics Teacher* 84 (September 1991): 454–55.

Presents a classroom technique to help beginning teachers: a student-sensitive approach to the first day of class using a questionnaire to assess students' attitudes toward mathematics and their interests.

10. **Clarke, David. "Quality Mathematics: How Can We Tell?" *Mathematics Teacher* 88 (April 1995): 326–28.**

Examines the need to clarify for students what is meant by "quality mathematics" in open-ended problem-solving contexts. Presents a process for negotiating a scoring rubric with students, and then shows how it is used by teacher and students.

11. **Clarke, Doug, and Linda Wilson. "Valuing What We See." *Mathematics Teacher* 87 (October 1994): 542–45.**

Offers guidance in conducting observational assessment, including what to look for, how to look for it, how to document it, and how to use it. Also offers hints from teachers who have experimented with observational assessment.

12. Clopton, Edwin L. "Summary Cards for Tests." *Mathematics Teacher* 85 (February 1992): 110.

Presents both the rationale and the policies for allowing students to use notes during tests in an advanced class.

13. Cramer, Kathleen, and Thomas Post. "Proportional Reasoning." *Mathematics Teacher* 86 (May 1993): 404–7.

Reports research findings regarding the learning and teaching of proportional reasoning. Presents four tasks devised to

---

Boldfaced titles in this bibliography indicate that the articles are reprinted in this book.

assess students' proportional reasoning and describes four solution strategies for solving these tasks based on the analysis of seventh and eighth graders' correct responses.

14. Crowley, Mary L. "Student Mathematics Portfolio: More than a Display Case." *Mathematics Teacher* 86 (October 1993): 544–47.

Describes the ways in which a portfolio may be used in a mathematics classroom. Explains what a portfolio is, what goes into one, how one can be organized, and how one might be assessed. Includes examples of junior high school portfolios.

15. Csongor, Julianna E. "Mirror, Mirror on the Wall... Teaching Self-Assessment to Students." *Mathematics Teacher* 85 (November 1992): 636–37.

Presents and discusses a way to help students conduct self-assessment and how to link this activity to testing.

16. Dodd, Anne Wescott. "Insights from a Math Phobic." *Mathematics Teacher* 85 (April 1992): 296–98.

The author's personal experiences in overcoming mathematics anxiety provide insights into how teachers can create a classroom environment that will help students develop self-confidence by assessing their feelings, using cooperative learning techniques, showing more patience, and having students write about their experiences.

17. Driscoll, Mark. "The Farther Out You Go...." *Mathematics Teacher* 88 (May 1995): 420–25.

Argues that a teacher's intended meaning and the students' constructed meaning may be at odds. Offers a vision of assessment that is integrated with instruction as a means to align intended and constructed meaning.

18. Edgerton, Richard T. "Apply the Curriculum Standards with Project Questions." *Mathematics Teacher* 86 (November 1993): 686–89.

Project questions are real-world problems that have multiple solutions and no obvious solution sequence, require hands-on data collection, and investigate topics within and outside mathematics. Discusses the evaluation of solution processes, describes a detailed example involving the trajectory of a baseball, and suggests nineteen other project questions.

19. Esty, Warren W., and Anne R. Teppo. "Grade Assignment Based on Progressive Improvement." *Mathematics Teacher* 85 (November 1992): 616–18.

Examines the consequences of assigning student grades using test-score averaging on course materials, tests, and learning. Proposes an alternative method of grading based on progressive improvement by the student that emphasizes the learning of concepts.

20. Gerver, Robert, and Richard Sgroi. "Retooling the General-Mathematics Curriculum." *Mathematics Teacher* 85 (April 1992): 270–74.

Presents four curricular alternatives and teaching strategies to improve the general-mathematics curriculum. Teaching strategies include reading mathematics, classroom discussion, an interdisciplinary approach, field trips, the use of manipulatives, varied assessment methods, cooperative learning, the use of technology, and team teaching.

21. Hoehn, Larry. "Problem Posing in Geometry." *Mathematics Teacher* 84 (January 1991): 10–14.

Presents an example of a typical geometry theorem that can be used to create geometry test questions and geometry contest questions. Thirteen problems are suggested.

22. Kenelly, John. "Implementing the *Standards*: Using Calculators in the Standardized Testing of Mathematics." *Mathematics Teacher* 83 (December 1990): 716–20.

Discusses the need for standardized tests and the changes that will be needed for their proper implementation. The use of calculators on tests is advocated. Computer- and calculator-delivered examinations are also discussed.

23. Klimas, Florence E. "Your Best Friend—Your Grade Book." *Mathematics Teacher* 85 (February 1992): 110–11.

Contains suggestions for color-coding a grade book, thus promoting efficient retrieval of information and easier analyses of students' progress or grades.

24. Kouba, Vicky L. "Self-Evaluation as an Act of Teaching." *Mathematics Teacher* 87 (May 1994): 354–58.

Presents techniques to help preservice and beginning teachers evaluate their own teaching, including concept maps and critical listening, analysis of videotapes and case studies, and cooperative teams and postobservation analyses.

25. Koss, Roberta, and Rick Marks. "The Teacher and Evaluation." *Mathematics Teacher* 87 (November 1994): 614–17.

Argues that effective evaluation of teaching must be done in a way that creates teacher ownership of the process. Suggests interviews and peer evaluation as possible techniques.

26. Kroll, Diana Lambdin, Joanna D. Masingila, and Sue Tinsley Mau. "Grading Cooperative Problem Solving." *Mathematics Teacher* 85 (November 1992): 619–27.

Discusses aspects of cooperative problem solving that include the selection of appropriate problems and the grading of group and individual papers using an analytical scoring scale. Offers six tips for grading cooperative problem solving. An appendix provides solutions to cited problems, potential follow-up questions, and an annotated bibliography.

27. Kuhs, Therese M. "Portfolio Assessment: Making It Work the First Time." *Mathematics Teacher* 87 (May 1994): 332–35.

Proposes strategies for teachers to use when they first use portfolios to assess mathematics learning in the classroom.

Boldfaced titles in this bibliography indicate that the articles are reprinted in this book.

Emphasis on Assessment

Includes a discussion of a collection with a purpose, student involvement in the process, criteria for evaluation, benefits and opportunities, and a sample focused holistic scoring rubric.

28. Leach, Eilene L. "An Alternative Form of Evaluation That Complies with NCTM's Standards." *Mathematics Teacher* 85 (November 1992): 628–32.

Describes an alternative form of evaluation that enables the teacher to assign a grade to students' problem-solving skills as they participate in a discussion to solve a problem. Discusses room arrangement, the role of the audience, grading, and secondary benefits of the method.

29. Leiva, Miriam. "Empowering Teachers through the Evaluation Process." *Mathematics Teacher* 88 (January 1995): 44–47.

For teacher evaluation to be an effective means for teacher growth, the teacher must play a central role in the evaluation process. Presents ideas for how a teacher portfolio can be used to document the teacher's evolving teaching.

30. Lester, Frank K., Jr., and Diana Lambdin Kroll. "Implementing the Standards: Evaluation—a New Vision." *Mathematics Teacher* 84 (April 1991): 276–84.

Four purposes of classroom assessment are described, providing a rationale for the use of alternative techniques. An overview of alternative methods of assessment focuses on four particular techniques: observing and questioning, assessing mathematics work, assessing writing, and assessing individual portfolios. A sample holistic scoring scale is provided, along with tips for getting started with alternative classroom assessment.

31. Levine, Deborah R. "Solving the Homework Problem." *Mathematics Teacher* 84 (September 1991): 455–56.

Presents a classroom technique to help beginning teachers. It is a suggestion on how to effectively review students' homework with their work at the chalkboard.

32. Manon, Jon Rahn. "The Mathematics Test: A New Role for an Old Friend." *Mathematics Teacher* 88 (February 1995): 138–41.

Suggests several ways in which traditional tests can be used in new ways as one of many assessment tools. Discusses their use in certifying skills, determining instruction, and stimulating higher-order thinking.

33. McLeod, Douglas B. "Affective Responses to Problem Solving." *Mathematics Teacher* 86 (December 1993): 761–63.

Presenting students with nonroutine problems is likely to produce affective responses from students unaccustomed to such problems. Discusses the theoretical background for evaluating students' emotional responses to problems, the relationship between problem solving and affect, emotions and beliefs, and techniques for dealing with affect in the classroom.

34. Meier, Sherry L. "Evaluating Problem-Solving Processes." *Mathematics Teacher* 85 (November 1992): 664–66.

Discusses problem-solving evaluation methods and describes the development of an instrument to evaluate an individual's problem-solving processes. Provides an example of the instrument.

35. Miller, L. Diane. "Begin Mathematics Class with Writing." *Mathematics Teacher* 85 (May 1992): 354–55.

Presents a technique used during the first five minutes of class that elicits from students written responses to questions about their understanding of mathematical content or their attitudes toward their mathematics class specifically or mathematics in general. Provides sample questions from algebra, geometry, and general mathematics.

36. Noble, A. Candace, and Kenneth B. Mullen. "The ACT Assessment in the 1990s." *Mathematics Teacher* 85 (January 1992): 22–25.

Presents a summary of the actions taken by American College Testing in response to calls for reform in standardized testing. The areas of reform discussed are test development, test content, skills levels, test criteria, and new testing initiatives, such as alternative-response-format questions and calculator use.

37. Schloemer, Cathy G. "An Assessment Example." *Mathematics Teacher* 87 (January 1994): 18–19.

Presents a scoring rubric to assess students' ability to communicate attempts at solving homework problems.

38. Schloemer, Cathy G. "Aligning Assessment with the NCTM's Curriculum Standards." *Mathematics Teacher* 86 (December 1993): 722–25.

Describes a series of eight project activities designed to increase students' communication and assess their understanding during a unit on functions and relations. Discusses different methods of evaluation and students' reactions to the activities.

39. Stallings-Roberts, Virginia. "Subjective Grading." *Mathematics Teacher* 85 (November 1992): 677–79.

Describes one teacher's implementation of subjective grading to assess students' achievement on mathematics tests. Reports students' and parents' reactions to the method. Shares five practices that developed with the experiences and provides an example of the grading policy used.

40. Wilson, Linda. "What Gets Graded Is What Gets Valued." *Mathematics Teacher* 87 (September 1994): 412–14.

Presents a fictionalized story based on a case-study research project involving a teacher who believes strongly in reform but whose efforts are largely thwarted by her grading system, which focuses on traditional activities.

Boldfaced titles in this bibliography indicate that the articles are reprinted in this book.

ANNOTATED BIBLIOGRAPHY

Journal for Research in Mathematics Education

1. Baxter, Gail P., Richard J. Shavelson, Sally J. Herman, Katharine A. Brown, and James R. Valadez. "Mathematics Performance Assessment: Technical Quality and Diverse Student Impact." *Journal for Research in Mathematics Education* 24 (May 1993): 190–216.

   This study developed performance assessments from hands-on instructional activities and examined their reliability and validity for obtaining individual achievement data. Ethnic-group comparisons indicated that Anglos scored higher, on average, than Latinos on all achievement measures. The magnitude of differences varied by the curricular experiences of students.

2. Cobb, Paul, Terry Wood, Erna Yackel, John Nicholls, Grayson Wheatley, Beatriz Trigatti, and Marcella Perlwitz. "Assessment of a Problem-Centered Second-Grade Mathematics Project." *Journal for Research in Mathematics Education* 22 (January 1991): 3–29.

   Describes a study of second-grade classes that participated in a yearlong project in which instruction was generally compatible with a socioconstructivist theory of knowledge and recent recommendations of the National Council of Teachers of Mathematics. Methods, results, and implications for mathematics instruction are discussed.

3. Hirschhorn, Daniel B. "A Longitudinal Study of Students Completing Four Years of UCSMP Mathematics." *Journal for Research in Mathematics Education* 24 (March 1993): 136–58.

   Compared the achievement and attitudes of students who had four years of the University of Chicago School Mathematics Project (UCSMP) secondary school curriculum to two distinct groups of comparable students (an age cohort and a mathematics course level cohort) at each of three different sites (one urban, two suburban). Instruments were an ETS Mathematics Level I Achievement Test, a 30-item Applications Test, and a 25-item Student Opinion Survey. At two of the sites UCSMP students outperformed both the age and course level cohorts by substantial amounts on both achievement and application tests. At the third site, both comparison cohorts outperformed the UCSMP students on the achievement test, but results on the application test were mixed. At all three sites, there was little difference in attitude.

4. Konold, Clifford, Alexander Pollatsek, Arnold Well, Jill Lohmeier, and Abigail Lipson. "Inconsistencies in Students' Reasoning about Probability." *Journal for Research in Mathematics Education* 24 (November 1993): 392–414.

   Examined inconsistencies in secondary school students' reasoning about the probability of equally likely events.

   Results of two studies suggest that the number of students who understand the concept of independence is much lower than the latest National Assessment of Educational Progress results indicate.

5. Lamon, Susan J. "Ratio and Proportion: Connecting Content and Children's Thinking." *Journal for Research in Mathematics Education* 24 (January 1993): 41–61.

   Twenty-four sixth-grade children participated in clinical interviews on ratio and proportion before receiving instruction in the domain. Students' thinking was analyzed according to mathematical components critical to proportional reasoning. Two components, relative thinking and unitizing, were consistently related to higher levels of sophistication in a student's overall problem-solving ability.

6. Marshall, Sandra P., and Alba G. Thompson. "Assessment: What's New—and Not So New—a Review of Six Recent Books." *Journal for Research in Mathematics Education* 25 (March 1994): 209–18.

   Reviews six books on assessment. All but one of the volumes are explicitly about assessment in mathematics education. The books are (1) *Changing Assessments: Alternative Views of Aptitude, Achievement and Instruction*; (2) *Assessment and Learning of Mathematics*; (3) *Assessment of Authentic Performance in School Mathematics*; (4) *Investigations Into Assessment in Mathematics Education*; (5) *Cases of Assessment in Mathematics Education*; and (6) *Mathematics Assessment and Evaluation: Imperatives for Mathematics Educators*.

7. Miller, L. Diane. "Teacher Benefits from Using Impromptu Writing Prompts in Algebra Classes." *Journal for Research in Mathematics Education* 23 (July 1992): 329–40.

   Examines the benefits to teachers who used impromptu writing prompts in first- and second-year algebra classes. An interpretive-research methodology was used to collect and analyze data. Concludes that teachers' assessment of students' understanding was enhanced by reading their students' responses to impromptu writing prompts, thus affecting their instructional practices.

8. Nagy, Philip, Ross E. Traub, Kathryn MacRury, and Roslyn Klaiman. "High School Calculus: Comparing the Content of Assignments and Tests." *Journal for Research in Mathematics Education* 22 (January 1991): 69–75.

   Compares the content of what is taught and what is tested in a high school calculus course. Results showed differences in content coverage across teachers and differences in the overlap between content taught and content tested. Methodological issues in the investigation of teachers' grading practices are discussed.

9. Research Advisory Committee. "Mathematics Education Reform and Mathematics Education Research: Opportunities, Obstacles, and Obligations." *Journal for Research in Mathematics Education* 21 (July 1990): 287–92.

Proposes the responsibilities of mathematics education researchers for the implementation of the NCTM Standards. Six areas that offer opportunities for standards-related research are identified: assessment, changes in curriculum materials, mathematics as communication, policy-related issues, the effects of technology, and the secondary school core curriculum.

10. Research Advisory Committee. "NCTM Standards Research Catalyst Conference." *Journal for Research in Mathematics Education* 22 (July 1991): 293–96.

Describes the Catalyst Conference convened by the Research Advisory Committee of the National Council of Teachers of Mathematics (NCTM) to stimulate research on the effects of the NCTM *Curriculum and Evaluation Standards* as a guide for change in mathematics education. Six focus areas were identified.

11. Silver, Edward A., and Patricia Ann Kenney. "An Examination of Relationships between the 1990 NAEP Mathematics Items for Grade 8 and Selected Themes from the NCTM *Standards.*" *Journal for Research in Mathematics Education* 24 (March 1993): 159–67.

Explores relationships between 137 grade 8 cognitive items used in the 1990 National Assessment of Educational Progress and selected themes from the NCTM's *Standards*. About half the items related to the four *Standards* themes (problem solving, reasoning, communication, and connections), with most of those being related to problem solving and reasoning.

ARTICLE-BY-TOPIC MATRIX

Arithmetic Teacher/Teaching Children Mathematics and Mathematics Teaching in the Middle School — Part 1

The following table displays categories under which an assessment article may be cataloged. Some articles have multiple listings. The articles reproduced in this book are indicated with an asterisk; others are marked with a checkmark.

Category / Article no.	1	2	3	4	5	6	7	8	9	10	11	12	13	14	15	16	17	18	19	20	21	22	23	24	25	26	27	28	29	30
Rationale	*				✓	✓			✓	*			✓		*					*					✓	*				
Classroom Testing					✓																									
Achievement Testing										*					*							✓				*				
Grading																				*							✓			
Scoring Rubrics				✓														✓									✓			
Portfolios										*		*																	*	
Journals												*											✓							
Writing																							✓					✓		
Observation							✓					*																		
Questioning			✓																											
Discussion								✓									✓													
Checklist										*		*																		
Interview												*																		✓
Cooperative Learning																										*				
Problem Solving							✓									✓			✓					✓		*	✓	✓		
Performance Assessment	*																													
Affect & Beliefs											✓																			
Technology											✓											✓								
Teacher Self-Evaluation																					✓									
Student Self-Evaluation										*	✓					✓														
Student Feedback																														
Misconceptions																			✓											
Diagnostic																														

ARTICLE-BY-TOPIC MATRIX

Arithmetic Teacher/Teaching Children Mathematics and Mathematics Teaching in the Middle School — Part 2

Category / Article no.	31	32	33	34	35	36	37	38	39	40	41	42	43	44	45	46	47	48	49	50	51	52	53	54	55	56
Rationale	√	√															√			√						√
Classroom Testing						*																				
Achievement Testing												√														
Grading																										
Scoring Rubrics																					*					
Portfolios																					*					
Journals								*													*					
Writing							√	*		√			√		√						*					√
Observation													√				√									
Questioning					√		√		√					√			√		*			√		√		
Discussion				√																			√	√	√	
Checklist											√					*										
Interview			*																							
Cooperative Learning					√	*	√																			
Problem Solving						*							√						*							√
Performance Assessment						*																				
Affect & Beliefs											√				√				*							
Technology																										
Teacher Self-Evaluation	√									√						*										
Student Self-Evaluation																										
Student Feedback																										
Misconceptions																										
Diagnostic			*															√								

ARTICLE-BY-TOPIC MATRIX
Mathematics Teacher—Part 1

The following table displays categories under which an assessment article may be cataloged. Some articles have multiple listings. The articles reproduced in this book are indicated with an asterisk; others are marked with a checkmark.

Category / Article no.	1	2	3	4	5	6	7	8	9	10	11	12	13	14	15	16	17	18	19	20	21	22	23	24	25	26	27	28	29	30
Rationale								√									*								*					*
Classroom Testing												√			*				*		√									
Achievement Testing					√		√															√								
Grading	√																		*				√							
Scoring Rubrics										*																*	√			
Portfolios			√											*													√			
Journals		*																												
Writing		*		√																										
Observation											*																			
Questioning																														
Discussion																				√										
Checklist																														
Interview																														
Cooperative Work		*				√										√														
Problem Solving										*			√					√								*		√		
Performance									√																					
Affect & Beliefs																														
Technology																						√								
Teacher Self-Evaluation																								*	*				*	
Student Self-Evaluation															*															

ARTICLE-BY-TOPIC MATRIX
Mathematics Teacher—Part 2

Category / Article no.	31	32	33	34	35	36	37	38	39	40
Rationale								*		
Classroom Testing		*							√	
Achievement Testing						√				
Grading									√	*
Scoring Rubrics				√			*			
Portfolios										
Journals										
Writing					*					
Observation							*			
Questioning										
Discussion										
Checklist										
Interview										
Cooperative Work										
Problem Solving			√	√						
Performance										
Affect & Beliefs	√		√							
Technology										
Teacher Self-Evaluation										
Student Self-Evaluation										

ARTICLE-BY-TOPIC MATRIX
Journal for Research in Mathematics Education

The following table displays categories under which an assessment article may be cataloged. Some articles have multiple listings.

Category \ Article no.	1	2	3	4	5	6	7	8	9	10	11
Rationale									√	√	
Classroom Testing								√			
Achievement Testing			√								√
Grading								√			
Scoring Rubrics											
Portfolios											
Journals											
Writing							√				
Observation											
Questioning											
Discussion											
Checklist											
Interview					√						
Cooperative Learning											
Problem Solving					√						
Performance Assessment	√										
Affect & Beliefs			√								
Technology				√							
Self-Evaluation											
Reasoning						√					
Book Review on											
Programmatic		√									